AF528651

Think New-Think Better:
Select Cases on Entrepreneurship

Think New-Think Better:
Select Cases on Entrepreneurship

EDITORS

Manoj Kumar Dash

Assistant Professor
ABV-Indian Institute of Information technology
and Management, Gwalior

Manoj Patwardhan

Associate Professor
ABV-Indian Institute of Information technology
and Management, Gwalior

Gaurv Kabra

ABV-Indian Institute of Information technology
and Management, Gwalior

SERIALS PUBLICATIONS
NEW DELHI (INDIA)

© Manoj Kumar Dash, Manoj Patwardhan, Gaurv Kabra

First Published – 2011

ISBN: 978-81-8387-460-1

All rights reserved with the Publisher, including the right to translate or reproduce this book or parts thereof except for brief quotations in critical articles or reviews.

Published by

SERIALS PUBLICATIONS
4830/24, Prahlad Street, Ansari Road
Darya Ganj, New Delhi-110002 (India)
Phone : 23245225 Fax : 91-11-23272135
E-mail : serials@satyam.net.in

Contents

Preface

Since entering the business dictionary, the term entrepreneurship has evolved with different meanings and perspectives. For many years, entrepreneurship was viewed as the equivalent of 'professionalism'. Across periods of time, some identified it as an economic function, while others related entrepreneurship with individual traits. Whether it is an economic function, a person with specific traits, or someone starting and successfully running a new venture, the one thing that epitomizes the entrepreneurial breed is the dream they chase - a dream to convert a vision into action and benefit from the rewards.

Entrepreneurs often bring to mind individuals who are innovative, dynamic, risk bearing, flexible and creative. Although every entrepreneur identifies an opportunity, utilizes the available resources and converts the opportunity into reality, no two entrepreneurs share the same entrepreneurial style. While, some might follow the promoter's style who takes advantage of an opportunity, irrespective of the resources available, others resemble the trustee's style, for which resources are of prime importance in order to execute plans. Whatever the style, all entrepreneurs chase a dream of converting their vision into reality. Since entering the business dictionary, the way entrepreneurs matter has changed. Earlier entrepreneurship was restricted to only small businesses. But with the rise in the need for being innovative, many large firms have also imbibed the virtues of entrepreneurship. Entrepreneurship generates new ideas, employment and increases productivity. Moreover, with social entrepreneurs seeking practical solutions to social problems, entrepreneurship has evolved beyond just profit making.

In the business world, innovation is the name of the game. To survive and remain ahead in the intense competitive struggle, businesses require being innovative. However, to successfully innovate is not an easy job. Not because a good idea is hard to find, but simply because converting an innovative idea into a profitable venture is just so much harder. Microsoft, Apple, Wal-Mart and Dell, have all managed to be successfully innovative. But how have these great companies done it? How could many of the fortune 500 companies remain on top for so many years? It is definitely not by accident. Be it Bill Gates, Steve Jobs, Sam Walton, or Michael Dell, there is a great entrepreneur behind every great company's success.

This book is the result of a study on Effectiveness of Entrepreneurship and innovation/change Management course delivered by author in the ABV- Indian Institute of Information Technology and Management, Gwalior. This is an important contribution to the scanty literature on entrepreneurship and change in the Gwalior. This book is a compilation of case studies of successful entrepreneurs from Gwalior Regions. This is a guidebook for those who want to talk up entrepreneurial activities and change agent as career option for self-employment. The book discusses reaction of Government official about Entrepreneurship, Successful of Young Web entrepreneur of India as well as produced by ABV-IIITM Gwalior, successful stories of Women Entrepreneur in India and above all the requisites information for web-Entrepreneur. This book is meant for new entrepreneurs who would like to lead in ever changing economy. Written in lucid language the book will also be useful for researchers, academics, planners and policy makers.

Acknowledgement

A large number of individuals have contributed in creating this book, *Think New Think Better: Select cases on Entrepreneurship*. We are thankful to all of them for their help and encouragement. Our writing in this book has also been influenced by a number of standard and popular text-books in this field. We express our gratitude to all of them.

We hereby express our gratitude to Chairman, ABV-IIITM Gwalior *Dr. M.N. Buch* for his invaluable guidance for innovating the idea for our book. Without his blessings this book would never have been a success.

We are indebted to the Director, ABV-IIITM Gwalior *Prof. S.G. Deshmukh* and Registrar, *Dr. Dilip Kumar* for how much we have learned from their guidance and insight provided. It was indeed a great honor and a great learning experience to work under such unerring personalities and having received their ever helping cooperation and wisdom.

We also sincerely thank the Faculty members of ABV-IIITM, Gwalior for their invaluable suggestions during the entire course of this book. Their feedback was a constant source of inspiration for us.

Our Overriding debt continues to students for their direct and indirect support. We are also grateful to Entrepreneurs of Gwalior for sharing their personal Experiences and providing their views on Entrepreneurship and the Government employees in Gwalior for providing their views on Entrepreneurship and also explain the way the government encourages entrepreneurs for their immense cooperation throughout the course of our book.

Finally, we extend our thanks to Director, IIM Lucknow *Prof. Devi Singh,* and Vice Chancellor, *Prof. Rajan Saxena* for their support, encouragement and suggestions.

We shall be forever in debt and grateful for all the support provided and the resource that were made available to us. We dedicate our project to the immense knowledge and expertise we got in this area without which the book would not have been completed. We eagerly look forward to receiving feedback from the readers for improving the book.

Authors

Foreword

Entrepreneurship is thriving in India today. Students are one of the drivers of this growth. They have a knack for spotting the opportunities available in various sectors, especially so in IT and IT enabled services. Cashing in on this trend are the students turning to business instead of opting for the security of a well paid jobs. There is an increasing array of entrepreneurship programs made available on the campus, especially in B-schools. ABV-Indian Institute of Information Technology & Management is no exception to this trend. Being the first IIIT in the country, the institute is engaged in conducting interesting programmes on entrepreneurship.

From a career perspective, entrepreneurship is always considered to be highly rewarding though challenging. A successful entrepreneur typically needs passion and belief in his vision and ideas, in addition to a risk taking capacity.

I am sure in the coming years; we will see a trail-blazing entrepreurs emerging from India's towns. They won't be typical suited-booted, valley funded entrepreneurs, but people with a home-grown, high impact vision. "Think new – Think Better" is an attempt to document such efforts. The book is also an attempt to share the inspiring vision of a band of home grown entrepreneurs from various domains. . This book will serve as a good resource material for a course on Entrepreurship. The authors, Dr Manoj Dash, Dr Manoj Patwardhan and Gaurav Kabra have taken painstaking efforts and energy in bringing out this excellent volume on select cases in entrepreneurship. Entrepreneurship also brings in change management. The book also documents case studies in change management. My special appreciation to the authors for bringing out this volume which is timely and highly thematic.

I am confident the book will act as a good companion in any entrepreneurship programme and will act as a motivator for young entrepreneurs.

Prof. S.G. Deshmukh
Director,
ABV-Indian Institute of Information
Technology & Management, Gwalior

1

The Entrepreneurial Perspective

Introduction

In the field of business, the people involved in the playoffs are called the entrepreneurs. They are also referred to as businessmen. They own and run their own businesses. The word "Entrepreneur' is a loanword from French. In French the verb "Entreprendre" means "to undertake', with "Intre' coming from the Latin word meaning "Between' and "Prendre" meaning "to take'. In French a person who performs a verb, has the ending of the verb changed to "eur", comparable to the "er" ending in English. Enterprise is similar to and has roots in the French word "Enterprise ', which is the past participle of "Entreprendre". Entrepreneur is similarly the French feminine counterpart of the "Entrepreneur".

No one is ever as enthusiastic and energized as someone propelled forward by a focused dream. But dreaming is not enough. Entrepreneurs are dreamers turned doers. Dreamers are those who envision a better product or an improved service. Dream struck entrepreneurs have created opportunities for improved living from the automobiles that we drive to the pizza we get delivered.

The only certain thing is that, entrepreneurs are very much involved in today's business arena. Tracing history back, it is said that the term entrepreneur has been conceivably recognized as an adamant part of the economic world only in the mid 1970s. The concept has then started to evolve with various meanings depending on the understanding of the society that gives meaning to it.

Entrepreneurs build a better way by risking ideas, money and countless hours in order to complete their mission. When the entrepreneur also creates a better life for themselves through financial gain and the self-esteem that comes from accomplishment, the dream has come full circle.

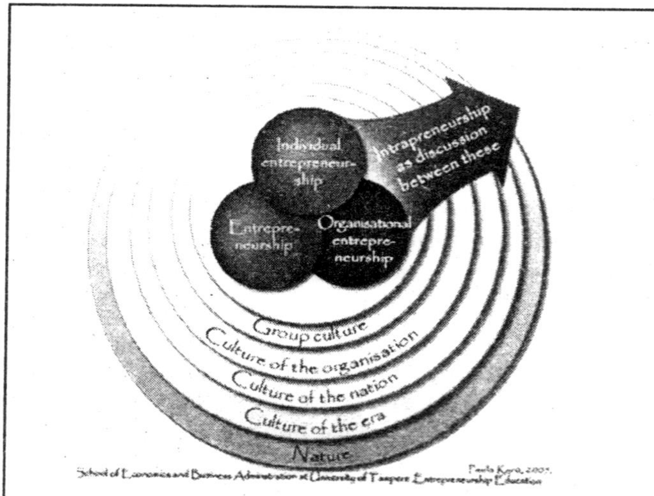

Figure 1: Various Aspects of Entrepreneurship

Definition of Entrepreneurship

Everywhere you turn nowadays, you always hear about venturing into entrepreneurship. But what is entrepreneurship exactly? In an online dictionary as defined by the Webster's Revised Unabridged Dictionary, in the year 1913, entrepreneur has been defined as the person who makes some products for his own benefit or account. This gives about the idea that the term has successfully evolved way back in the year 1913. Now such definition may quite be blurry.

How can a person be called an entrepreneur when he does nothing with that product aside from creating it? What term will be labeled to a person who takes other people's products and make a success out of them? Will they be not branded as entrepreneurs too? According to Merriam-Webster dictionary, an entrepreneur is someone who organizes, who manages, and who assumes the risks posed by the business or enterprise world. Now this definition of an entrepreneur is richer in content compared with the first one. Risks-these are literally faced by entrepreneurs as they pursue with any type of investment in the market.

In a much formal definition of Ashoka, an entrepreneur goes to refer to an organizational society that promotes nothing but social change. Social entrepreneurs are those individuals who open up some new and major possibilities in the areas of health, education, environment, and all other areas of the human needs.

To drive a stricter point, the business entrepreneurs are those who lead the innovations in the world of commerce while the social entrepreneurs are those who drive social change in the society. In more ways than one, such definition all the more points out that those business entrepreneurs not only start with any type of business but they do promote change within the business range.

Moving from formal definitions, Ashoka, an organization which promotes social change, calls for "social entrepreneurs", people who open up major new possibilities in education, health, the environment, and other areas of human need, "just as business entrepreneurs lead innovation in commerce, social entrepreneurs drive social change." The concept of business entrepreneurs leading innovation is appealing because it denotes more than just starting a business.

Dale Tucker, a personal entrepreneur, goes to define the term as an individual who decides to take hold and control of his own future and therefore become a self-employed person either by creating his own business or by working with a team just like what multi-level marketing means. On the other hand, Mark Hendricks suggests that for one person to be called an entrepreneur, he needs to be particularly daring. He must be able to meet the challenge of either winning or losing in the business. He therefore must be open to the possibilities of the results of the competition. Entrepreneurship is collectively defined as exhibiting one's vision, taking action, and pursuing that vision as a goal to be achieved in life as service to reality. In the meaningless definition, it's getting your butt out of that couch and doing something rather than fulfilling your life's destiny of being a couch potato.

Mark Hendricks takes Tucker's definition a step further, acknowledging innovation, but also providing alternatives. Hendricks suggests that to be an entrepreneur you don't particularly have to be daring. Many entrepreneurs are perfectly content to sell tried-and-true products, bringing a steady income without the intensity of launching a new product. He labels these lifestyle entrepreneurs. They want to be their own boss and make a good living, but they don't need to be on the cutting edge, which entails living where one wants, working with people one likes, and doing work one wants to do.

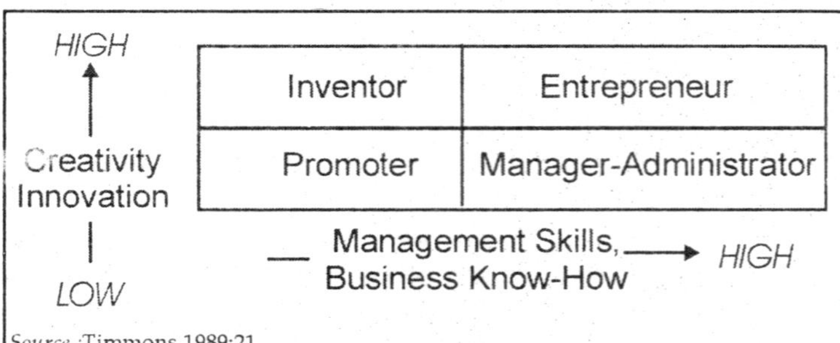

Source :Timmons 1989:21

Figure 2: Entrepreneurs- More than an Owner/Manager

In the early 16th century, the Frenchmen who organized and led military expedition were referred to as 'entrepreneur'. Around 1700 A.D, the term was used for contractor of public works. The term Entrepreneur was firstly applied to the business by the French Economist Cantillon in the 18th century. Cantillon developed one of the early theories of the Entrepreneur and is regarded by some as the founder of the term. He has viewed the entrepreneur as a risk taker, observing that merchant, farmer, craftsman and other sole proprietor.

"Buy at a certain price and sell at an uncertain price, therefore operating at the risk."

Entrepreneur a person, who has initiative in investment and decision to the enterprise; seeking all resource of factor of production, resources of Management, Behavior, Cultural, Economical and Political factor for establishing, innovation and founded enterprise, having assumption of risk, profit and future growth.

It is actually a process wherein a group or an individual makes an effort to pursue opportunities to satisfy needs and wants through uniqueness and innovation. Some people have the misconception that entrepreneurs are gamblers in the sense that they take risks and invest in industries that have no record of success. However, the truth is, these entrepreneurs take calculated risks that have the potential to provide them with huge returns.

Entrepreneurship Feeling

Dreaming is the easy part; doing is the challenge. Building a business will impact how you live. Your energy, stamina and supportive family and friends will be important elements in your business venture. Entrepreneurs have personal characteristics which enable them to forge ahead and take on challenges. You will explore the characteristics of the successful entrepreneur and see for yourself how you stack up.

The key factors you need to remember about entrepreneurship are opportunities, innovation, and growth. An entrepreneur sees opportunities in environmental trends and changes that nobody has seen before and pursues this opportunity with whatever resources he has at hand. The second theme in entrepreneurship is innovation which involves transforming and revolutionizing existing products or services to cope up with the changing global environment. The third theme is growth; this involves the continual efforts of an entrepreneur to expand his business locally and internationally.

Where do entrepreneur find an idea for a successful business venture? How does an entrepreneur know if it will work for him?

Entrepreneur starts first with the areas of your life you enjoy the most. What hobbies and interests do he have? What are those activities which he enjoys so much that time flies when you are involved? Working on cars, sewing, teaching others, art, negotiating or putting together complex projects? Do he draw pictures of buildings, create new recipes, develop computer programs or take pictures? All of these interests are a clue to his real talents and capabilities.

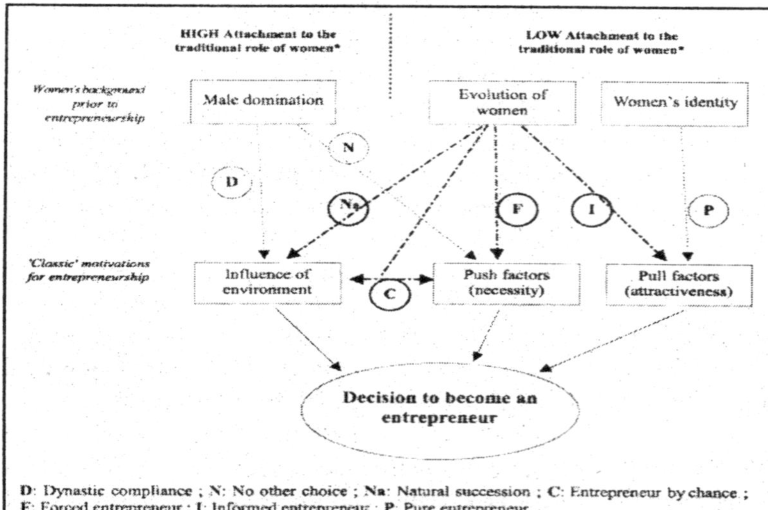

(*Source:* Classification appeaing as well in a typology developed by Gofee and Scase 1985)

Figure 3: Factors Affecting to be an Entrepreneur

Being in business for oneself will involve hard work and sacrifice. Successful entrepreneurs can make the sacrifice because they believe in and are motivated by the product or service they deliver. They gain satisfaction from sharing their interests with others.

- What are some products and services that you know of that are currently available in your area of keen interest?
- How could these products and services be improved?
- Are there products and services you wish were available in your area of keen interest?

An entrepreneur is on the constant look out on how to create new approaches to make his business grow and become a huge success. Building a business requires more than a belief in a product or service It also requires a belief in you. A belief is that you are capable and know how to solve problems. A belief that what you don't know today you can learn in order to help your business succeed. A belief that you will be able to do what ever it takes to create and deliver your product or service. This belief in our self is the foundation for being a successful entrepreneur. It will open up creative thoughts and pick you up when you are down. You create your own belief system. You build it, nurture it and turn it into reality.

Entrepreneur Motivation

Wherever you turn, you see the results of entrepreneurship. Productive entrepreneurship is now one of the main drivers of economic growth. It is associated with the ability of individuals to begin new ventures, the quantity and quality of start-up firms, and the ease with which enterprises can enter and exit the market. In a churning process, new establishments are created, some existing ones expand, and others dissolve operations. The entry and exit of firms shifts market share from the less to the more efficient, self-selects winning firms, and leads to knowledge and technology spillovers.

People that were unheard of before are becoming some of the riches names in the world and it is all because they have taken risks and have succeeded. So whether we realize it or not, it is the entrepreneurs who drive the global environment nowadays.

These themes are the key factors which businesses are founded upon. The largest corporations we find today did not start out big, rather they started out as small enterprises by visionaries who want more than what is offered to them. We can see from the history of some of the most successful business today that the founders of these businesses have taken great leaps of faith and incredible amounts of risks in order to be what they are today.

Entrepreneurship plays an important role in the economic growth and development of nation. It is a purposeful activity includes in initiation, promotion and distribution of wealth and service. An entrepreneur is a critical factor in economic development and an integral part of the socio-economic transformation. It is a risk taking activity and challenging tasks, needs utmost devotion, total commitment and greater sincerity with fullest involvement for his personal growth and personality. The entrepreneurial career is not a one day job nor is it bed of roses. Prosperity and success never come easily. It takes time and needs hard work.

(*Source:* Hyungrae Jo and JinJoo Lee 1999)
Figuere 4: Entrepreneurs Mind to Generate New Idea

Therefore, before choosing this path one should be very careful in knowing about his own self. This introspection process helps him in knowing about himself. Every person has his own potentiality and resource. How he looks in to this aspect. If the person cans understand or identify his inner traits then it help him choosing the right path for which he should look into his beliefs, faith values etc. For an entrepreneur it is of great importance to know about him on the basis of above mentioned individual consideration. These consideration give him ample scope to face his own self by asking the question "Who I am?" If he can given meaning answer to this complex question with exemplary courage and utter personal disregard to being exposed, then it helps him in getting a fair idea about himself. On the whole it helps him to making the right decision in choosing the right path for getting involved for deciding the future course of action. This is nothing but a self-identification process. After having being proper identified his strength, weakness and ability, he can make a decision of his choice, whether he will take up entrepreneurship as a career or not. If yes, then in which entrepreneur.

They are the ones who are always seeking out opportunities and taking risks to improve our world and profit from it in return.

Entrepreneur Background

The relative profit tends to be high when an entrepreneur has more education and experience in the line of business. On the other hand, the profitability tends to be low when the entrepreneur has only start-up, managerial and high-growth experience without an educational background.

A similar effect is shown in the growth of the firm. The positive effect is on growth if an entrepreneur has a professional knowledge of the product, which is gained through previous work experience related to that product. If the entrepreneur

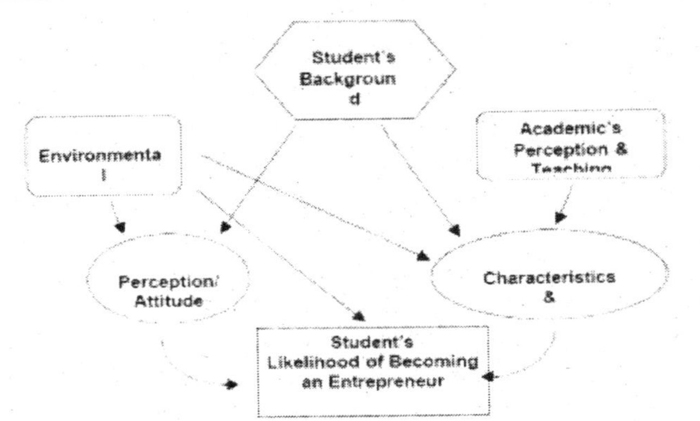

(*Source:* Hyungrae Jo and JinJoo Lee 1999)

Figure 5: Entrepreneurial Background

has start-up, managerial and high-growth experience, but lacks knowledge of business, this results in a rather negative effect on the growth.

The implications are that a good understanding of the product is essential to the success of the venture, whereas starting a new business with only limited previous experience related to the management dimension can be dangerous and may lead a firm to be unsuccessful. *Background of entrepreneurs* provides insights into high-growth founders' motivations and their socio-economic, educational, and familial backgrounds.

A Survey was conducted By Entrepreneurship Development Institute (EDI) Ahmadabad for finding the background profile study of entrepreneur in 2009, and it was found:

- More than 90 percent of the entrepreneurs comes from middle-class or upper-lower-class backgrounds and were well-educated: 95.1 percent of those surveyed had earned bachelor's degrees, and 47 percent had more advanced degrees.
- Seventy-five percent of the respondents ranked their academic performance among the top 30 percent of their high school classes, and 52 percent said they ranked among the top 10 percent. In college, 67 percent of the founders ranked among the top 30 percent of their undergraduate classes, and 37 percent ranked their performance among the top 10 percent.
- Founders tended to be middle-aged—40 years old on average—when they started their first companies. Nearly 70 percent were married when they became entrepreneurs, and nearly 60 percent had at least one child, challenging the stereotype of the entrepreneurial workaholic with no time for a family.

Entrepreneurs identifies prior work experience, learning from previous successes and failures, a strong management team, and good fortune as the most important factors in their success.

Further some other interesting results are derived which are as follows:

- Professional networks were important to the success of their current businesses for 73 percent of the entrepreneurs. In comparison, 62 percent felt the same way about personal networks.
- Only 11 percent of the first-time entrepreneurs received venture capital, and 9 percent received private/angel financing. Of the overall sample, 68 percent considered availability of financing/capital as important. Of the entrepreneurs who had raised venture capital for their most recent businesses, 96 percent considered financing important.
- Eighty-six percent of Ivy-League graduates ranked university education as important, as compared with 70 percent of the overall sample. Only 20 percent of entrepreneurs and 18 percent of Ivy-League graduates ranked university education as extremely important.
- Most company founders (86 percent) ranked state or regional assistance as slightly or not at all important.
- In identifying barriers to entrepreneurial success, the most commonly named factor by 98 percent of respondents – was lack of willingness or ability to take risks. Other barriers cited by respondents were the time and effort required (93 percent), difficulty raising capital (91 percent), business management skills (89 percent), knowledge about how to start a business (84 percent), industry and market knowledge (83 percent), and family/financial pressures to keep a traditional, steady job (73 percent).

Environment of Entrepreneurship

A work environment can be identified as the place that one works. i.e. in an office building in a cube, at home at the kitchen table, from a car or truck, at a construction site. Environmental strategies are a key aspect of organizational change. Across industry, enterprises are taking a more pro-active stance in addressing sustainable development concerns and becoming good corporate citizens. Many enterprises in both manufacturing and services are developing environmental strategies to reduce negative impacts on ecosystems. Improving performance through eco-efficiency, realizing new commercial opportunities, improving public image and complying with corporate codes of conduct are driving these strategies. Governments can

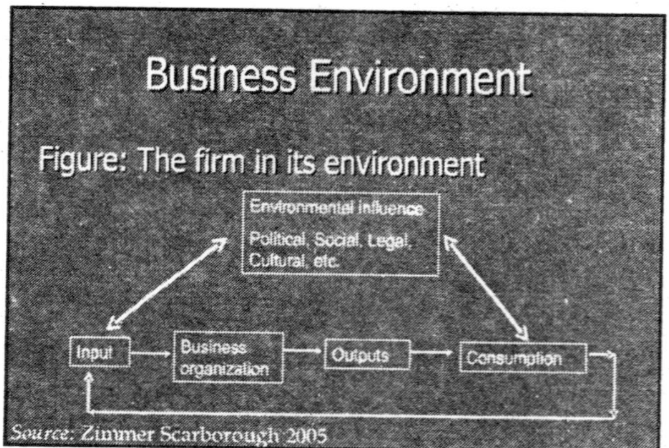

Figure 6: Business Environment

reinforce such behavior through promoting adoption of environmental management systems, better environmental reporting, and links to assessments by the financial community. Through diffusing information to consumers and stimulating environmental innovations, governments can help catalyze

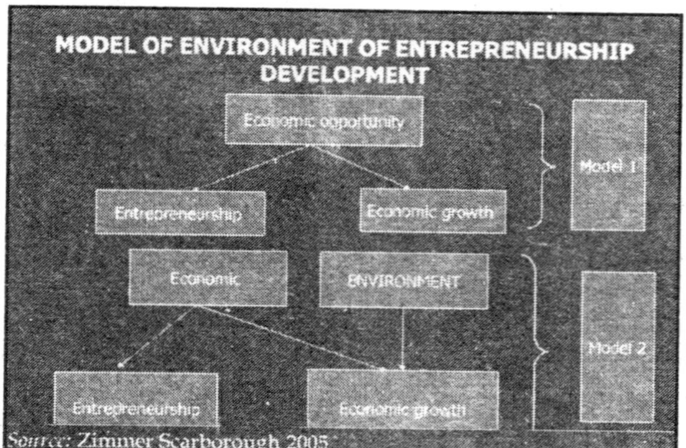

Figure 7: Model of Environment of Entrepreneurship Development

markets and drive the development of new and more sustainable industrial processes and products. The following figure represents how the environment affects a firm by means of inputs, processing and outputs.

Characteristics of Good Entrepreneurs

Before a doctor diagnoses a specific disease, his patient must undergo a series of laboratory exams and assessments. He has to know the history of his patient and how lifestyle affected his present health problem. As results come in, that would be an indication of the time when a physician gives specific drugs and therapies for maintenance. This will eventually contribute to the level of optimum health for that individual. If all else fails, the process will be repeated again. Similar to what the abovementioned situation has stated, an entrepreneur's responsibility would be pretty much the same. It's just that, he should see his customers as his patients and what they must have to survive a present predicament or a need. He must follow certain steps before doing anything irrational that could contribute to the downfall of his business. He should have certain characteristics innate in his personality for if he lacks one of these, he's most probably doomed to fail.

Some characteristics of a good entrepreneur include determination, intelligence, and the ability to think outside the box. These characteristics will help any good entrepreneur think of and find a solid niche to fill and see the business through the tough times as well as the good times. A good entrepreneur also has characteristics of running their business as easily as possible.

Common Traits in a Successful Entrepreneur are:

1. *Good Health:* Successful entrepreneurs must work long hours for extended periods of time. When they get sick, they recover quickly.
2. *A Need to Control and Direct:* They prefer environments where they have maximum authority and responsibility and do not work well in traditionally structured organizations. This is not about power,

though. Entrepreneurs have a need to create and achieve by having control over events.

3. *Self-confidence:* Findings showed that as long as entrepreneurs were in control, they were relentless in pursuit of their goals. If they lost control, they quickly lost interest in the undertaking.
4. *Sense of Urgency:* They have a never-ending sense of urgency to do something. This corresponds with a high energy level. Many enjoy individual sports rather than team sports. Inactivity makes them impatient.
5. *Comprehensive Awareness:* They have a comprehensive awareness of a total situation and are aware of all the ramifications involved in a decision.
6. *Realistic Outlook:* There is a constant need to know the status of things. They may or may not be idealistic, but they are honest and straightforward and expect others to be the same.
7. *Conceptual Ability:* They have superior conceptual abilities. This helps entrepreneurs identify relationships in complex situations. Chaos does not bother them because they can conceptualize order. Problems are quickly identified and solutions offered. The drawback is that this may not translate well to interpersonal problems.
8. *Low Need for Status:* Their need for status is met through achievement not through material possessions.
9. *Objective Approach:* They take an objective approach to personal relationships and are more concerned with the performance and accomplishment of others than with feelings. They keep their distance psychologically and concentrate on the effectiveness of operations.
10. *Emotional Stability.* They have the stability to handle stress from business and from personal areas in their lives. Setbacks are seen as challenges and do not discourage them.

11. *Attraction to Challenges:* They are attracted to challenges but not to risks. It may look like they are taking high risks, but in actuality they have assessed the risks thoroughly.
12. *Describing with Numbers:* They can describe situations with numbers. They understand their financial position and can tell at any time how much they have in receivables and how much they owe.

Characteristics of the Successful Entrepreneur

Every entrepreneur is unique. Every entrepreneur has his or her own set of strengths, weaknesses, talents and abilities. However, entrepreneurs who have stood the test of time and have made a difference in their communities and industries do share common characteristics.

Optimism

Taking risks and paving new paths can only be accomplished with optimism. Optimism is a belief in the future, a view of what is possible rather then what is impossible. The ability to envision possibilities not yet proven. When you are optimistic you look for solutions rather then reasons for problems. You strive for ways to get things done rather then excuses to explain why it wasn't possible.

Tenacity and Courage

Sticking to the goal, even when it means doing things differently, is tenacity. Many entrepreneurs speak of break-through which came only when they were told it couldn't be done. "Dare me" is the underlining theme of many successful entrepreneurs. Facing opposition, and those who believe it couldn't be done, only drives the successful entrepreneur to try harder. Risking your ideas, as well as your money requires courage and determination.

Well Defined Ethics and Values

The successful entrepreneurs know what they stand for. They have a strong sense of values and business ethics which are guiding forces in their decisions. They know being true to themselves is more than just a cliché - it's a way of operating. It will be important for you to determine what values you will stand behind in your business. What values you will use to make decisions and set direction.

Ability to Listen and Learn

Whether from customers, employees, advisors or the public, the successful entrepreneur is hungry to learn. Learn more about their product, marketplace, possible innovations and trends which will affect their business. They are quick to admit what they do not know and even quicker to seek the information needed to stay on track.

Self-control and Discipline

Staying focused on the vision and managing the details means self-control and discipline. Principles of time management and positive work habits are important to the long term success of your business. Setting objectives and action plans which are essential to accomplishing important goals and insuring the accomplishment of those targets by you and others in the organization takes discipline and focus.

Self-confidence

A key characteristic of any high performer, including the successful entrepreneur, is a positive sense of self-confidence. It's confidence that enables people to try new things and effectively manage risk. It's confidence that will be needed to sell your plan to the bank or investors. It's confidence that will give your sales presentations the power of influence. Confidence is the result of programming your mind with positive and optimistic thoughts and plans. The support of friends and family can add to that sense of self-confidence.

Some of the Other Characteristics of an Entrepreneur are:

- *Creativity*- is thinking outside the box. Expanding one's mind of what is beyond the ordinary through fine research and collection of data.

- *Stability-* either physical, mental, social or emotional, a leader must possess a stable life which means he could handle tough situations during tough times.
- *Charismatic-* intelligence of communicating with different walks of life. Who says a charming man is less than an intelligent one? A good entrepreneur must have the certain magic glistening in his eyes and could convey enchanting words to get hold of that convincing power no one dare resist.
- *Risk-taker-* as someone beginning his own dream, he should be stern and must have the guts and the balls to take the big leap of plunging into his own doom or success. He should not be afraid of taking chances when opportunity strikes.
- *Energetic-* willing to do whatever it takes to reach to the finish line. His drive must always be at its highest level for being an entrepreneur would make you work overtime. His enthusiasm must prevail the next best thing.
- *Time bound-* like a written report in a newspaper, an entrepreneur must be on the top of every innovation. By looking at our past, we could predict our future.

So how can an entrepreneur be tailored to be one? What business skills are required in order to become an entrepreneur? There are pointers that must be looked into before someone may divulge into any business venture. These include the setting up and the attainment of specific goals, qualification to enter into a commitment, and then being able to keep up with work schedules. The following are some of the qualifications to look into Planning and organization.

The capacity to handle money- Budget must be carefully determined, loans must be secured, funds must be raised, and all of the finances must be recorded. For all these things, an entrepreneur must be an expert.The selling of products and ideas- An entrepreneur should be acquainted with the proper way of selling. In the world of business, the products whether they take the form of materials or ideas need to sell out in order to gain profit.

Management- Anyone who does not have the management skills is not fit to be an entrepreneur. The ability to work with people- A good rapport is always needed in an entrepreneur. If he is unable to influence people then he will not likely succeed.

Conclusion

In the field of business, the people involved in the playoffs are called the entrepreneurs. They are also referred to as businessmen. They own and run their own businesses. In the strictest sense, the definition of what a real entrepreneur is varies.In an online dictionary as defined by the Webster's Revised Unabridged Dictionary, in the year 1913, entrepreneur has been defined as the person who makes some products for his own benefit or account. This gives about the idea that the term has successfully evolved way back in the year 1913. Now such definition may quite be blurry.

How can a person be called an entrepreneur when he does nothing with that product aside form creating it? What term will be labeled to a person who takes other people's products and make a success out of them? Will they be not branded as entrepreneurs too? According to Merriam-Webster dictionary, an entrepreneur is someone who organizes, who manages, and who assumes the risks posed by the business or enterprise world. Now this definition of an entrepreneur is richer in content compared with the first one. Risks-these are literally faced by entrepreneurs as they pursue with any type of investment in the market.

In a much formal definition of Ashoka, an entrepreneur goes to refer to an organizational society that promotes nothing but social change. Social entrepreneurs are those individuals who open up some new and major possibilities in the areas of health, education, environment, and all other areas of the human needs.

To drive a stricter point, the business entrepreneurs are those who lead the innovations in the world of commerce while the social entrepreneurs are those who drive social change in the society. In more ways than one, such definition all the more points out that those business entrepreneurs not only start with any type of business but they do promote change within the business range. So how can an entrepreneur be tailored to be one? What business skills are required in order to become an entrepreneur? There are pointers that must be looked into before someone may divulge into any business venture.

No one is ever as enthusiastic and energized as someone propelled forward by a focused dream. But dreaming is not enough. Entrepreneurs are dreamers turned doers. Dreamers who envision a better product or an improved service. A solution for an age old problem or a convenience to make life a little better for others. Dream struck entrepreneurs have created opportunities for improved living from the automobiles that we drive to the pizza we get delivered.

Entrepreneurs build a better way by risking ideas, money and countless hours in order to complete their mission. When the entrepreneur also creates a better life for themselves through financial gain and the self-esteem that comes from accomplishment, the dream has come full circle. In the pages to follow, you will further define your dream. Even if you have not yet decided what you business should be, by exploring your interests and capabilities you can uncover a business idea right for you.

Dreaming is the easy part; doing is the challenge. You will also become aware of the things which are important to know and decide in order to make your business succeed. Building a business will impact how you live. Your energy, stamina and supportive family and friends will be important elements in your business venture. Entrepreneurs have personal characteristics which enable them to forge ahead and take on challenges. You will explore the characteristics of the successful entrepreneur and see for yourself how you stack up.

Are you ready for the challenge? Let's go...

2

Gwalior: An Overview

Madhya Pradesh economy largely depends on agriculture, industries and minerals. About 70% of the total work force of the state depends directly or indirectly on agriculture. Mines and industries play important roles in economic development of the state. There are many flourishing textile mills in the state and artificial silk manufacturing plants located at Ujjain, Nagda, Indore and Gwalior. Public sector industries including the Bhilai Steel plant, the Heavy Electrical and the Bailadilla are the major achievements. The Nepa Mills produces newsprint for the country. Diesel engines are manufactured at Indore and attractive pottery and carpets are produced at Gwalior.

A sizeable population in the villages makes traditional crafts such as chanderi sarees, leather and clay toys. Secondary industries such as dyeing, calico printing and bleaching have also tended to concentrate in areas producing handloom cloth, silk and wool products. The state's wood work and lacquer-ware are also very famous. Important minerals found in M.P. are coal and iron. High quality iron-ore is found in Bastar, Jabalpur and Gwalior. The Panna region is famous for its diamond belt and is well known for the production of diamonds. Bauxite and marble are also found in several districts of Madhya Pradesh.

Agriculture: Madhya Pradesh is one of the leading producers of pulses like urad, mung and arhar. About one-fifth of the country's total production of pulses comes from this state. Other crops produced in Madhya Pradesh are wheat, soya bean and mustard.

About Gwalior

Gwalior has kept pace with the times and has not rested on its past glory alone. A wave of industrialization and enterprise has been sweeping across and around this vibrant city of Madhya Pradesh, as indeed throughout the state capital, excellent infrastructure, and abundant resources the city has attracted many major corporate houses, Today it is home to world majors like Cadbury, Kodak, Hotline, SRF, Crompton, Godrej, Flex and Atlas among others.

Facilitating this revolution is the Madhya Pradesh Audyogik Kendra Vikas Nigam, which has set up seven industrial Growth Centers in the area. The purpose of these industrial areas and zones is to provide all infrastructure facilities at one place for development of a particular industry. AKVN Gwalior has proposed ten such centers which are: Food Parks at *Gwalior, Banmore, Chainpura, Nadantola and Morena, Apparel Park at Banmore, Transport Complex at Chainpura and Banmore and IID Centres at jaderua (Morena) & Pratappura*

The City of Gwalior in Madhya Pradesh is designated as Counter magnet city in the National Capital Region (NCR) plan- 1989. It is one at the counter magnet cities which are to play a role in reducting pressure on the growth of the Capital Region and the City of Delhi. The city of Gwalior with its size, distaning from Delhi and potential for growth is poised as a major economic player in the region.

Gwalior has also been declared as priority urban region of Madhya Pradesh. The city is the largest urban centre in the Gwalior Agra Region, Which comprises the Districts of Gwalior, Bhind, Morena, Sheopur, Guna, Datia and Shivpuri. The basic economic activity of the town in trade and commerce and Gwalior acts as the principal collection and distribution centre of the region. The city has a significant sociocultural status and rich architectural heritage. Gwalior town with its strategic location on the Delhi-Agra-Bombay route coupled with the presence of the majestic Gwalior fort makes it an important tourist town of India.

As a counter magnet, the city of Gwalior is expected to play two major functions:

- To stem the migration from less developed area of Madhya Pradesh to the capital city of Delhi.
- To act as regional growth centre and to help attain a balanced pattern of urbanization in the sub region.

For implementation of the counter magnet project, the Government of Madhya Pradesh in the year 1992, Constituted a Special Area Development Authority (SADA). The jurisdiction of SADA covers an area of 30,000 hectares of which 6,500 hectare is Government property; app. 9,000 hectare is privately owned; and over 14,500 hectare is reserve forest. This SADA area is hereafter referred to a Gwalior West because of its location of the western side of the City of Gwalior.

Gwalior City is a District in Madhya Pradesh State near Agra. The new section of the city called Lashkar. Lashkar is few miles south from the old city. It is the site of factories producing cotton, yarn, paint, ceramics, chemicals, and leather products. The nucleus of Gwalior is a citadel crowning an isolated rock about 91 m (300 ft) high, 3.2 km (2 mi) long, and 823 m (2700 ft) wide. The rock is said to have been a strong hold for more than Ten Centuries and Old city is located in the Eastern base of the rock. The old city is covered with white sandstone Mosque, Palaces, rock temples and statues of archaeological and architectural interest. The Jiwaji University was built in Gwalior in the year 1964. Gwalior City was the Capital of the princely State of Gwalior until 1948 and the summer Capital of Madhya Bharat State from 1948 to 1956. When Madhya Bharat became part of Madhya Pradesh, it becomes separate District. According to Census 2001, population of the District is 1629881.

Gwalior's history is traced back to a legend in 8th century AD when a chief tain known as Suraj Sen was struck by a deadly disease and cured by a hermit-saint Gwalipa. As a gratitude for that incidence, he founded this city by his name. The new city of Gwalior became existence over the centuries. The cradle of great dynasties ruled the city Gwalior. With different Dynasty, the city gained a new dimension from the warrior kings, poets, musicians, and saints who contributed to making it renowned throughout the country. The city is also the setting for the memorials of freedom fighters such as Tatya Tope and the indomitable Rani of Jhansi. Today the old settings stand side by side with the trappings of modernity.

Business in Gwalior

Business in Gwalior is influenced by two major forces. The first being the 'need' for the trade whiles the second reason being the potential for the stimulated demand. The 'need' for the trade caters to the consumption of the product by the residents of Gwalior; whereas the 'potential' looks after the additional trade activities taking place within the town. The need for trade in most of the growing towns in India is estimated to be about 1 square meter per person. Gwalior being a part of India cannot be an exception to this. Statistics prove that there is a scope for further development in the trade and commerce of Gwalior. The growth in the business in Gwalior has largely supported the agriculture and handicraft industries of the town.

Moreover, trade and commerce at Gwalior is also known to tap the international cargo trade. With the saturation of the commerce in Delhi with respect to the international cargo trade, Gwalior is emerging as one of the principle centers of the international cargo trade. Gwalior is situated in the Delhi-Agra-Bombay corridor; therefore, the town holds immense potential for the development of containerized or non-containerized cargo. Besides, the goods that are bound for the international market, as well as those sourced in the industrial towns are currently produced at Delhi. But, with the development of the infrastructure in Gwalior, the production of the goods can be initiated in Gwalior.

Demographic Characteristics of Gwalior

Table 1
Total Area Details of Gwalior

Total Area Details	
Total Area	5214.00 sq kms.
Forest Area	1091.79 sq kms
Net sown area	2601.42 sq.kms
No. of Households	209.12 thousands
Net irrigated area	911.93 sq.kms

Source: District Information office Gwalior

Table 2
Population Details of GwaliorPopulation Details

Total Population	
1412.61 thousands	Total Literates 661.59 thousands.
Total Males 770.85 thousands	Total Females 641.76 thousands.
Urban Population 830.45 thousands	Rural Population 582.16 thousands
Total Workers 436.73 thousands	Main Workers 403.58 thousands

Source: District Information office Gwalior

Table 3
Population Details of Gwalior City Wise

Town/Urban Area/ Urban City	*Status of Civilian in Town/Urban Area*	*Male*	*Female.*	*Total*
Gwalior (Nagar Nigam)		442484	384435	8269192
Morar (Cantt)	Cantt Area	22904	15977	388813
Antri	Nagar Panchayat	5061	4473	95344
Billaua	Nagar Panchayat	6115	5407	11522
Tekanpur	Populated town	8527	4292	128196
Pichore	Nagar Panchayat	6209	5516	117257
Dabra	Nagar Palika	30107	26558	566658
Bitarwar	Nagar Palika	8183	7083	15266

Table 4
Male/Female Ratio of Total Population

	Male/Female Ratio of Total Population		
Name of the District/Tehsil	*Total*	*Male*	*Female*
Gwalior	847	833	857
Gird	849	819	860
Pichore (Dabra)	839	850	820
Bhitarwar	847	843	873

Source: District Information office Gwalior

Table 5
Population Details on the Basis of Tehsil and District

District/Tehsil		Population			Literacy				
		Total	Male	Female			Male	Female	Total
District Gwalior	Total	1629881	882258	747623	964234	604587			
	Rural	646550	352668	293882	285269	202568	359647	82701	276946
	Urban	983331	529590	453741	678965	402019			
Tehsil Gird	Total	1177055	636484	540571	738523	450876			
	Rural	311255	171096	140159	133534	95485	287647	38049	249598
	Urban	865800	465388	400412	604989	355391			
Tehsil Pichore	Total	270028	146819	123209	139644	93578			
	Rural	177297	95861	81436	78980	55633	46066	23347	22719
	Urban	92731	50958	41773	60664	37945			
Tehsil Bhitarwar	Total	182798	98955	83843	86067	60133			
	Rural	157998	85711	72287	72755	51450	25934	21305	4629
	Urban	24800	13244	11556	13312	8683			

Source: District Information office Gwalior

Table 6

Male Female Ratio of Total Population, Region wise

Name of the District/Tehsil	*Male/Female Ratio of Total Population*								
	Total			*Rural*			*Urban*		
	Total	*Male*	*Female*	*Total*	*Male*	*Female*	*Total*	*Male*	*Female*
Gwalior	69.79	80.83	56.76	53.72	69.70	34.40	79.83	87.91	70.44
Gird	73.38	82.96	62.13	52.26	67.85	33.15	80.56	88.24	71.68
Pichore (Dabra)	62.41	76.49	45.43	54.51	70.60	35.33	76.92	87.14	64.33
Bhitarwar	56.87	73.19	37.49	55.69	72.35	35.78	64.37	78.57	48.07

Table 7
The Statistics of Gwalior

Head	Units	District	State	India
Relative CMIE Index of Development	Index	114.00	73.00	100.00
Population Growth per annum	%	2.48	2.40	2.14
Population Density (persons/Sq. Km.)	Nos.	270.93	149.24	273.60
Urbanisation	%	58.79	23.18	25.73
Literacy	%	57.70	44.20	52.21
Male Literacy	%	70.81	58.42	64.13
Female Literacy	%	41.72	28.85	39.29
Urban Literacy	%	71.04	70.81	73.08
Rural Literacy	%	37.91	35.87	44.69
Forest area as % of reporting area	%	20.92	31.78	21.82
Net sown area as % of reporting area	%	49.85	4.39	46.30
Gross irri. area as % of reporting area	%	37.93	13.42	30.72
Average size of operational holding	Hect.	2.86	2.91	1.69
Fertilizer consumption per Hect.	Kgs.	62	38	72
Value of output of major crops / hectare	Rs.	3321	2170	3576
Value of output of major crops / capita	Rs.	667	755	758
Per capita food grains production	Kgs.	203	208	173
Road length per 100 Sq. Km.	Kms.	–	28.37	60.14
Rai' 'ay route length per 100 Sq. Km.	Kms.	–	1.33	2.04
Post . fices per lakh population	Nos.	–	16.70	17.93
Telegraph offices per lakh population	Nos.	–	5.01	4.93
Telephones per lakh population	Nos.	–	460	800
Bank branches per lakh population	Nos.	8.21	6.67	7.30
Per capita bank deposits	Rs.	3697	1427	3269
Per capita bank credits	Rs.	2142	890	1978
Per capita bank credit to agriculture	Rs.	147	181	222
Per hectare bank credit to agriculture	Rs.	730	521	1046
Per capita bank credit to SSI	Rs.	315	97	185
Per capita bank credit to industries	Rs.	1021	317	705
Data Source	–	–	–	GISTNIC

Source: District Information office Gwalior

Tourism in Gwalior

The Fort Standing on a steep mass of sandstone, Gwalior Fort dominates the city and is its most significant monument. It has been the scene of momentous events, imprisonment, battles and jauhars. A steep road winds upwards to the fort, flanked by statues of the Jain tirthankaras, carved into the rock face. The magnificent outer walls of the fort still stand, two miles in length and 35 feet high, bearing witness to its reputation for being one of the most invincible forts of India. This imposing structure inspired Emperor Babur to describe it as "the pearl amongst the fortresses of Hind ".

Gujari Mahal

Within the fort are some marvels of medieval architecture. The 15th century Gujari Mahal is a monument to the love of Raja Mansingh Tomar for his intrepid Gujar Queen, Mrignayani. The outer structure of Gujari Mahal has survived in an almost total state of preservation; the interior has been converted into Archaeological Museum housing rare antiquities, some of them dating back to the 1st century A.D. Even though many of these have been defaced by the iconoclastic Mughals , their perfection of form has survived the ravages of time. Particularly worth seeing is the statue of Shalbhanjika from Gyraspur, the tree goddess, the epitome of perfection in miniature. The statue is kept in the custody of the museum's curator, and can be seen on request.

Man Mandir Palace

Man Mandir Palace is built between 1486 and 1517 by Raja Mansingh. The tiles that once adorned its exterior have not survived, but at the entrance, traces of these still remain. Within the palace rooms' stand bare, stripped of their former glory, testifying to the passing of the centuries. Vast chambers with fine stone screens were once the music halls, and behind these screens, the royal ladies would learn music from the great masters of the day. Below, circular dungeons housed the state prisoners of the Mughals. Emperor Aurangzeb had his brother, Murad imprisoned, and later executed here. Close by is Jauhar Pond, where in the Rajput tradition, the Ranis committed mass sati after their consorts had been defeated in battle. At Man Mandir Palace, a poignant ambience of those days of chivalry and heroism still lingers in the silent chambers. A superbly mounted Son-et-Lumiere here brings it all alive everything.

Ghaus Mohammed's Tomb

The sandstone mausoleum of the Afghan prince, Ghaus Mohammed, is also designed on early Mughal lines. Particularly exquisite are the screens which use the pierced stone technique as delicate as lace. It is on the way to Gwalior fort near Hazira from Railway Station.

Gopachal

Gopachal Parvat - situated on the Mountain Area at slopes of Gwalior Fort carries uniquestatue of Jain Tirthankars. The largest Idol of Bhagwan Parshwanath on Lotus is the largest statue (in single stone piece) in the world, being 47 feet high and 30 feet in width. 26 Jain statues in a series give a beautiful and attractivce picturescue. Built between 1398 to 1536 by Tomar Kings .These Jain Tirthankars Statues are a species of Architecture and a treasure of Old Indian heritage and culture.

Sun Temple

Located near the Residency at Morar, the newly constructed Sun Temple takes its inspiration from the famous Konark Sun Temple in Orissa. Distance from Railway Station/Bus Stand: 5.00 Kms. Approx.

Sarod Ghar

This Museum of Music has been set up in the old ancestral house of the legendary Ustad Hafiz Ali Khan. It houses ancient instruments of the great Indian Masters of yesteryears. It also houses an impressive collection of photographs and documents. Sarod Ghar is a unique institution devoted to promoting Indian classical music, heritage and culture. Through this 'window' to the past, music lovers can gain a better understanding of the evolution and history of our classical music and a deeper perspective and insight into the context of the art as it exists today.

Jai Vilas Palace and Museum

A splendor of a different kind exists in the Jai Vilas Palace, current residence of the Scindia family. Some 25 rooms have been turned into the Jivaji Rao Scindia Museum, and in these rooms, so evocative of a regal lifestyle, the past comes alive. Jai Vilas is an Italianate structure which combines the Tuscan and Corinthian architectural modes. The imposing Darbar Hall has two central chandeliers weighing a couple of tones, and hung only after ten elephants had tested the strength of the roof. Ceilings picked out in gilt, heavy draperies and tapestries, fine Persian carpets and antique furniture from France and Italy are the features of these spacious rooms. Eye catching treasures include: a silver train with cut glass wagons which served guests as it chugged around the table on miniature rails; a glass cradle from Italy used for the baby Krishna each Janmashtami, silver dinner services and swords that were once worn by Aurangzeb and Shah Jahan. These are, besides, personal mementoes of past members of the Scindia family: the jeweled slippers that belonged to Chinkoo Rani , four-poster beds, gifts from practically every country in the world, hunting trophies and portraits. The Scindia Museum offers an unparallel glimpse into the rich culture and lifestyle of princely India.

Gwalior Industries

Gwalior industries have earned the status of a counter magnet in NCR in India. Gwalior is one of the vibrant industrial bases that are known for its strategic location. The industries at Gwalior are emerging as industrial estates that are managed by independent industrial development corporations. The independent industrial development corporations are working towards developing the industries of Gwalior. In fact, any development that is conceived for strengthening the counter magnet role of Gwalior would lead to the industrial development of Gwalior as a potential sector.Moreover, the potential for the industrial development of Gwalior lies in the establishment of integrated industrial estates. The industrial estates in Gwalior are replete with the common facilities that are required by the industries of Gwalior. It is noteworthy in this context that the existing industrial areas are responsible for the proliferation of the industries in Gwalior. According to AKVN, 1994, about 60% of the total industrial areas (33222 acres of land) in Malanpur Ghirongi Industrial Areas is to be allotted for the expansion of the industries in Gwalior. Statistics also prove that about 142 industrial units would be needed by 2010. The industries at Gwalior include the textile mills and the artificial silk manufacturing plants. The handicraft and hand loom industry also form an important part of the industries in Gwalior. Morar is said to be the center of local trade. It is also known to house the tanning industry in Gwalior.

Industries

There are 67 small scale industries are operational in the Industrial development Centre Banmore of Morena district. 23 small scale working industries are operational elsewhere in the district. 8 medium & 3 large scale industries are also operational in Industrial development Centre Banmore. There are 2 exports units.

Table 8
Medium and Large Scale Industries in Industrial Area Banmore

Name of the Industry	*Name of the Product*	*No. of Employees*
J.K. Industries (tyre plant) Ltd.	Automobile nylon and radial tyre	1610
Gwalior milk centre	Butter,ghee,skimmed milk	5783
Punj Layad Ltd.	Heavy basels noyan control system	58
Phorcein rubber Ltd.	Automobile tube	
Consolidated steel and alloy Ltd.	Steel products	161
Sterling Malt and food Pvt. Ltd.	Warle Malt	
M.P.Cellulose Pvt. Ltd.	Nitro Cellulose	
Gwalior Steel Pvt. Ltd.	Steel Casting	35

Source: District Information office Gwalior

Table 9
Medium and large Scale Industries in Morena (Other than Banmore)

Name of the Industry	*Name of the Product*	*No. of Employees*
Morena mandal sehkari shakkar karkhana	Sugar	200
Rajya parivahan tilhan sehkari sangh	Oil cake	125
K.S. oils Ltd.	Solvent Oil D oil cake	50

Source: District Information office Gwalior

Table 10
Industries Industrial Development Centre Banmore

Particulars	*In Industrial Development Centre Banmore*	*In Distt. Other Than Banmore*
Small Scale Industries(working)	67	23
Medium large Scale industries(working)	04	03
Export units	02	

Source: District Information office Gwalior

Table 11
Export Units in Morena District

Name of the Unit	Name of the Product	No. of Employees
J.K.Industries Ltd. Industrial area Banmore	Tyre, Tubes	1040
K.S. Oils Ltd. Industrial area Morena	Oil	50

Source: District Information office Gwalior

Malanpur & Ghirongi are the Twin Industrial Growth Centers

These centers are being promoted and managed by AKVN Gwalior. The industrial areas have attracted more than 100 manufacturing units. Included in these are some of India's most reputed corporates. Though a part of district Bhind these centers are virtually suburbs of Gwalior, being only 10 kms from the city limits. Gwalior is easily accessible from both Delhi and Bhopal. The city lies on the main North-South railway track of Northern Railway. National Highway 3, the Agra-Bombay road also passes through Gwalior. The city is connected to Mumbai, Indore, Bhopal and Delhi via air route too. Malanpur & Ghirongi already house 117 Large, Medium and Small manufacturing units of which 10 are Export Ortiented Units and 1 is 100% Export Ortiented Unit.

Estate Features

Area

- Malanpur 625. Hechares. Ghirongi 833 Hectares
- 320 MVA on 220 KV and 6OMVA on 132 KV supply.
- Power available on LT, 11 KV, 33 KV. 132 KV and 220 KV. Power cut relaxation is available

Water

- Water is in surplus. Total availability of water is 6 MGD. At present, 1.5 MGD water is being consumed in the Industrial Area. 1 MGD Treatment Plant is in full operation.

Transportation

- Indian Airlines connects Gwalior with Delhi, Indore, and Mumbai & Jabalpur. Malanpur-Ghirongi IGC is just 10 minutes drive from the Gwalior Air Port. Helipad is also available at Malanpur.

- Gwalior is 110 Km. from Agra & 317 Km. from Delhi on NH-3.
- Gwalior is on the Delhi-Chennai and Delhi-Mumbai broad gauge line. It is very well connected by rail to Delhi, Mumbai and major South Indian cities.

Banmore

This is one of the major growth centers in Madhya Pradesh and is located strategically just 18 kilometers from Gwalior in the Morena district on the Agra-Mumbai National Highway. It has attracted large and medium scale projects and another 82 small scale projects with an aggregate investment of over Rs.300 acres. It is home for the well known JK Tyres. Facilities like street-lighting, shopping complex, telecommunications links with Gwalior have also been created.

Estate Features

- Only 18 kilometres from Gwalior on the Agre-Mumbai National Highway.
- 4 large and medium scale projects
- 82 small scale projects
- Aggregate investment of over Rs. 300 crores
- Available Area 289 hectares
- 239 hedares for industrial projects
- 189 hectares already allotted
- Water availability of 15 lakh liters per day.
- Street Lighting
- Shopping complexes

Main Industries in the Region

1. National Fertilizer Limited, Vijaipur,Guna
2. Gas Authority of India Limited, Vijaipur, Guna
3. Solvent Extractions Units

4. Sugar Industry
5. J. B. Mangaram Company Limited, Gwalior
6. Grasim (Birla Group)
7. Potteries
8. Leather
9. Railway Spring Factory
10. Rubber Products
11. Food Processing
12. Bina Power Supply Company Limited (Grasim Group), Bina (Proposed)
13. Bharat Oman Refinery Ltd. Bina (Proposed joint venture of BPCL & Sultanate of Oman).

Development Perspective of Gwalior

The existing city of Gwalior has a rich history and distinct character of its own. Serving as the seat of the powerful Maratha kingdom - the city wielded its influence in a large region around it. Many of the economic activities in the region (mostly agriculture) have traditionally been traded here. The city continues to be the predominant centre for trade and commerce till date. Additionally, it has also maintained its role as the seat of administration.

The Marathas were powerful and a wealthy dynasty-as a result art, education and cultural flourished in the city. Till date, the city continues to attract a large number of tourists to its magnificent monuments that stand testimony to its glorious past. The standards to education in the institutes established by the earlier monarchy compete with the very best in India.

In terms of physical growth, Gwalior is a tri-nodal city consisting of - Old Gwalior settlement around the fort, Lashkar-area developed by the marathas and Morar-the British cantonment. These were established at different periods in history. In recent decades, all three settlements have witnessed increase in size and population resulting in almost contiguous urban growth.

The population growth in the city has been sluggish in the recent decades (between 1971-1991) growing at a uniform rate of 3.5% annually. On the other hand, growth in neighbouring towns of Morena and Bhind has been phenomenal during the same period reflecting a potential for overall growth of the region.

The occupational pattern for Gwalior city indicates a slight shift from the manufacturing sector to the commercial sector during the same period. While the industrial growth within the city limits seems to have slowed down, there is further increase in the trade and commerce activities. The trend also indicates that large increase in industrial workforce has apparently been absorbed in the neighboring towns of Morena and Bhind.

The current economic base of the city remains commerce. There is a large component of the workforce in the service sector too which includes tourism. However, it has been observed that tourist infrastructure in the city is not present in proportion to the tourist potential of the town. There is thus a large scope for growth in this sector.

The Gwalior Development Plan 2005 (Draft) prepared by the Directorate of Town and Country Planning, Madhya Pradesh proposes to retain the traditional economic activities of the city, i.e. Commerce and Industry. There is an equal allocation of land for industrial and commercial activity for the horizon year with total increase of 75% in the land area for these sectors. While the stated sectors do have potential for growth in future, further diversification in the economic base of the city is required for the city to emerge as an effective counter magnet to the NCR.

The Development Plan for Gwalior has proposed to retain the existing form of the city as a combination of three sub-cities by integrating them physically without letter them loose their individual identities. The Plan proposes to develop a number of relatively self-contained planning units with each unit meant to function as a distinct entity in respect of local level shopping, primary education.

A total area of 4331 Ha. Presently is proposed to be increased to 7481 Ha for development of urban uses. However, the real increase in population is proposed to be absorbed within existing areas through redensification. The present ratio of 5.4 persons/1000 Ha is proposed to be increased by almost 40% to 7.0 persons per 1000 Ha.

In light of development trends and proposals for Gwalior city, the role and function of the new settlement (Gwalior West) needs to integrate it existing city as well as complement and boost the functions traditionally related to Gwalior.

Market Potential for Proposed Sectors

In order to investigate the potential for new sectors, a need and demand analysis was carried out. This section summarizes the results of the Techno Economic Feasibility Study and Demand Analysis for the proposed sectors. In case of Gwalior West, the demand analysis was carried out for the following urban uses based on the regional economic indicators as well as the traditional roles and functions of Gwalior that can provide a fresh impetus to growth in the city.

Tourism

Gwalior holds the potential of emerging as a major tourist centre due to its historic background, strategic regional setting and multi-functional character. The Majestic Gwalior Fort located in a region also known for tourist sports such as Agra, Orchcha, Khajuraho provides appropriate setting for promotion of heritage based tourism. Also, the plan of the Department of Tourism, Government of India, proposes to promote five major tourist circuits in the country one of which is the Agra-Gwalior-Jhansi-Orchcha-Khajuraho circuit. The terrain of the region and the presence of wildlife in the region present vast opportunities for the promotion of adventure tourism in the region. The Tighra Reservoir with its idyllic natural settings holds potential for development of large-scale tourist complex comprising holiday resorts, water sport, sports complexes etc. This can form an extension to the existing Madhav National Park, which is already part of the national nature and wildlife circuit.

The annual trade fair held in Gwalior is a major event in the Gwalior Region and presents opportunities for further growth and expansion, If combined with the existing industrial base of Gwalior.

It may be concluded, thus, that the twin cities of Gwalior and Gwalior West together can attract a large number of tourists, in all three categories of : (i) heritage and culture, (ii) Adventure, and (iii) Business tourism. It is estimated that with improved tourist facilities and services, the average daily accumulation may increase to 8669 to 2010 from the present levels of 2712 (1994), but is subject to expansion of appropriate hotel facilities.

Education

Gwalior has traditionally served as a seat of learning and has a rich heritage of quality education established by the Scindias. It is strategically located along major north south, and northwest corridors of the country. Currently, there are a large number of applicants for medical and engineering studies each year. In the northern states, the number of such applicants every year is above 40,000. However, the distribution of professional colleges in the country is skewed with the number of colleges in the southern states exceeding those in the north. As a result every year, a large number of students in the north who are not able to obtain admission, choose to apply to colleges in the south especially the private ones where admission is available on payment. According to studies carried out by the consultants, there are about 25,000 to 30,000 students who migrate to colleges in south each year. Considering Gwalior's proximity to Delhi and strategic links to the north coupled with growing industrial base of the region, it is possible to attract a large number of students by offering good quality technical education. At even very conservative estimates, the number of students could vary between 1400 and 14373 as per current growth trends.

Industry

Industries are now coming up in a planned manner in integrated industrial estates which are developed and managed by independent industrial development corporations. The importance of Gwalior as a vibrant industrial base lies its strategic location and the status given to it of a counter magnet to the National Capital Region. It is imperative therefore that any development envisaged as part of its counter magnet role should consider industrial development as a potential sector that could offset much of the primacy effect of Delhi.

The potential for industrial development lies in establishment of integrated industrial estates which are industry specific replete with common facilities required by the industry. The existing industrial areas of Gwalior are likely to absorb the growth of industry in the next few years as large areas are still left to be allocated. (Out of 33222 acres of land in Malanpur Ghirongi Industrial Areas, 60% is still available for allotment, source-AKVN, 1994). As such the growth of industry in Gwalior West may pick up only after the existing areas are completely saturated. Based on current growth trends, there would scope for development of small Scale Industries and Large & Medium Scale in Gwalior West. It is estimated that by 2010, land for 142 industrial units would be required.

Trade and Commerce

This sector considers the development of trade and commerce in a new town as influenced by two major forces: basic need for trade in the town, and potential for induced demand. While basic need is that which caters to the day to day consumption requirements of the town's inhabitants, induced demand potential is that sector which covers scope for additional trade activities in the town as a form of economic base.

It has been recorded that in the medium sized growing towns, the need for basic commerce is in the range of 1 sq.m per person. It is expected that the need arising for resident population of Gwalior West would also be in this range. There is a market potential for further developing Gwalior as a regional market centre. Such a role is being played by Gwalior already, however the scope can be further increased to meet specialized needs of agriculture, handicraft and industries in the region.

In addition to the regional needs, there is scope of tapping international cargo trade, as the current capacity of Delhi is reaching saturation levels as cargo traffic continues to grow. Being located on the Delhi-Agra-Bombay corridor, Gwalior can attract a portion of the containerized/non-containerized cargo by establishing Freight complex facilities. Goods bounds for international market and sourced at industrial towns such as Moradabad, Ferozabad, Kanpur and other which are currently packed and dispatched from Delhi can be diverted to Gwalior if adequate infrastructure is provided.

The sector considers the possibility of Gwalior West being able to attract offices of few public sector undertakings currently located in Delhi in compliance to the National Capital Region Plan and the Master Plan for Delhi. The National Capital Region Plan - 2001 has identified the decentralization of economic activities in the region as one of the driving factors towards the success of the entire plan. This decentralization not only aims at shifting of industrial limits from the National Capital but also a number of central government (subordinate officers) and offices of public sector undertakings which have been functioning from Delhi for the last two to three decades.

If adequate facilities are provided in Gwalior West, it may be able to attract Public Sector Officer as per the NCR plan. High levels of service in terms of convenient connectivity to Delhi Housing and Social infrastructure and a strong labour base can provide conditions for setting up integrated Public Sector Officers cum Residential complexes within Gwalior West. Out of the total of 18 Public Sector Offices with a total employee strength of 13343 (SCOPE, 1995), which have been listed for shifting out of Delhi, at least 25% of these may be attracted to relocate in Gwalior West. This can be accomplished with an aggressive promotional Programme.

Housing

Housing is proposed to be developed as a major activity of the new city offering variety both in terms of size and quality promoted through private initiatives. The major demand is expected to be from the development of use functions within

Gwalior West and spill over of housing requirement from Gwalior City.

It was observed that the current rate of supply of housing is decreasing, even if current rate is maintained at supply of 2000 dwelling units annually, there would be an estimated net demand of 68579 units by 2005. The real demand for housing in Gwalior West, however, would be from the economic opportunities that would emerge in the city. By combining the two demand sources (I) spillover of demand from Gwalior, and (ii) demand from the labor force of the economic activities of Gwalior West, it is estimated that housing would need to cater to approximately 174000 households by 2010. The results of the demand analysis have, on the basis of the potential dean, classified the above sectors in form of Growth Stimulators, Growth Accelerators and Growth Sustaining Factors. The analysis by providing a projection of economic activities has enabled in arriving at the level and type of employment for Gwalior West. This exercise has formed the core of the planning exercise.

Integration with Gwalior

The study of the market potential, while providing specific growth indices for Gwalior West has treated both cities as an integrated whole where the old and the new city complement each other functionally. Considering the basic role and function of Gwalior city region-Commerce, Industry, Tourism and Education; the plan for Gwalior West provides for activities in the same categories. The Development Plan for Gwalior 2005 provides a major boost to Commerce and Industry within Gwalior Planning Area; the plan for Gwalior West envisages enhanced growth of Tourism and Private Education sectors which would act as stimulators to growth. The new city promises an improved quality of life through better housing (in form of low density plotted development) and state of art decentralized infrastructure system. In order to facilitate functional integration of the two settlements, the plan proposes direct road linkages between Airport, Existing CBD of Gwalior through improvement of existing road links (Tighra Road).

Conclusion

To make better understanding to the Students, who are very eager to become Entrepreneur the needs, support, resources and risk related to starting a new venture in detail it is necessary to provide them some practical college. To give a first experience of students we assign a opportunity to meet local Entrepreneurs and to find out their entrepreneurship style and attitudes towards business and by doing so, it was aimed that students gained some basic knowledge about Entrepreneurship as they may perceive in future. Since Gwalior has its own Advantages not only in Tourism but also in Industries, it is a big opportunity for Students to meet different types of entrepreneurs in the Gwalior. So our Next chapter is explaining the details of case study that our Students have done.

3

Case Study on Social Entrepreneurs and their Entrepreneur Style

Since time immemorial, the Indian business segment has been dominated by family-run businesses, with most of them hailing from traditional, money-lending or trading communities, known for their sharp business acumen. Moreover, entrepreneurship in the Indian scenario has long been associated with the 'Tatas', 'Birlas' or 'Ambanis'. However, with many first-generation entrepreneurs bombarding the Indian business sector in the recent years, this trend has taken a back seat. Although these legendary business houses have played a major role in the country's business scenario, majority of the Indian start-ups in the recent past, are the brainchild of first-generation, middle-class entrepreneurs. The economic reforms and liberalisation have rekindled the latent entrepreneurial streak of the Indian people, making entrepreneurship a desired choice of career. Further, easy access to resources and growing social acceptance has encouraged many Indians to jump on to the entrepreneurship bandwagon. Driven by the aim of creating ventures based on feasible business models and backed by innovative ideas, these new entrepreneurs are not leaving any stone unturned.

Nevertheless, this sudden splurge in entrepreneurship has also given rise to many apprehensions. Are these entrepreneurs dedicated towards building world-class companies which shall weave long-term success stories? How many of these entrepreneurs will be able to make a mark like the legendary business firms of the Tatas and Birlas? The numbers of businesses per thousand residents in an area is known as the enterprise rate and the difference in the rate between areas is known as the enterprise gap. The enterprise gap is at its maximum in some inner city areas. Small business ownership can be a route out of unemployment and exclusion. It can also offer a more flexible way of working. Women and people from ethnic minorities have much lower levels of entrepreneurship than would be expected however. Setting up a business requires certain skills and experiences which people in deprived areas can be more likely to lack.

The case studies that follow each have a number of common features. Each case study deals with design and development issues and each highlights the importance of developing sound marketing strategies including market research. The hurdles which they face and their future plans are also covered.

Case No 1.
Mr. Parminder Singh (Volga Restaurant)

Mr. Parminder is an example of those kinds of persons who did not follows market strategies; they derive strategies on their own and follow them. Mr. Parminder Singh did his graduation in Commerce. His father is matriculate and he had experience about the trade due to his inheritance. His father moved to Gwalior from Indore and started the business in 1961.

Business Idea: Mr. Parminder started the business with a small amount of Rs. 9000. He chooses the business in which his father is already involved but changed the whole setup and acquired land at a different place. One day he was sitting in a restaurant and he was really dissatisfied with their service, then he decided to open up a new restaurant and his restaurant will ensures Quality to his customers.

Initial Phase: Mr. Parminder started the business with a small amount of Rs. 9000.he did not faced any major problems that may be faced by others during the startup of the business. This is all possible due to his dedication and hard work for his business and knows how to take advantage of his father's experience.

Strategy: Mr. Parminder greeted each and every customer with a sense of responsibility and he ensured that his customers get a good service and timely delivery of orders. In the initial days of his startup his customers are general residents, college students and office working, Quality and Transparency has been his motives in order to put the restaurant in its place

Hurdles: Mr. Parminder Singh did not faced any major problem since, everything was well planned and carved out in correct manner but the Biggest hurdle he faced was he had to close his shop for a year due to a judicial case on asset at Patenkar bazaar but he remained calm and moved the restaurant and started to grow again..

Future: The future plan of Mr. Parminder reflects his dedication and his hard work. He is planning to expand his restaurant. The construction work is going on at present too. He hopes to increase the market capitalization by increasing the goodwill of his place. He also wants to open chain of his restaurant in Gwalior and when he had enough capital with him then he will go for branding of his restaurant like as McDonald. In future he also wants to do business on internet, that order your items on internet and they will deliver these items at your home within half hour of your placing the orders.

Views on Entrepreneurship: "Honesty and quality are the best policies, Patience and Persistence would also be the key virtues to be looked upon."

Case No 2.
Mr. Rajat Bhamri (Junk yard PhoolBagh)

Mr. Rajat Bhamri is a true example of young Entrepreneur. He was born in 1984 at Gwalior. He completed his childhood education that is from 1 to 8 from Carmel Convent Higher Secondary School Gwalior and then he joins Kendriya Vidyalaya No. 2 at Gwalior. After completing his 12th education he wants to gain business Knowledge but due to family constraint he did Engineering. He did his job for 3-4 years then he starts his own business.

Business Idea: Mr. Rajat Bhamri was not from a high business family but he had already decided to do his own business. Firstly he told his older brother Karan Bhamri that he wants to start business of their own and they decide to open a show room which can provides lots of different quality which can make it different it from the other show room at Gwalior.

Initial Phase: Mr. Rajat was doing job before starting his own business. So he had already good amount in his own account to start his own business but he got full support from his family members also. They together start business .Firstly they start from their home. They used to sell lots of stocks at their home then after open a single Showroom at Shivaji Tower Gwalior name as Junk Yard. At that time they had enough money to run their own business.

Strategy: Mr. Rajat opened multipurpose showroom. First thing he is trying to make his showroom totally different from other showrooms. So he starts his business with a little stock. He brought those items by which he can make more and more customers. For it he did lots of advertisements and a lots of add so that he can attract more and more people. After some time there was enough people who can know, what basically JUNK YARD is and for what purpose.

Hurdles: Mr. Rajat Bhamri was mentally strong to start his business but at the same time he was not too confident about the resources so he did job first to make some money and after getting enough money he start his own business. When he plan to open a showroom the main problems there were where will be the suitable place to open, rent of the building, funds and how to manage all those things as well as the political issues like to tax etc.

Views on Entrepreneurship: "When a new business is started then it takes some time in getting customers, we have to build a trust with the customer and when that happens our customers increase and so our profit."

Case No 3.
Mr. Neeraj Singh Tomar (Tomar Electronics)

Mr. Neeraj Singh Tomar is an example of self made entrepreneur and a kind of person who never gives up. he started the business on his own and today results shows that his hard work has really paid him. He was educated up to high school from his childhood; he had the intention of setting up his own venture. He tried many business such as lottery, woolen clothes etc but they failed. After the failure of business he had only experience left with him.

Business Idea: Mr. Neeraj has no one with him after failures, but his dedication and passion forced him to continue with the work and he started trying himself to gather knowledge about recent electronics. Since there was no other electronic shop in the vicinity, he acquired sufficient knowledge and then he started to set up his electronics shop. That time he merely started it with coolers and radios and now he offers full range of appliances.

Initial Phase: Mr. Neeraj started his venture in 2005 with an initial capital of Rs 30,000. He somehow managed to gather the capital for the shop and equipments from his friend and brother. Initially he is not getting many customers, but gradually his Customer base increases at a very good pace due to his Quality Service and his marketing strategies.

Strategy: Mr. Neeraj utilized his networks and adopted a very good selling policy on installment basis due to which he was able to get initial base of customer. He gave customer profit sharing on referring the customers to him. In order to have a large customer base he is laying all efforts in ensuring quality services to the customers.

Hurdles: Mr. Neeraj faced many hurdles in his life. After the failure of his starting business of Lottery and woolen clothes, his friend stopped working with him and relatives also not having good feeling for him. Mr. Neeraj faced some problems at first regarding his new startup in terms of money and establishment, but after these he never looked back.

Future: The future Plan of Mr. Neeraj reflects passion, hard work and willingness to do something on own in proper direction. He is planning to establish chains of his shops in different localities in Gwalior and after this he wants to expand his business outside Gwalior and wants to make his shop as Brand.

Views on Entrepreneurship: "Good knowledge in one's field is an essential component of entrepreneurship, first set up priorities and then uses knowledge in order to achieve those priorities."

Case No 4.
Mr. Sumit Agrawal (Ashok Radios)

Mr. Sumit Agrawal was very dedicated towards electronics and was always enthusiastic to experiment new things. He was born in a middle class family. His father is running the electronics shop so he was very much attached to this business from starting and and now he runs his father's electronics shop and he has also set up his own laboratory at home for research work.

Business Idea: Mr. Sumit Agarwal did his engineering from NIT Jaipur in Electronics. but still he is not getting handsome package in any company, so he decided to join his father's shop as it was his passion to always do something research oriented as he was brought up in that environment.

Initial Phase: Mr. Sumit joined his family business, so he didn't required to invest money at starting but to expand his business he invested approx. 4-5 lakhs initially and this money was saved by him when he worked as a junior engineer at a private firm before he joined his family business and now he is also working as a faculty in private colleges to raise funds for investing more in his shop and take it to new levels.

Strategy: Mr. Sumit knows that generation is changing and now everyone is attracted towards new electronic gadgets. The strategy used by him was so simple, he uses electronics waste material to prepare something useful for others. This will reduces the cost and everyone wants electronics items it at minimum cost. His major customers are of age 16-25 as this is the age when people want to get more at less cost so they can easily get here on his shop. He also helps Students from various colleges to develop their projects.

Hurdles: Mr. Sumit did not face any big hurdles till now, since he is still on phase of developing his business. And he has always got his family support if any problem has ever occurred to him. He was taking care of his family business, so he had not face any problems related to money and establishment of shop which is the common problems faced by the Entrepreneurs.

Future: The future plan of Mr. Sumit is to make his shop nationally famous and he wants to provide new technology to India at cheaper rates and he is ready to do as much hard work required for it. His main aim is that India should never be behind in technology and technology should touch the very common people of India.

Views on Entrepreneurship: "you should be hard working dedicated towards your work for achieving anything."

Case No 5.
Mr. M.M. Moondra (Tanishq)

Mr. M.M. Moondra is currently owner of TANISHQ (Franchise of Tata Enterprise) and TITAN EYE + (Franchise of TITAN). Before starting this business he was an industrial distributer of jewels for many companies. Mr. M.N. Moodra took this Tata franchise in 2003. He did graduation in Hindi and English both but due to his family jewellery business, he was interested in it.

Business Idea: Mr. M.M. Moondra is very inventive kind of person. He realizes in the early phase, that after some time peoples go for branded jewellery instead of local. So he took the franchisee of Jewellery. It took some time to establish this franchisee but after some time Customers realizes that "branded jewellery is not very costly".

Initial Phase: Mr. Moondra invested approximately 3-4 crores in starting the business. Mr. Moondra had business background, financially they were very strong but it was a big venture so they took some loan from bank to meet financial needs. During that time skilled labor are not available easily, so He hires Good labor and then trained them and now they are growing very rapidly.

Strategy: Mr. Moondra focused on first class of customers because these high class customers were always fond of branded jewellery and new type of designs. So Mr. Moondra understood their needs and served good quality with new designs. After maintain the good business they focused on middle class customers also. They tried to sell jewellery that was at good price.

Hurdles: In the career of Mr. Moondra finance was not a hurdle for him. Main problem they faced was "managing the business" because his brothers were living in Mumbai so he was not able to help him directly and after some time they opened another franchise of Titan. The business of Mr. Moondra is growing at a good pace but on the other hand problem of "managing the business" is also increasing.

Future: The future plans of Mr.Moondra reflects his ambition to grow big and bigger. His future plans include expansion of business in jewellery and to open up another franchise related to this business. He is also trying to provide latest designs for Gwalior's people form various part of India.

Views on Entrepreneurship: "Honesty, Quality of service you providing, *Dedication* for hard work, *Passion toward your business."*

Case No 6.
Mr. Manoj Yadav (Yadav Enterprises)

Mr. Manoj Yadav runs a local computer centre and computer printing centre at moti-ramani complex lashkar kampoo Gwalior. He completed the graduation in 1993 and completed his 1 year PGDCA in 1994 and immediately started the business at home. he achieved success in his work only due to his hard work and his to become boss of your own.

Business Idea: Mr. Manoj started this business as a hobby which later became his need as the time progressed. He started his business with two computers and starting getting work form banks and government Offices. After 3 years in 1997 he got a rented shop in a residential area in year 2003-04.

Initial Phase: During Start up of the business Mr. Yadav requires finance, man labour, computer appliances to run the business. Mr. Yadav invested around 50 thousand rupees in 1994. He acquired all finance form home and took no loan or any other kind of partnership.

Strategy: Mr. Yadav targeted customers are mainly students of colleges and school. Students have to submit their reports and other paper work and some school gives him some paper work. Some of customers are the local offices in the vicinity and also gets some work from public and government offices.

Hurdles: The major hurdles which come across Mr. Yadav are related to finance and stiff competition. Since many computer and printing centre are now available in the city. he overcomes these hurdles by making strong bond with its customers and making many permanent customers and also started a side business of stock brokerage.

Future: The future Plans of Mr. Manoj Yadav includes maintain of the current status of firm, upgrading in services and expanding his business. He also wants to achieve remarkable success in Stock Brokerage. He has a vision to expand his shop to other locations of Gwalior and in other cities. His aim is to open the chain of his shop and website for his shop.

Views on Entrepreneurship: "start a business not at very large scale but still earn small profits and make it expand and not without taking any help from outside either in form loan or partnership."

Case No 7.
Mr. Ashok Agarwal (Mufti Outlet in DD Mall)

Mr. Ashok Agarwal was very keen to explore new things and to meet strangers. He always wanted to go new places and wanted to make new things out of trash things. His father was a government servant. In his childhood he had to face a big tragedy, he lost his father in his early age. Now circumstances were like he had to grow up quickly. Some he had completed his graduation (B.Com.) from Bhim Rao Ambedkar University, Agra. His childhood passed in Agra but now he is in Gwalior.

Business Idea: Mr. Ashok Agarwal did B.Com. He knew about commercialization, one thing was clear in his mind that he is going do his own business. So one day he was just sitting and thinking how to start our business. Now he got an idea in his mind that he will open a ready-made garment shop in some mall. So he collected money somehow and took a shop in DD Mall and opened a franchise shop 'Mufti'. He contacted 'mufti' and then opened a outlet in DD Mall.

Initial Phase: Mr. Ashok Agarwal spent 50 lakh initially to hire the shop and he is paying them 10 thousand per month. The entire garment they are getting their merchandise from different companies like mufti, Denim and some others. Thus still he is not franchisee. His business is based on LLC (Limited Liability Company).

Strategy: Mr. Ashok Agarwal targeted young generation, because style shoots them, they always try to look smart, beautiful and attractive; they are actually interested in their own appearance. So Mr. Ashok Agarwal always tries to get best garments for them. He already had selected such places for his shop that there is no need to advertise because that place is always full of youths and so his business is working fine. To attract more and more customers, time to time he gives them offers like '50% flat off' or 'buy one get one free'.

Hurdles: Initially Mr. Ashok Agarwal had a big problem in managing this whole thing, to get merchandise here itself and then arranging it, quantity should be optimized in stores not too low not too high. Customer satisfaction is also very much necessary; everything which we are delivering them should be high quality within price limits.

Future: The Future Plan of Mr. Ashok agarwal reflects his dedication and his hard work. Mr. Ashok Agarwal is gaining more and more experience by interacting with other company partners and sellers. Mr. Ashok Agarwal would like to open a bakery shop just like 'Crisp Corner' and one day he would like to have his own trademark which will be recognized world wide.

Views on Entrepreneurship: "Be crazy about your work, never give up and keep thinking, never let your brain to become mush".

Case No 8.
Mr.Rajesh (Govind General Stores)

Mr. Rajesh is a normal business man living in Gwalior. He did his education up to 10th Standard. The idea to start a business came from his father who also a grocery store owner. He took over his father's business after his father. He has a vast experience of 38 years in the current business.

Business Idea: Mr. Rajesh father's was owner of Grocery store, So he realizes that if they provides general items which are essential for daily needs under the same roof then it will increase their popularity in the market and ultimately profits. There were no other General Store at the time of inception of his General Store.

Initial Phase: Mr. Rajesh did not face any problems for his startup in terms of money and location, as was faced by others. The initial capital invested for the startup of business was given by his father, this is the main reason he was risk averse kind of person. As the prices may fluctuate daily, investment should be done up to a certain level. The funding of this business comes from the money that got by selling the products daily.

Strategy: Mr. Rajesh believes that Customer Satisfaction is the key strategy for the success of business. Mr. Rajesh believes in laying all efforts in ensuring quality services to his customers. Coming to the funding options, there is no need for a partner or a thing like that as it is a small business and should manage the capital available wisely depending up on the factors like season, geographical area, people's lifestyle etc.

Hurdles: As of such Mr. Rajesh didn't face any big problems. It's a risk less business which goes on flat without any instant increase in the profits. The biggest hurdle which he faces is during festive seasons.. He had put in many efforts to overcome these hurdles. He himself without the help of any other person had to work very hard to manage his business during tough times. He did carry all the goods himself and also had to take care of his family.

Future: The future plan of Mr. Rajesh is very big which includes expansion of his small general store into a small kind of super market. He wants that his supermarket includes all of the features which are present in any Supermarket. He has a vision to expand his shop to other locations of Gwalior and in other cities. His aim is to open the chain of supermarket and website for his supermarket.

Views On Entrepreneurship: "Commitment to the business and efficient use of available capital are the two important milestones to become successful."

Case No 9.
Mr. Salahuddin Khan (Salt 'N' Pepper Restaurant)

Mr. Salahuddin khan is an example of self made entrepreneur. His hobbies of gardening and interior decoration are clearly embedded in the ambiance of his restaurant that makes it very distinctive among all the others in the city of Gwalior. There were no Chinese restaurants at the time of inception of his restaurant (2000). He started his restaurant as a Chinese restaurant and invested all his earned money from PCO to initially raise the restaurant (initial capital was Rs 10,000).

Business Idea: Mr. Salahuddin khan had experience of PCO owner before 2000 which was quite popular among students he started a Chinese Restaurant in City of Gwalior. Due to his interest in Interior decoration and gardening he provided a peculiar ambiance to his PCO which was quite a distinctive feature that made his name and good will among college students. The very idea of opening a Chinese restaurant came to Salahuddin khan mind when he realized that college students have to move far away from that place for fast foods, since there was no restaurant in the vicinity.

Initial Phase: Mr. Salahuddin khan faced some problems at first regarding his new startup in terms of money and place of restaurant. His savings, money borrowed from friends and some bank loan was the source of initial investment for his startup and he invested all his earned money from PCO to initially raise the restaurant (initial capital was Rs 10,000).

Strategy: Mr. Salahuddin khan greeted each and every customer with a sense of responsibility and he ensured that his customers get a good service and timely delivery of orders. In the initial days of his startup he specifically targeted college students, couples, birthday's parties and other family occasions. With his sincere efforts and timely service he expanded his customer base with quite a fast pace..

Hurdles: In initial phase he is having some initial problems of fiancé, location of restaurant, but he really uses his mind and due to his hard work he is successful. there were no big hurdles as everything was well planned and carved out in correct manner but once there was a fire in the restaurant and he had to face heavy financial and psychological setbacks.

Future: The future plans of Mr. Salahuddin khan reflect his ambition to grow big and successful. He emphasizes on improving the service quality, time to even better standards. He wants to increase the number and variety of items available in his restaurant in near future .He has a vision to expand his shop to other locations of Gwalior and in other cities.

Views on Entrepreneurship: "Customer satisfaction and quality are topmost priorities and always welcomes suggestion from customers and likeminded people."

Case No 10.
Mr. Shiv Kinger (Planet Books)

Mr. Shiv Kinger is an example that Entrepreneurship is not dependent on age. In fact, some times it is enriched by person's long years in a trade. He completed his 12th in 1970 and then he moved to Cuttack, Orissa to his relatives where he learnt the basics of Book marketing business. In 1974 he came to Gwalior and does a job of Book Stall Agent at Gwalior Railway Station. Being in this trade for about 30 years, he finally decided to open his own Book Shop.

Business Idea: After an experience of about 30 years Mr. Shiv Kinger resigned from Wheeler's & Co. The very idea of having his own book shop came to Mr. Shiv Kinger's mind when he realized that there was no book shop in the nearby market and people were facing a lot of problems in getting the books they want..

Initial Phase: In the initial phases of his new startup, Mr. Shiv Kinger faced many problems related to money, space availability & attracting customers etc. In the initial days there were not many customers and most of the time he spent sitting idle in his shop because the shop was not so popular. After some initial days of startup, when the business grew due to his hard work and experience, he appointed an employee for his shop to take care of the inventory/stock of books and sales.

Strategy: Mr. Shiv Kinger greeted each and every customer with a sense of responsibility and he ensured that his customers get a good service and timely delivery of orders. In the initial days of his startup when there were not many customers coming to his shop, he specifically targeted students of reputed schools, IAS and IPS officers and Doctors. With his sincere efforts and timely service he expanded his customer base with quite a fast pace.

Hurdles: Mr. Shiv Kinger faced some problems at first regarding his new startup in terms of money and establishment. His savings, money borrowed from friends and some bank loan was the source of initial investment for his startup. With this investment he managed to get a shop in *Parasmani Mall* and utilized his 30 years of experience to create a successful establishment and got the business on track

Future: The future plans of Mr. Shiv Kinger reflect his ambition to grow big and successful. He wants to increase the number and variety of books in his shop in near future. He has a vision to expand his shop to other locations of Gwalior. His aim is to fulfill the requirements of the people of Gwalior in such a manner that no one has to go anywhere else for a book that he/she wants.

Views on Entrepreneurship: "There is no such thing as a failed entrepreneur. You are a failed entrepreneur only when you quit. Until then, you are simply not successful."

Case No. 11
Mr. Praveen Kumar (Ashish Shopping Center)

Mr. Praveen Kumar is an example of self made entrepreneur. He is true example of a kind of person who can do anything if he wants to do. He did Bachelor of Science form Gwalior. He is successfully running his shop from past 26 years.

Business Idea: Mr. Praveen Kumar wanted to set up a business of his own, he decided to come up with something new, a shop which could cater to different needs of the people which was base for his idea. He was the first person in his family to do so, to set up a business where as all his paternal generations were into service. So, he came up with an innovative idea to have a gift and novelties shop which had different kinds of cards, greetings, plastics, small accessories, some stationery stuff, and a wide range of gifts to choose from.

Initial Phase: Mr. Praveen Kumar faced some problems at first regarding his new startup in terms of money and place of shop. He had to invest around '25000 so that he could set up a shop which first consisted few items of all different kinds of gifts and greetings, and some stationery. His father had funded him with the capital that he needed and with his support Mr. Praveen Kumar was able to set up his Business.

Strategy: Mr. Praveen Kumar ensures that his customers get a good service .His shop had customers from all different ages of people who come around to buy gifts and greetings for their friends or family members for all different kinds of occasions. The shop experienced peak sales during the New-year, Christmas, and other special occasions. In addition to these, this shopping center also undertook semi-wholesale orders for marriages or other similar occasions. He offers discounts to the customers on various occasions.

Hurdles: Mr. Praveen said that he had faced many problems in undertaking his business. He had put in many efforts to overcome his hurdles. He himself without the help of any other person had to work very hard to manage his business during tough times. He did carry all the goods himself and also had to take care of his family.

Future: The future plans of Mr. Praveen reflect that Mr. Praveen Kumar is a kind of person who only believes in hard work. He wanted to expand his business much more and wanted to take up bigger wholesale orders. In the long run, he said that he wanted to convert his shop into a Shopping Mall kind of a shopping center.

Views on Entrepreneurship: "strong determination and will is required to run business even during tough times and fight hard to win over all the hurdles that confront."

Case No. 12
Mr. Rajesh Sharma (Panchvati Restaurant)

Mr. Rajesh Sharma is an example of The Entrepreneur who is basically an *Intrapreneur*. He embodies all characteristics of an entrepreneur. These characteristics include conviction, passion, drive and high risk taking. He is from Village Deogarh at a distance of 80 km from Gwalior. His father was a farmer. He is educated up to class eight. Due to some misunderstandings at home he had to leave the home. That was a huge risk taken by him. He worked in Indore for 8 - 10 years. After that he came to Gwalior Mr. Harishchandra Jain told him to run panchvati.

Business Idea: Mr. Rajesh Sharma started working in a restaurant in the utilities department. While working, he thought that if he is doing this work he should do it in a better way. He started learning and working a lot about and in this field. He acquired some good knowledge in this field. After an experience of 30-35 years he went on to become a chef. He travelled in the whole country. He did job as a chef in various restaurants and five star hotels. He has been successfully running Panchvati for 7 years. That's how he became an *Intrapreneur.*

Initial Phase: Mr. Rajesh faced some problems at first regarding his new startup in terms of money and place of shop but he overcome all his problems with his smartness.

Strategy: Mr. Rajesh Sharma followed traditional ways of advertisement to attract customers initially. He advertised in newspaper, television and used hoardings to attract his initial customers. Today customers are high class Families of Gwalior. He said food is of high quality and tasteful. In order to have a large customer base he is laying all efforts in ensuring quality services to the customers.

Hurdles: His biggest hurdle was that he didn't know anything when he came in to this new field. He solved that problem by his dedication and hard work. Now he knows to cook various types of foods that make him highly skilled person in the field of hotels and restaurants. His thinking, abilities and a right road will lead him to success.

Future: The future plans of Mr. Rajesh Sharma reflect his passion and ambition to grow big and successful. He emphasizes on improving the service quality, time to even better standards. He wants to increase the number and variety of items available in his restaurant in near future. He still wants to work a lot and want Panchvatis to spread over whole Gwalior in future.

Views on Entrepreneurship: "one should have a belief in himself. No work is difficult if one think that he has to do this work."

Case No. 13
Mr. Abhinav Garg (Career Launcher)

Mr. Abhinav Garg is an example of entrepreneur who becomes entrepreneur due to his knowledge and experience. He completed his education as an Engineer and MBA and start working as lecturer in Indore .He saw several Engineers who got passion of studying MBA like him and at the same time, he got irritated by college atmosphere.

Business Idea: Mr. Abhinav Garg found out that there was a great opportunity and future for MBA and the no. of students preparing were constantly increasing. Hence he decided to start a MBA coaching center and he felt that he can't cope since already there are several coaching centers. Then he bought Franchise of CL which already established and got its own reputation.

Initial Phase: Mr. Abhinav Garg started with initial capital of 6 lakhs rupees borrowing from his near and dear. Since starting preparation center doesn't need much capital as that of other industries, as its capital is mainly knowledge of the subject which he already got by his experience. He recovers this money back in 18 months as he succeeded well. The major hurdles are like Gwalior doesn't have much technical experts as needed for him and locating them from other place to Gwalior is also a difficult task ahead.

Strategy: Mr. Abhinav Garg targeted students who want to do MBA. He runs various types of courses in CL which will help the students to crack management Exams. As the main goal of this project is to make students clear the MBA entrance exam, so he make sure that top students from top colleges in Gwalior like IIITM were given more intense coaching and he succeed in getting good no. of ranks .So CL reputation got increased.

Hurdles: In initial phase he is having some initial problems of fiancé but the main hurdle is that Gwalior is not having good teachers who can really guide the students to crack management Exams. So he brings the efficient teachers from outside. Presently CL is running very successfully with so many students and then he also focused on law entrance which is also similar type of exam as that of the MBA.

Future: The future plans of Mr. Abhinav Garg reflect his Experience and Knowledge in this field. The future appear to him very brightly as Engineering, Medical and Civil are also going to change into aptitude pattern very soon in which he is very successful and expert. He wants to start coaching for Medical, Engineering and other courses also.

Views on Entrepreneurship: "Experience & Knowledge can make you an Entrepreneur and to become an Entrepreneur it is necessary to believe on yourself".

Case No. 14
Mr.Vishal Jain (Vishal Opticals)

Mr. Vishal Jain owns an optical shop named "vishal opticals "at gole ka mandir in Gwalior. As soon as he completed his graduation and got a degree in Bachelor of Arts (i.e.BA), He started his business as he has passion towards business ventures. He overtook his father's business and it has been 8 years since he has come into this field. He doesn't have any previous job experience and the initial capital that he took was Rs 40,000 which came from his father.

Business Idea: Mr. Vishal Jain had a passion about business, he tried to explore his qualities in that particular direction .As we all know almost for every 10 people we see around ,at least 3-4 people are equipped with spectacles, so his idea were basically of manufacturing the spectacles as per user requirements , repairing them and preparing fancy spectacles for youth.

Initial Phase: Mr. Vishal Jain fully owned his business as such there were no partners with him I that business .As vishal optical has a wide range of customers ranging from age group15-20 to old people, he had to maintained those ranges and for which his family members supported him .Even he solitary managed his shop, it was remarkably simple to get established as this was his own business.

Strategy: Mr. Vishal Jain believes that Customer Satisfaction is the key strategy for the success of business. Mr. Vishal Jain believes in laying all efforts in ensuring quality services to his customers .He regularly offers attractive discounts. As Mr. Jain knows most of his customers personally and has good relations with them, he has a loyal customer base.

Hurdles: Mr. Vishal Jain does not notice any major hurdles for his business .Only in the initial phase he faced some problems regarding managing the customer's needs on shop, as he is the single person on his shop but as the time went, he managed everything successfully.

Future: Mr. Vishal Jain future Plan is to expand his client-network and to make sure that he doesn't lose his grip on his customers. He wants to expand his business and ensure a bigger profit margins, this reflects his ambition to grow bigger and more successful. Currently his shop is simple, but In future he wants that his shop will convert into a showroom kind of place, where all types of frames and glasses are available and his shop will become brand in Gwalior.

Views on Slogan Entrepreneurship: "Hard work, belief in oneself and compassion for ones work along with sound knowledge can work wonders in any field of business".

Case No. 15
Mr. Anurag singh (Super Gallery Studio)

Mr. Anurag Singh is a studio owner named *"Super Gallery"* which is located at the Gole ka Mandir market in the outskirts of the city of Gwalior. He did his education up to intermediate level then he had no job and neither had he done any work. But, he always had the intention of setting up his own venture.

Business Idea: After completing intermediate he had no work. He got some experience from his friend who used to do work related to photography. He had a discussion with friend regarding photography shop, since he has no experience of running a business so; He indulged himself in his brother's business and started gathering knowledge related to marketing of gifts.

Initial Phase: After acquiring sufficient experience, he started his own shop. Mr. Anurag Singh faced some problems at first regarding his new startup in terms of money and establishment. He somehow managed to gather capital for the shop and products from his friend and brother. With this investment he started his shop and utilized his experience to create a successful establishment and got the business on track He, along with his brother on a fifty-fifty partnership, started the venture in 2006 with an initial capital of Rs. 35,000.

Strategy: Mr. Anurag Singh believes in ensuring quality wok to his customers. He utilized his networks and adopted a very good advertising policy due to which he was able to get three-four customers on the first day itself. In order to have a large customer base, he laid all efforts in ensuring quality services to the customers.

Hurdles: Mr. Anurag Singh faced many hurdles while he was gathering knowledge on gifts and in the starting he could not make ends meet. But his dedication and passion forced him to continue with the work and he started trying himself to gather knowledge. He faces many hurdles in terms of money place work force but he managed all these by his dedication for the shop.

Future: The future plan of Mr Anurag Singh reflects his ambition to grow bigger; he is planning to have a much larger variety of gift products in his own shop and plans to gather all the investments required for it from his savings. He also wants to open his studio at other places of Gwalior.

Views on Entrepreneurship: "give first priority to Customers".

Case No. 16
Mr. Vishambhar Guru (Relish Baker)

Mr. Vishambhar Guru was the founder of Cobra Pen. This product got great success in Madhya Pradesh but after some time he changed his mind due to some reasons and joined his nephew's business. Presently, Relish Baker is running robustly under his guidance which initially was run by his nephew Mr. Ravi Guru.

Business Idea: Mr. Vishambhar Guru was always keen to stat his own business but he was told by his family members to start such a business in which family reputation should be maintained. First he started manufacturing Pen and he got great success in Madhya Pradesh but after some time he changed his mind due to some reasons and entered into the business of Relish bakery.

Initial Phase: Mr. Vishambhar Guru faced some problems at first regarding his new startup in terms of money and establishment, to overcome this problem he had taken a loan of Rs. 2 lakh to start his business. Initially, he sold things at a lower price to retain customers. As a result of his efforts, he could start his franchise in Gwalior.

Strategy: The first priority of Mr. Vishambhar Guru is quality and customer satisfaction, these are interrelated. If quality is good then customer will already satisfied. By selling at lower price first he tries to connect customers to create effect of his taste in their mind so next time they themselves come to his shop. At present, Mr. Vishambhar Guru has approximately ten franchises in Gwalior, still he does not feel that he is earning a good amount of profit. According to him, quality maintenance is difficult with such a low amount of sales, but he never wants to compromise with quality. According to him, hard work and quality production is the key to success.

Hurdles: Mr. Vishambhar Guru faced some problems at first regarding his new startup in terms of money and establishment but The biggest hurdle, he faced, was that he couldn't get any customer till two years after starting his business and then he promoted his brand with poster flags, ads discount schemes and by offering some sample for free. Once people tasted his product they became his permanent customers.

Future: The future plans of Mr. Vishambhar Guru reflect his ambition to become superior in his field by expanding his brand. He had also applied for catering in many institutes this year. He also wants to be associated with ABV-Indian Institute of Information technology and management Gwalior.

Views on Entrepreneurship: "You need to work hard and honest in order to grow"

Case No. 17
Mr. Arun Upadhyay (the Road Chef's)

Mr. Arun Upadhyay has a bachelor's degree in Commerce. Initially, he looked after his family business but he derived no joy from it .He wanted to be his own boss so he talked to his brother who gave him advice to open up an independent business for himself.

Business Idea: Mr. Arun Upadhayay's brother who is currently pursuing hotel management course in London advice him to open up an independent business. After that, he came across the idea of caravan to start his business which is a common pattern of fast food stalls in London. Then he decided to open up his own shop "THE ROAD CHEF'S" in the year 2009.

Initial Phase: Mr. Arun Upadhyay faced some problems at first regarding his new startup in terms of money and establishment. The initial Investment was a bit high due to the idea of caravan who he got made from Delhi. There were no other people involved except his family. He slowly grows his business, never tried to make profit from the very first day of start of his business.

Strategy: Mr. Arun Upadhyay targeted customers are students as well as families. His idea is to attract the customers by giving them quantity food in fewer amounts. As his business is in initial stage only so his network has not grown much till now. But in spite of that, within one year, he has started two corners in Gwalior one is at BADA and other is at ACHLESWAR.

Hurdles: Mr. Arun Upadhyay faced some problems at first regarding his new startup in terms of money and establishment but the biggest among this is establishment phase, came from Nagar Nigam and Government but he handled them patiently. This shows that he never surrender against the situation. He employs ten helpers which includes chefs as well. His annual turnover is Rs 3-4 lakhs.

Future: The future plans of Mr. Arun Upadhyay is to extend the business but he is also looking for new food items which may revolutionize his business. He concentrates on new food product which is not being served in Gwalior so far.

Views on Entrepreneurship: "Start business at low level with a small budget. Do concentrate on the quality of the product. Never start the business by spending a lot of capital as starting a new business involves many risks and risks and there is always a chance that you may not succeed".

Case No.18
Mr. Prateek Bhargav (Member of Board of Director and Entrepreneur)

Mr. Prateek Bhargava was very sincere since his childhood. He was born in a very rich family. His family had been in business, since the last 50 years .He completed his graduation and post graduation from a reputed college. He then completed his masters in commerce. He was very passionate towards business because of his family lineage.

Business Idea: During the course of college life, Mr. Prateek Bhargava was made up in his mind to do something for his own ton, and came up with the great idea of a Mall in Gwalior. His basic education was more than sufficient for this kind of idea. Moreover, it was easy for him to get established and work on his idea in a full swing.

Initial Phase: Mr. Prateek Bhargav did not face any problem related to money for his startup but the problem is related to the place of mall. Initially, his efforts were directed towards achieving the required capital needed for the venture. This he could get using his friend and family network. Some capital also came from banks loans.

Strategy: He believes in laying all efforts in ensuring success. He used his friends and business network to get various company franchisees for acquire a hub like orientation for his business in Gwalior. His entire family supported him. But the biggest help came from his uncle Mr. Dindayal. He required nearly Rs.60 crores which he got from his friends, family business and by bank loans. He also set up a 5 crores company in medical business.

Hurdles: He has made a long journey to achieve success in his venture by weeding out many hurdles, obstructions and difficulties during the project completion. According to him, .getting the correct idea was never a hurdle, but good planning was required to maintain the growth of business. The most typical problem was promotion of his ventures. So he started saving money to give ads on newspapers, hoardings etc.

Future: In the near future, Mr. Prateek Bhargav plans to start a wider chain of malls .This reflects his ambition to grow bigger and be more successful. His emphasis is more towards quality service and maintaining customer relations. His plans also reflects his diversification behavior, since he is also planning to expand his business in other related fields like real estate business etc.

Views on Entrepreneurship: "Establish your own venture, work hard, be dedicated and passionate and be willing to do something on your own."

Case No.19
Mr. Arvind Arharia (Lakhshya Institute)

Mr. Arvind Arharia owns a school, a training institute and a cybercafé. His school "Shri Keshwanand Vidhyalaya "and training institute " lakhshya institute" are located in sarafa bazaar, Gwalior and cybercafé in hazira, Gwalior. He graduated from MITS, Gwalior as a Bachelor of Science .Initially, he was in a private school teaching children but he used to found something missing in life.

Business Idea: Mr. Arvind Arharia knew that there are so many colleges in his area like "Bhagwatsa Mahavidyalaya" and "Navin Kanya Mahavidyalaya" which had many students.

He choose computer sector because it was an upcoming field and there were more students coming into it every year. After some years he opened a cybercafé with two computers in hazira sensing that all families cannot afford computer. He got some experience from private school so he opened a school by managing the initial capital somehow.

Initial Phase: Initially he started a school which he got affiliated from MP government. Initially, there were only two rooms in his school. After some years he opened a cybercafé with two computers in Hazira. The problem was seed money as computers used to cost much. Initially his budget was 1 lac, but somehow he managed.

Hurdles: Mr. Arvind Arharia path was not a simple as it seems because finding a good teacher was not an easy job. The other problem was getting the initial capital. The most typical problem was promotion of his ventures. So he started saving money to give ads on newspapers, hoardings etc.

Strategy: Mr. Arvind Arharia follows simple strategy of giving Quality service to his customers. His main customer is students from schools in the locality. Some are also from Indra Nagar and Prasad Nagar. He believes that the real meaning of the word "entrepreneur" is not easy as buying a candy; you need to be passionate and dedicated. But if you got these qualities, no one can stop you.

Future: The future plan of Mr. Arvind Arharia is to expand his business as much as he can and provide quality education to students. He wants his students to become successful. . Presently, he is opening a new branch in Shinde ki Chawni which is located in the center of Gwalior.

Views on Entrepreneurship: "Be innovative and walk in proper direction and success will come at your feet".

Case No. 20
Sandeep Maheshwari (Dava Ghar)

Mr. Sandeep Maheshwari was in a private job but wanted to explore his potential by being his own boss. So he opened an independent business for himself. He did MSc from Gwalior. His brother and father were also in the business line. Since they were not the owner of any business, they decided to open their own business in 2006.

Business Idea: Mr. Sandeep Maheshwari started his business with an investment of Rupees1 lakh by taking a loan from Punjab National Bank. There was no other person involved in his business apart from his family member. They were the independent owner of the store. The notion of starting a new shop came in the mind of Sandeep by analyzing the environment as there was no shop like that in the vicinity.

Initial Phase: In the beginning of the journey of his business he had to face some problems in terms of money to start up the business and to find the appropriate place for his business. The problem of money was resolved by taking loan of Rupees 1 lakh. But still he faced problem of gaining popularity. He tried hard to get the first few customers. For the customer patients he had to visit the doctors in locality to direct the patients to him in lieu of some commission.

Strategy: In his business the usual network is the network of Medical Representatives. His network included 10-15 Medical Representatives, 30-40 doctors and few medical retailers. Two prominent were Maheshwari Traders and a retail shop in Lucknow. His strategy was to start the business at low level with small budget and then take it to a faster pace.

Hurdles: The biggest hurdle faced by Sandeep was during the establishment phase. Money was tight, so he could not afford any helpers. As a result all the business tasks, even the petty ones like confirming medicines by taking appointments were to be carried by him. This resulted in delaying of his regular business and hence has to suffer a bit.

Future: The future plan of Mr. Sandeep Maheshwari is to open an AYURVEDIC MEDICINE shop in the vicinity. He got an idea that starting a new job can be way too risky and you have got to have a lot of connections with various people in key positions to get success. Hence his future goals do not include further expansion but prospering business from those two shops and becoming a wholesale medical dealer.

Views on Entrepreneurship: "Business plan with all the estimated budgets provides for the foundational land pillars you need to succeed in business."

Case No.21
Mr. Praveen Kumar (Gift Shop)

Mr. Praveen Kumar was a person who believed in hard and smart work. He wanted to serve people from the bottom of his heart. He knew that an innovative idea could change his fate. So he came up with the idea of setting shops of gifts and novelties. His father also supported him in the best way he could. Mr. Praveen Kumar was a bachelor of science from Gwalior. Because of his novel idea and father's support, Mr. Praveen Kumar could start his business with less trouble.

Business Idea: After his graduation he wanted to do something which would cater the needs of the people. So he came up with the innovative idea of setting up a shop which could provide greetings, plastics, small accessories, some stationary stuff, and a wide range of gifts to choose from.

Initial Phase: Mr. Praveen Kumar invested Rs. 25,000 to set up his shop, although it was easy for Mr. Praveen Kumar to stand in his new profession, but he had to do all things by himself. The sales were good with a profit around 10-20%. His shop provided gifts, greetings, and some stationary to serve the general needs of the people of all age hence they used to visit his shop for various purposes. The sales used to go up in festival seasons.

Strategy: Mr. Praveen Kumar's strategy was very much clear. He felt that only an idea was required which could sustain the market competition instantly when it will be implemented. One should have strong determination to face both profit and loss and to face the heat. Mr. Praveen Kumar also felt that one cannot be successful if he/she is dull or not smart. Also a strategic plan has to be made for how much capital is required to carry out his business.

Hurdles: Mr. Praveen Kumar had faced several problems while establishing his business but didn't loose his determination and gave them a good fight. He himself without the help of any other person had to work very hard to manage his business during busy routine. He not only did all the work of his business himself but also took care of his family.

Future: The future plan of Mr. Praveen Kumar comprised of expanding his business much more then what it was initially and wanted to take up bigger wholesale orders. For the long run his plans were of converting his shop into a shopping mall and to extend his business to every kind of item related to a common man.

Views on Slogan Entrepreneurship:"Hard work, believe in one's own self and love for one's own work along with sound knowledge can work wonders in any field of business".

Case No. 22
Diwakar Chaturvedi (Embro Computers)

Mr. Diwakar Chatturvedi of Embro Computers did his graduation in commerce in 1984 from Madhav Science College, Gwalior. He began his business in the year 2000. He has worked for many other big companies in these years which include supreme locker; as such he has enough business experience.

Business Idea: Mr. Diwakar Chaturvedi did not want to do job under anyone and wanted to explore his potential by being his own boss. His elder brother who is a software engineer actively helped him to start a computer hardware and software firm. At that time there was a boom in the IT industry and this helped them take off.

Initial phase: Mr. Diwakar Chatturvedi invested Rs. 2 lakhs for the startup of his business.. He had a shop of his own so he didn't have much difficulty establishing his business. He got some money from his father and took the rest of the amount from bank as loan. With all these he set up an IT firm which deals in computer hardware and software, laptops, etc.

Strategy: Mr. Diwakar Chatturvedi used his contacts with those persons who are in need of PCs, software, etc. To make his offers more attractive he put discounts like providing free accessories such as mouse, keyboard, pen drive, etc. with the purchase of laptops, and PCs. The biggest strategy he followed was every time don't focus on profit maximize sales and satisfy your customers.

Hurdles: Initially, Mr. Diwakar Chatturvedi faced some problems regarding Finance, but these problems are solved in short period of time by his dedication to become own boss. During starting period of business sales suffered a lot and meaningful profits could be achieved only after a year. Sometimes, he even has to work with no profits for three or four months. Financial problems were very common. The problem of money was resolved by taking loan from banks. But he still faced problem of gaining popularity.

Future: The Future plans of Mr. Diwakar Chatturvedi reflects his ambition to grow big and bigger. His plan includes expansion of his business at different places in Gwalior and also from outside Gwalior and try to take distributor agencies of maximum number of IT dealers. His plans also reflects his diversification behavior, since he is also planning to expand his business in other related fields like mobile, invertors, etc.

Views on Entrepreneurship: "Make your strategies according to the competitors and market environment. Be ready to make flexible changes from time to time."

Case No. 23
Mr. Praveen Dubey (Bharti Stationary)

Mr. Praveen Dubey was a graduate in commerce from MLB College, Gwalior. Since his childhood he wanted to do a kind of job which can serve the needs of a common man. He had an intension of setting up his own ventures and hence started a business of Stationary with his father. His father's experience helped him a lot whose work was related to note-book manufacturing.

Business Idea: Mr. Praveen Dubey had an idea of opening a bookstore and stationary shop as his father was in the relevant field of note-book manufacturing. He started to work hard in this field. He gradually tried to improve the quality of products to increase his customers. He doesn't believe in short term profit and gave a discount on most of his products to gain the customers confidence in his business.

Initial Phase: Initially he had to face the problems related with the place for his shop and money for starting his business. He believed in first analyzing the market and then produced his product according to the requirement of the market. He had invested approximately 2 lakh in his business by borrowing from his father.

Strategy: Mr. Praveen Kumar's strategy to increase the customers was to improve the quality of products, and selling the products at a small more discount then other distributors. He supplied his copies to different parts of Gwalior and nearby cities and towns. In order to have a large customer base he is laid all efforts in ensuring quality services to the customers. Entrepreneurship wants hard work, effort, dedication and the passion out of you. If one has awesome knowledge in any field and has the innovative idea and courage to implement, the success is sure to come.

Hurdles: Mr. Praveen Kumar initially faced some financial difficulty but his smart business decisions and hard work helped him in handling these problems. Initially he had to manage whole of his business himself and no one was there to help him in his daily work. Later, he employed some workers for the same. With the time, he overcame every hurdle with ease and now was counted as in one of the successful entrepreneurs of his locality.

Future: The future plans of Mr. Praveen Kumar reflect his ambition to set up his vast empire of his own. His plans comprised of setting different binding machines to increase the production and laser printers for improving the quality of his products. He will continue doing hard work in future also to achieve his goals.

Views of Entrepreneurship: "Entrepreneur is a proper mixture or in chemistry language is a solution of intuition, ambition, hard work and willingness to do something".

Case No 24
Mr. Manoj Kumar (Indian Shop)

Mr. Manoj Kumar was a kind of person who never let any hurdle to come in the way of his progress. He has done his education up to B.com (2nd year).Although he was not very educated which was the basic motivational factor for Mr. Kumar as he started a business related to students of various schools and colleges. No one from his family was in business line. Even he does not belong to a business background then also he gave a shape to his dream of starting a business by starting it in the year 2006.

Business Idea: Mr. Manoj Kumar always wanted to achieve high in his life. He wished to establish his own Business. He started his own business by targeting the students of various schools and colleges situated in the city itself. He started his business with Rs 1 lakh Rs. His total revenue amounted to Rs 5 lakhs annually.

Hurdles: He faced the biggest hurdle during the establishment phase itself. He could not get much help from anyone. With mere 1 lakh Rs he started his small business but slowly and gradually gave a way to expand his business. Now he has afforded some employees to work in his shop which he has started to provide the basic accessories to the students.

Initial Phase: Mr. Manoj Kumar initial phase was not so smooth .He had to struggle a lot to get on track. He initially invested Rs 1 lakhs. There were no other people involved with him to render any kind of help to start his business. He has to see all the process of his business himself. As a result he could not give much time in market survey to find out or cater the needs of the market. But slowly he managed with it and cope up with all these problems with his hard work and determination.

Future: Mr. Manoj Kumar had big plans in his mind. Within few years, he had opened another shop in the mall. His future goals do not include future expansion but growing on the existing business. He wants to be a leader in his own field of providing all kind of accessories items related to the students of various colleges and schools.

Views on Entrepreneurship: "Before starting our own business it's better to work as to get experience with the outside world. Its risky profession as an entrepreneur, so we must be cautious and always we must be thinking about the future aspects which influence our business and how to tackle them or how to make changes in our business accordingly and also regarding our business expansion."

Case No. 25
Mr. Arun Sengar (Mama Bhanja Mobile Store)

Mr. Arun Sengar was from a good educational background with an MBA from Jiwaji University and an MA in geography. He is a prime example of self confidence and Independence. He do not wanted to work under any one, hence his main motive was to be Independent and to earn at regular basis by his own efforts.

Business Idea: Mr. Arun Sengar had an idea of possessing an independent mobile store as he saw the growing market of telecommunication and invested the whole amount in it at his own risk about six years ago. He also had a work hawk eye over the place where he got the students of not less than five colleges at one spot.

Initial Phase: Mr. Arun Sengar started his business on his own with a mere amount of roughly Rs 25,000. Initially, he got the starting money from his friends and relatives which he promised to return with interest to them as soon as possible. This business does not demand much of an initial infrastructure cost apart from the furniture and the decorating.

Strategy: Mr. Arun Sengar was indeed a mastermind and chooses the location of the shop with full calculation. He targeted the college going students from ABV - IIITM, MITS, GEC, Agricultural College and Birla College, as Gole ka Mandir was the nearest one shop market for them. He cultivated his relationships with the initial customers who let to the attraction of their friends automatically and thus ultimately lifted up his business. He feels the customers are everything that a businessman has.

Hurdles: Mr. Arun Sengar initially faced some financial difficulty but his firm decisions and strong relations were too strong to be broken by such small interruptions. He also had faced a time when he had handsome amount of assets with him but was left with no money in his hand. But as the time passed he overcame every hurdle with ease and now can be counted as the moist successful entrepreneurs of his locality.

Future: He sees himself as the major owner of the mobile stores in the entire Gole Ka Mandir area. He is also planning to establish chains of his shop in different parts of Gwalior and adjoining areas. But he doesn't forget to mention the shopkeeper and customer relationship as the primary focus He believed that business is not only about establishing one's own venture but is his will to win. If one has sound knowledge in any field and has the confidence of properly utilizing that knowledge in terms of a venture, than success is sure to follow.

Views on Entrepreneurship: "No body is a born Entrepreneur what matters is how one follows his dreams."

Case No.26
Mr. Ravi Rajalka (Rajalka Enterprises)

Mr. Ravi Rajalka was born in a normal middle class family with His father was in service in a private textile manufacturing unit and His was a housewife. He did Bachelor of Commerce, but his eagerness for study forced him to do MBA (finance) in 1993. Mr. Ravi Rajalka with his brother running his business very smoothly.

Business Idea: Mr. Ravi Rajalka entered into business in 1993 after passing from college, he got the distributorship of vadilal which was then followed by a number of vadilal outlets in Gwalior. He then took the dealership of Honda and Mahindra gensets .His next idea was to open up a discothek cum bar in Dindayal mall, Gwalior's one and only mall located at very heart of city. The latest idea of his was from his observation of discotheks running successfully in other major malls of India. This idea of his culminated in DND discothek becomes operational on 1st August 2010.

Initial Phase: Initially, Mr. Ravi Rajalka's business was much smaller and didn't require much financial assistance. It was entirely financed by his family .His brother entered into a partnership with him and then, the pillars of this great business were raised.

Strategy: Mr. Ravi Rajalka had planned a very effective strategy. He invites famous artist for performing in his discothek so that the discothek becomes more and more popular in the city. Also he got his promotional banners at the entry gate of the mall so that the people visiting the mall are aware of his discothek.

Hurdles: Mr. Ravi Rajalka faced some problems at first regarding his new startup in terms of establishment, he did not faced any problem related to finance since initially he requires small amount for starting his business that amount is managed by himself. Mr. Ravi Rajlka has never faced any major obstacles in his business till date .He was smart enough to properly invest his profits so that he never faced any financial or any sort of hurdles.

Future: The Future plan of Mr. Ravi Rajalka is quite bright because he has entered into ventures keeping in mind the future trends. He is a kind of person who never surrenders due to situation and he never wants to stop at any place if that place is achieved then try for next place.

Views on Entrepreneurship: "Entrepreneurship helps to imbibe in us the spirit of innovation through interactions with customers."

Case No. 27
Mr. Praveen Kumar (Praveen Enterprises)

Mr. Praveen Kumar was a person who believed in hard and smart work. He wanted to serve people from the bottom of his heart. He came up with innovative idea of setting shops of gifts and novelties. Mr. Praveen Kumar was a bachelor of science from Gwalior. Because of his novel idea and father's support, Mr. Praveen Kumar could start his business with less trouble.

Business Idea: After his graduation he wanted to do something which would cater the needs of the people. So he came up with the innovative idea of setting up a shop which could provide greetings, plastics, small accessories, some stationary stuff, and a wide range of gifts to choose from.

Initial Phase: Mr. Praveen Kumar invested Rs. 25,000 to set up his shop, although it was not easy for Mr. Praveen Kumar to stand his new profession, but he had to do all things by himself. His shop provided gifts, greetings, and some stationary to serve the general needs of the people of all age hence they used to visit his shop for various purposes. The sales used to go up in festival seasons. He also used to take up contracts for serving on occasions like marriage etc.

Strategy: Mr. Praveen Kumar's strategy was very much clear. He felt that only an idea was required which could sustain the market competition instantly when it will be implemented. One should have strong determination to face both profit and loss and to face the heat. Mr. Praveen Kumar also felt that one cannot be successful if he/she is dull or not smart.

Hurdles: Mr. Praveen Kumar had faced several problems while establishing his business but didn't loose his determination and gave them a good fight. He himself without the help of any other person had to work very hard to manage his business during busy routine. He not only did all the work of his business himself but also took care of his family.

Future: The future plan of Mr. Praveen Kumar comprised of expanding his business much more then what it was initially and wanted to take up bigger wholesale orders. For the long run his plans were of converting his shop into a shopping mall and to extend his business to every kind of item related to a common man.

Views on Entrepreneurship: "Hard work, believe in one's own self and love for one's own work along with sound knowledge can work wonders in any field of business".

Case No. 28
Mrs. Chandra Gupta (Medical and General Store)

Mr. Gupta was in this business from past 11 years. He has two brothers. One is a chemical engineer other one did his Graduation in electronics and computers and he did his education up to class 12th only and now he is in Business of Medicine.

Business Idea: Mr. Gupta had a medical store, but he noticed that if he kept certain items such as soaps, toothpaste, creams etc. he could increase his sales. If the customer can get all the necessary items of his use at one place at good price then he does not prefer to go to other place

Initial Phase: Mr. Gupta buys a shop with some initial investment and he invested that money himself. Then he collect the information about the whole sale medicine market because the medicines are bought from there and one should have good knowledge about where we could get the medicine at the cheapest price because the prices varies from dealer to dealer.

Hurdles: When he opened the new shop there were very few customers. It took about 5-6 months to build the trust and then only customers increase slowly overtime. Often there is a problem that the medicines expire and if he did not return them to the company at the proper time then he has to bear the loss himself. In procuring medicines he prefers to give advance payment which earns him an additional profit of 3%. But in this there is a risk of money getting jammed till he is not able to sell them. This creates a problem for getting them in the future because often there is a money shortage.

Strategy: Mr. Gupta had a medical store, so he does not require other place for starting a general store; he has enough experience of business. So he utilizes his experience for increasing his business that if a single shop is satisfying customer daily seeds then why will customer move to other shop. Most of this profit is from the medicines but other items which he keeps help him in adding new customers.

Future: The future plans of Mr. Gupta reflect his ambition to become successful in life. He will always keep a watch over those items which might help him to increase his business. He wants to become wholesaler of Medicine and General Items.

Views on Entrepreneurship: "When a new business is started then it takes some time in getting customers, we have to build a trust with the customer and when that happens our customers increase and so our profit.

Case No. 29
Mr. Vijay Khandwani (Bombay Saree House)

Mr. Vijay Khandwani was in his parental business and today his his hard work has really paid him. After being educated up to 10th grade he had no job,he had the intention of running his father's business. He got some experience from his father who uses to do work in the shop. He indulged himself with his father and started gathering knowledge related to the quality of garment materials and design.

Business Idea: Mr. Vijay Khandwani always wanted to achieve high in his life. He wished to establish his own Business. He started his own business by targeting the women section of society i.e. students of various schools and colleges situated in the city itself. He knows that women's are more conscious about their dressing sense, so by offering variety to them it is quite easy to gain profit.

Initial Phase: Mr. Vijay Khandwani faced some problems at first regarding his new startup in terms of money and place of shop. He had to purchase a shop which first consisted few variety of all different kinds of sarees, and some other dresses. His father had funded him with the capital that he needed and with his support Mr. Praveen Kumar was able to set up his Business.

Strategy: In order to have a large customer base he is laying all efforts in ensuring quality services to the customers. He always offers drinks to his customers, whether the purchase the clothes from his shop or not. He thinks that this drink will create a soft corner in the customer mind for him and eventually he is attracted towards the shop.

Hurdles: The business is running smoothly but hurdles came in his way as his father passed. Now he is the only one who has to look after the shop. But his dedication and passion forced him to continue with the work and he started trying himself to gather knowledge. He received many hurdles in the course of learning but came out of them bravely. After acquiring sufficient knowledge he started to set up his bigger shop in better place. He somehow managed to gather the capital for the shop and equipments from his friend and brother.

Future: The future plans of Mr. Vijay Khandwani is to establish chains of his shops in different localities and if possible even outside Gwalior. He had one other plan in his mind that he wants to open a shop for men also.

Views on Entrepreneurship: "Gaining knowledge is important but it is also important to apply it properly in order to reap benefit."

4

Case Study on Techno-Entrepreneurs and their Attitudes

Introduction

The term entrepreneur is being redefined by the increasing number of young and even teenage entrepreneurs out there. These young people are proving that age really is just a number, and being an entrepreneur is all in the mind, or at least it begins there. Entrepreneurs, of all ages, know that the only person who can prevent you from succeeding is yourself; and these individuals are proof you can do anything that you put your mind to.

You are never too young to have a dream, and with hard work and determination you can turn your dream into a reality, and possibly an income producing business. Don't get me wrong, opening and successfully running your own business is not easy, the competition can be fierce, depending on the field you choose. On the other hand, if a person has a vision or dream and creates a workable plan which can give life to their dream, whatever that may be, the opportunities are endless. Let me introduce you to some young entrepreneurs who have followed their dream and who are now their own boss! You may be surprised at the list of major companies that have been founded by minors.

Some of the worlds most famous and profitable businesses were started by students. Microsoft began in Bill Gates' Harvard dorm room, Google got its start on the Stanford campus as the computer science project of doctoral students Sergey Brin and Larry Page and thousands of other student companies thrive in every industry. Even if you're not aiming to be another Bill Gates-maybe you just want to earn some extra cash with a summer landscaping business-you'll have to navigate some unique challenges as a young entrepreneur testing the business waters. Here are the some resources for young Entrepreneurs.

Resources for Young Entrepreneurs

One of the biggest challenges for any entrepreneur is finding the funding to launch his or her new business. This is even more of a challenge for the young entrepreneur. The financial institutions that are ready to loan money to someone who has many years experience in the business world aren't too keen to take a chance on the young and those who are wet behind the ears.

Not to fear, though! With a little determination and grit, and knowledge of the right places to check, even the youngest business owner can find cash to help get started. Here are the most likely places you'll find funding for your new enterprise.

- *Yourself:* Nobody said that you can start a business without a little sacrifice. The fastest way to come up with the cash is to pull some out of your own savings and/or to sell things that you can live without. Which is more important—that plasma TV and Play station 3 or the vision for your new business? If you can live without it and need the cash for your business, sell it!
- *Smaller Businesses:* This kind of a process in which you move up a business ladder. For instance, if your vision is to operate a DVD kiosk but you can't afford it, start with a more affordable business: Perhaps making and selling sandwiches at lunch time to the employees at local businesses. Once you've made enough money there, move up to another business that will likely bring in more money. Continue this process until you have the money needed to buy your first kiosk.

- *Friends and Family:* Some of the most successful business people started by getting cash from people they already know. Suggestion: This works better if you can tell them something specific that you need to get with it. Instead of telling them, "I need my money to start a business," tell them, "I'm starting a business but don't have the money for newspaper advertising. Can you help with that?"
- *Banks and Lenders:* Yes, this is the hardest place for the young business person to get a loan, but it's not impossible. This is very doable, especially if you have a unique concept that you can demonstrate has a real potential for immediate profit (since immediate profit means being able to quickly repay the loan). You'll be able to improve your chances if someone with money and property will agree to co-sign the loan request with you.

Brief Profile of Some Young Entrepreneurs

Murugavel Janakiraman– Murugavel Janakiraman launched BharatMatrimony.com in 1997. Today it is the premiere Indian matrimonial portal on the Internet. The Asia Indian Chamber of Commerce has honored Janakiraman as one of the top five Asian Indian businessmen in the United States. Janakiraman, 38, is the CEO of Consim Group. With a master's degree in computer science, he has worked as a consultant on software projects for several leading U.S. companies.

Vijay Shekhar Sharma– Vijay Shekhar Sharma is the founder of One97, a telecom products and Services Company founded in 2000. With an Electronics and Communications degree from Delhi College of Engineering, he is the quintessential entrepreneur with many successful ventures. Sharma is a leader in his industry, and his many "firsts" include groundbreaking business models and customer communication products.

Yangdup Lama– Yangdup Lama, a certified bar and beverage trainer, is a bar consultant for several international spirit brands in India. He received his formal bartender training in Spain in 1996 and 1997. Shortly thereafter, he was named the winner of the Asia Pacific 30 under 30 for being one of the outstanding bartenders in Asia. Lama launched a bar and beverage Management Company in 2003 that currently runs three bartending schools in Delhi, Mumbai, and Kathmandu.

Rouble Nagi– A resourceful artist, Rouble Nagi has worked in various media including paint, sculpture, ceramics, metal, stone carving, and mosaic. Nagi has one of the largest mural companies in Asia, with more than 600 murals to her credit worldwide. "Life inspires my art. Art has given me my life," says Nagi. She shares her passion with the next generation, as an organizer of art camps for the underprivileged children of India.

Nalin Khanduri– Great Indian Outdoors In 2000, Nalin Khanduri founded Great Indian Outdoors, a leading outdoors company destined to become India's first adventure/outdoors corporation. A chemical engineer with an MBA degree, Khanduri's love of the outdoors is evident from his twenty years of experience with wilderness trips. Great India Outdoors offers programs to individuals, families, schools, and corporations.

Mark Zuckerberg– Facebook Mark Zuckerberg, twenty-five, co-founded the world's largest social networking site- Facebook. This internet icon is not just for kids, but offers networking tools for everyone. The numbered of registered users to this site grows each day, with currently over 300 million active users.

Sasikanth Chemalamudi– CEO: Habits. A graduate with honors from the Birla Institute of Technology & Science in Pilani, Chemalamudi turned down an offer from outsourcing powerhouse Infosys to pursue his passion for entrepreneurship. He co-launched Habits, a creative learning resources company that encourages more creative thinking with the aid of educational materials such as musicals, plays, and interactive games. Habits is also involved with projects in rural India to encourage self-employment.

Vikas Kedia– Founder & Partner: MobiTrail. The next big platform shift in online gaming will be to mobile handsets, and Kedia thinks his company is positioned to capture that growth. This 25-year-old programmer based in Bombay is founder of MobiTrail, which develops and delivers games to mobile phone users. Its games and applications can run on networks using J2ME, Symbian, and BREW operating systems. The company is developing some hot games of its own and has such clients as Reliant Online Gaming in India and Hong Kong-based Mobile2win, as well as other international customers.

Atul Prakash Khekade– Co-Founder: Innovation Trip Khekade launched his first business, a Web technology and software applications company, at 17, and has written a book on graphical user interfaces. Now the University of Mumbai-trained engineer and scholarship recipient is trying his hand at the business tourism market. Last year he co-founded Innovation Trip, which sets up U.S.-based workshop-and-trip combos for senior executives in the developing world interested in the latest best-business practices in the States.

Vishal Sampat: Founder: Convonix. Sampat caught the entrepreneurial bug early in life. While still in his teens, he launched his first venture, a streaming online music radio service featuring Indian tunes. His latest venture, launched in 2001, is Convonix. It is an Internet marketing firm with more than 35 employees that helps clients enhance their online traffic and get better placement in search engine results. The company has also developed its own Web analytics and campaign management programs.

Divyank Turakhia: Co-Founder, President & Director: Directi Group. Turakhia tried his hand at Internet consulting in high school at age 14 and, two years later, launched Directi Group with $600 borrowed from his parents. In the first month of operations, the business managed to generate enough revenues to return the borrowed amount and get the company rolling. Today, the company is debt-free, has more than 1 million customers for its array of domain name registration, Web hosting, and site building services, and employs more than 250 people. It is one of the fastest-growing domain registration companies in the world. When Turakhia isn't running the show, he pursues hobbies such as sky diving, paragliding, and flying airplanes.

Young Entrepreneurs of IIITM Gwalior

Puneet Chandra (Director Bcube IT Services)

He is interested in Social Networking from his childhood. He think that he don't want to discourage jobs at any time in my life, the only difference is that you are not trying to get employment; you are in fact trying to create employment. Some people start businesses after doing job for a couple of years. he always believed in is to make people believe in your idea and that they can grow with you, that's how you will form a team and it is the team that make a dream come true. he did well to encourage my team that this idea can work.

As a matter of fact my first two start ups failed completely due to some or the other reasons. It is the learning which got successful and finally we are over300 employees now. Some major bottlenecks initially were:

- Funding was a major bottleneck.
- Managing government related work (bribes)
- Lack of long term mentorship.

The major Break through as an Entrepreneur is that Taking a loss of over 30 lacs without any borrowings from anyone and still sustaining. Bringing Bcube back into profits this year employing 300 people.

Nikhil Gupta and Rohit Gupa (C.B.I Solutions)

An entrepreneur gets more freedom in industrial life. He always has a chance to apply his ideas. He can do things in his manner. He not only works on a pre-decided schedule but also plans that schedule. In job you have to follow a pre-decided schedule and that's all. But entrepreneur's life is more stressful, successful and more risky.

They initially worked for BDISYS for 1 year. It gave them enough experience and presented our business-plan to venture investors. Then we started our company on 13-04-2008 in end of our 3rd year.They started with a very low amount and also found mentorship from BDISYS.

They began as consulting company. IT consulting, investment consulting, financial consulting is our field. They design business-plans and provide investment and financial consult to SME of FDI. We are registered from LMU Internship Munich/German.

Now They are just moving on market research. We are currently working on calculation of carbon graded and green product development for SME.The main problem they faces was time management. Commitment is must for an entrepreneur. If you initiate something risk factor is always there. So self-confidence is must.According to them Any student should not be forced to be an entrepreneur because commitment is a very important quality for an entrepreneur. And a forced one does not have this.

Deepak Raj, Ravi Prakash, Shialendra Tripathi and Amit Singh (Quad Infotech)

These are trying to establish in the Market. Four students of IPG - 8th semester dejected by their failure to catch up any internship due to great bear figures on every market sensex decided not to trade off their talent and zeal for small firms. Instead they started creating their own web networks and this was when Quad InfoTech was born.

Instead waiting to grow stronger in terms of legal/technical knowledge or capital, they decided to come across what may and to continue with the resources available. In the beginning working as service providers, gradually as they developed networks and learned intricacies of marketing, they developed their own products.

Their ERP (enterprise resource planning) that includes every aspect of administration in a college is already running successfully in SPIT&M and Sahjaha Singh Maha Vidyalya in Hardoi (U.P.). They have also been contracted for govt. projects; GI's (Geographical Information system) which are an ambitious project by up Jal Nigam. VOIP (voice over internet protocol), a sixth generation web application are also in their list of tasks. When talking about future perspectives in more detail a mix up of ideas come through which could be focused in to three different areas in which they would like to direct their company:

- *Cloud Computing:* As Mr. Deepak Raj's area of research in cloud computing he said the world is wide eyed towards this concept and definitely one could hit the market if they are successful players in this field.
- Mr. Shailendra Tripathi and Mr Amit Singh are looking forward to E-governance in which govt. is funding entrepreneurs for creating, advertising as well as implementation of software/hardware based platforms for various tasks such as payments of bills, bank loans, IT education in villages, managing public portals etc. Mr. Tripathi says that this would help creating awareness among peoples and would help eliminating indiscipline in govt. sector at various levels.

  Mr. Ravi Prakash as an MBA student is more interested in E-marketing sectors which include product details, e-shopping, advertisements etc. and revenues are generated from firms contracting them. He also added this would really be a hard nut as there are already big names in this sector and to venture into this wild competition they would have to be unique and innovative in their approach if they want to set up their own mile stones.

The hurdles which they faces were that Mr. Deepak points out that lack of capital was a major issue. Then also various governmental intricacies of setting up business from registering company to creating their own customers was not at all ways full of roses. Mr. Ravi added that their project mylucknow.com which was next generation yellow pages concept; include the details of every shop, landmarks, public places, and any places of commercial importance at one place in their website. But due to various factors which also comprises lack of data & advertisements the plan was postponed.

Gaganpreet Singh(GPS) (Managing Director Realty Apple Pvt. Ltd)

The idea came to my mind for the first time in 2002, but it was in the year 2006 when he actually decided to become an entrepreneur. It was just by taking the right decision at the right time by which he managed to start up enterprise. He faced many difficulties like firstly he had no background, there was no guidance from seniors or the relatives and no one in my relation was as such in business, next problem was that the real-estate market at that time was in recession, and at last but not the least during the start-up you have to take out the maximum output out of minimum resources.

He believe that his dreams are getting fulfilled as he expected. Due to well taken decision and planning my dreams grew exponentially well. The only message to all start early as possible-the only thing which can help anyone in building entrepreneur struggle only, the sweet fruit.

It is not the number of entrepreneurs that matters, what actually matters are how successful your entrepreneurs are which really add to the growth of status of the institute. If you are giving hundreds and hundreds of entrepreneur then it is not going to help if they are constantly struggling for many years. It is the level of success that your entrepreneurs achieve which actually does matter.

Online start-up businesses run by young adults are an increasingly common phenomenon. A commonly overlooked demographic, however, are the real youth—those under 18 years of age. With online businesspeople facing very low barriers to market entry, many tech-savvy kids are getting in on the act and taking advantage of the opportunities that abound. While these entrepreneurs are more the exception than the rule, some of their successes are highly notable—myyearbook.com was initially founded by two high-school students, yet at one stage was the third-most popular social networking site in the United States, behind MySpace and Face book. Of course, Face book's Mark Zuckerberg was still in college when he established one of the most popular social networking sites in the world.

Sadly, these successes aren't as common as they could be. While the world has countless enthusiastic young people with ideas and technical skills, there are many challenges facing these youthful entrepreneurs. These range from the natural—Venture Capitalists (VC) disputing their expertise, for example—to artificial (such as the age restrictions placed on credit card services that might otherwise be used to pay for start-up resources). Here are some tips for the technically-minded young entrepreneur—both the aspirant service provider and the ambitious salesman—to help them overcome these challenges and succeed in their ventures.

1. *Be Ready to Handle the Challenges of a Business:* Running a business isn't easy. With customers to deal with, clients contacting you at any hour of the day, products to maintain and possibly even staff to manage, operating a business is very intensive. Before you begin anything, consider whether or not you really want to be in business. Running a business isn't for everyone—you may be technically minded, but running a profitable business is a different thing altogether. Look at the market leaders—Google, for example, is managed by three people: two technically minded founders, plus an experienced professional in the business-oriented role of CEO. Still, if you have an idea, and you really want to go into business with it, don't give up now. You just might it make it big!

   Another important issue you will have to deal with is time, or a lack thereof! With school, work, and everything in between, you could soon find yourself trying to get through 30 hours of work every day. Running a business is more often than not a full time job, and at some point, something's got to give. Think about where you want to go in life, and make your decisions accordingly. For example, you could be part of a sporting team, or you could go into business, but you probably can't do both. Often co-curricular and non-school (where applicable) involvements are the first to go; to maintain your social involvement, consider attending user groups, where you can also network and create opportunities for your business.

2. *Plan Your Idea on Paper and Be Ready to Explain It to Others:* When you're running a small business, opportunities can come up at the most unexpected times. You may run into a potential client at a party, a conference, or even a bus stop. You can't let everyone know about your new product or service but the more people who do know, the more opportunities you're likely to get, and therefore the better your chances of making it through your first few months in business. Get the word out—you might just chance on a recommendation to a potential client!

   Work out your business model and the most useful, concise description you can come up with for your goods or services. Let me take this opportunity to recommend my ingenious patent-pending project management system—I call it Pen and Paper. Working out a plan with pen and paper is often far more effective than typing it up, and gives you more time to think it out while you write. Be ready to explain your business to anyone at any time; with this plan in hand, you shouldn't have any problems. Without a plan, your explanations can end up being inconsistent, sounding unconfident, and achieving little or no effect.

   Get business cards printed and carry them around. I've been handing out cards since I was 13, and they're very effective client-winners. At the very least, they give you something on which to scribble the contact details of potential clients. If you bump into anyone who might be in the market for your goods or services let them know what you do; briefly explain your business using the plan you prepared earlier and give them a card. When you meet in person, some people simply won't take you seriously; a business card demonstrates that you're serious about what you do.

3. *Make Good Use of All the Resources Available to You:* Often, young entrepreneurs don't have a lot of capital, but there are still many resources available to you. For example, if you're building a web application for the financial services industry, do you (or more likely, your parents) know any accountants of economists? If you need to quickly undertake a photo shoot for an advertising campaign that a friend has offered to help out with, could you set something up in your parents' garage? For some, imposing on friends and family to help get things moving can be awkward, but learning to take advantage of the available resources is going to give you a huge advantage as a young entrepreneur.

   Lack of access to capital can often become a challenge for young entrepreneurs – basic business development resources such as ad campaigns can become a problem if you don't have a budget. With a bit of thinking, however, many of these problems can be alleviated by taking advantage of the resources at hand.

4. *Build Your Product to be as Complete as Possible before Seeking Financial Assistance:* So, you're developing your whiz-bang product, and suddenly you realize that the Flash charting library you've been using in your application actually costs $1200 for commercial use. You pick up the phone, call Uncle Rob and ask if he can lend you the cash. He politely declines. A series of calls to your other relatives end in a similar fashion.

   As an entrepreneur, you have ideas with a lot of potential. Just as you will eventually sell your product to potential customers, selling your product to potential financial backers is even more important, and this makes explaining and clarifying those ideas a priority. Develop your product as much as you can before seeking financial support; if possible, put together a demonstration video. The more you can demonstrate your idea, the more convincing you'll be. Building on the advice that we discussed in point 2 above, potential financial backers—especially venture capitalists—are very important to the success of your business, and deserve an appropriate amount of your attention.

5. *Maintain a Professional Communication Channel:* When dealing with clients, you may find yourself working with mature professionals who are high up in their respective corporate hierarchies. Getting them to take you seriously is the tricky part.

   If at all possible, live locally, but work globally. Run your life in your local neighborhood, but until you're older and feel confident to deal with clients in person or over the phone, you might consider restricting your customer base to offshore clients (although for US-based entrepreneurs this isn't always an option). Assume the role of a mature industry professional, and you'll be treated like one. When you go professional, age won't matter unless you make it matter. Preparing stunning introductions and speeches always helps for the times when you have to work locally; keep a standard speech in mind and make sure you can deliver it confidently as needed.

   When you're working globally, keep communication to email—definitely don't offer instant messaging as a method of communication. With email, you have a chance to gather your thoughts, and to work out how to respond to clients. As a young entrepreneur, you often have to tread carefully and make sure you don't lose anyone from your limited customer base. With email, you can take the time to prepare a professional response that conveys your intended image. Instant messaging should be avoided at all costs, especially if you plan to contact clients using the same instant messaging profile you use to contact friends — this creates all sorts of opportunities for revealing your lack of experience.

6. *Monitor Progress and Keep Track of Tasks:* The last thing clients want is for you to miss a deadline because you were out on a date or partying with friends. Keep a reasonable separation between your professional and social lives — the so-called work/life balance — but keep track of your progress in your life as an entrepreneur, and maintain a close eye on your daily operations.

   Often a dedicated calendar and marker pen are sufficient, but develop a system that works for you and allows you to keep track of deadlines, pending tasks, and goals. Importantly, establish many goals, and give each a definite deadline; then make sure you achieve these goals within the time frame you have given yourself. Of course, this is easier said than done, and requires a lot of self-discipline.

   Make sure you keep an eye on the big picture, of course. Work out when you expect to start generating revenues, when you want your products and services to be ready, when you aim to secure your first customer, and so on. If you see progress in general sliding, consider putting in a few extra hours here and there, or (if possible) hiring some help — reliable offshore freelancers are plentiful, and the kid next door might not mind helping you out here and there in return for a bit of pocket money (although again, this might be a bit too close to home).

7. *Be Prepared to Fail:* Let's be honest — most start-ups just don't take off. However, this eventuality shouldn't be confused with "failure." Every time you start a business, you gain a new raft of experiences, extend your skill set, and learn valuable lessons for your future enterprising.

   In the event that your business doesn't make it big, and you end up pulling out of it, look back on what you've learned and consider what you plan to do next time. Chances are that you intend to start another business in your lifetime; when you do, you'll be one business the wiser, and ready to deal with new challenges. There's always another opportunity; dust yourself off and keep on going! You haven't failed; you've progressed.

8. *Have Fun!:* You might have built a fantastic product and sold it to half of your target market. Perhaps it even made you rich and famous and put you on the cover of *TIME* magazine at 16! But at the end of the day, the question is: did you have fun?

   It may be the case that your product doesn't take off, you can't find any suitable buyers, or the world simply isn't ready for your product or service. In any case, always keep an eye on the big picture, and make sure you enjoy what you're doing. Entrepreneurialism requires a lot of enthusiasm—you can face some serious challenges if you don't take pleasure in your daily business activities.

   The following advice to young entrepreneurs came from 14 self made members of the Forbes 400. (Source: forbes.com). Sharing its cause its worth reading and it gives you the courage to go on. Achieve what you want to achieve.

Advice to Young Entrepreneurs

You are the next wave, and all of our shoes will be filled by someone. It may as well be YOU. Never give up trying.

- Identify where you have or can create an edge over the rest of the world and doing something you enjoy. Then push that advantage to extremes.
- Everyone has the will to succeed; only those with the will to prepare do.
- Never give up, and have a positive reaction to failure.
- Be curious. And ... the more you give, the more you get. It's as simple as that.
- Learn the business from the ground floor up–not from the top floor down.

- Have a passion for what you do, work hard, have great people with good personalities, enjoy the ride, but balance work and family.
- Identify and affiliate with creative talent. Brainstorm concepts and analyze constantly, but at the conceptual level, not the spreadsheet level
- Ask lots of questions! And, when and if you get the chance to travel, always look for new ideas to bring home! Set your goals and never give up!
- Accumulate a lot of singles and gradually get into the doubles and triples before you try for the home runs.
- To succeed, you have to put in the hours and when you think you are there, put in more.
- Have great focus, set high but achievable goals and work EXTREMELY hard at achieving them. Be flexible and ready to adapt to change.
- Listen to yourself. Be guided by your real passions and convictions, not just by what you think might get you ahead in life
- Find and follow your passions; develop a culture and live it. Positive financial results will flow from that.

5

Case Study on Women Entrepreneurs and their Entrepreneurship Style

Introduction

A large number of women around the world have set up and managed their own businesses. It was not easy for these women to succeed in business. They had to face a lot of difficulties and overcome a number of barriers to become successful in their ventures. They had to deal with discrimination and withstand the skepticism of society, and also put in more effort than men to prove their credibility to others. The entrepreneurial style adopted by women was different from that of men. Studies have revealed that women focus more on intuition and relationships for running businesses, while men emphasize logic and efficiency. The ability that women have to look beyond the obvious and identify hidden opportunities sometimes helped them gain an edge over men. The entrepreneurial style of some of the successful women entrepreneurs of India are featured in this case. All the women featured in this case came from different backgrounds and worked in different fields. Ekta Kapoor, the daughter of a successful film star, started her television software business at the age of 19 and became immensely successful by the time she was in her early 20s. Kiran Mazumdar Shaw had no educational qualifications for running a business

She did not even have an active interest in setting up a business. A chance meeting with the CEO of Biocon International, however, changed her career plans forever. She became India's first lady biotechnology entrepreneur. Shahnaz Husain came from a royal family of conservative Muslims. Her business intention was to draw the attention of the world towards the natural system of ayurveda, which she managed to do successfully. The women of Shri Mahila Griha Udyog Lijjat Papad inculcated a spirit of entrepreneurship among semi literate women. These women were able to overcome social and educational constraints to establish an extremely successful business model. By so doing, they set an example for other women.

Ekta Kapoor

Seeing your own production being aired is a great kick and the fact that most of them figure among the top ten TRP rating makes me feel wonderful."

Ekta Kapoor was said to be the face and brain of Balaji Telefilms Limited (BTL)1, and was almost solely responsible for the phenomenal success of most of BTL's serials. According to Ekta, her childhood was "materially easy but emotionally difficult." As a child she was extremely obese and suffered from low self esteem. She was a poor student and was happy to get by with the minimum pass marks. Even as a child she was an avid television watcher and spent most of her free time glued to the TV. She felt guilty about letting her parents down, but was unable to do anything about it. The turning point in Ekta Kapoor's life came in the early 1990s when a non resident Indian, Ketan Somayya, approached her father and requested him to make some software for the channel he wanted to start. Ekta's father asked her to take up the responsibility of making the software. Consequently, Ekta Kapoor made six pilots, of about three episodes each, at a cost of about Rs 0.5 million. The proposed channel, however, did not fare well and had to be sold to Zee TV not wanting to waste her efforts; Ekta Kapoor started looking for other buyers for her pilots.

She was not successful in finding buyers for the first pilots, but her father came to her rescue and gave her more money to make more pilots. BTL was set up in 1994 by her father. Mano Ya Na Mano, (Believe It or Not) BTL's first serial was telecast in 1995. This was followed by Dhun Dhamaka (Musical Explosion), a music based show aired on Doordarshan, which was moderately successful. The first major success came with Hum Paanch (We Five), a comic sitcom about 5 girls and their harassed parents, which ran for 5 years on Zee TV. BTL came out with an initial public offer (IPO) in October 2000 to set up an integrated studio in Mumbai and to buy advanced equipment. A day prior to its listing on BSE, BTL entered into negotiations with Nine Network Entertainment India Pvt. Ltd. (a wholly-owned subsidiary of Nine Broadcasting India Pvt. Ltd.) for a merger in the ratio of 65:200 through an all-share deal.

The merger was later called off. In its first year as a public company, Balaji showed a net profit of Rs 646 million on net sales of Rs.3.45 billion for the nine month period ending in December 2000. The initial years in the business were not very easy for Ekta Kapoor. There were times when she used to have 5 or 6 pilots ready but none of them would get approval from the channels. People did not take her seriously. Experienced writers would try to force her to accept sub-standard scripts as they thought she was the "brainless daughter of a moneyed father." She was able to overcome these barriers through sheer grit and determination. She worked relentlessly, even foregoing holidays, to make a mark for her. Her time was completely occupied with thinking out stories, finalizing scripts, deciding on sets, costumes, casting, etc.

Her hard work and commitment eventually paid off, and by the early 2000s she had two highly successful serials, Kyunki Saans Bhi Kabhi Bahu Thi (KSBKBT, because the Mother-in-law was also a Daughter-in-Law) and Kahani Ghar Ghar Ki (KGGK, The Story of Every Home) to her credit. She was called the lady with the Midas touch as she hit gold with almost all her projects. By the end of 2002, she had about 35 programming hours per week on television - no mean task for a person in her late 20s. Her hold on television viewers was very strong. She had shows on almost all channels telecasting Hindi programs, as well as some on regional channels. BTL became the biggest name in television and every offering of Ekta Kapoor was lapped up by eager viewers. Ekta Kapoor believed that her initial failures contributed a lot to her success at a later stage. As a novice, she made too many presumptions about the tastes of her audiences. But after her first few projects failed, she became more careful. She started watching television carefully to analyze the programs that were succeeding and those that were failing to understand the likes and dislikes of the viewers. She said that her study of TV programs helped her understand viewers' preferences.

Ekta Kapoor was responsible for introducing a number of changes in Indian television. She was credited with introducing Indian viewers to daily soaps when weekly soaps were the order of the day. She felt that weekly serials could not hold the interest of the audience because of the time gap between episodes. When people missed an episode, they lost interest and stopped watching the serial altogether. Daily serials, however, not only captured and sustained the interest of the viewers; they were also more remunerative for the producer. Ekta Kapoor also introduced the genre of family-based serials in India. She understood that the average Indian was very family oriented and loved to be surrounded by members of their extended families. She capitalized on this characteristic by making serials that showed the life of large joint families.

People welcomed this theme as they were fed up with stories about extramarital affairs. They wanted feel-good serials with which they could identify, and Ekta Kapoor gave them what they wanted. Most of BTL's serials featured regularly in the top ten programs and, almost without exception, enjoyed high viewership ratings. Ekta Kapoor managed to change the concept of prime time television when she made 10:30 pm a prime time slot. When she chose 10:30 as the slot for KSBKBT, Ekta Kapoor did not expect the serial to become so popular. Till then, prime time on television was between 8:00 and 9:30 pm. After that, people had their dinners and went to bed. But after KSBKBT became popular, people changed their television viewing habits and 10:30 pm became a high viewership slot. Since Ekta Kapoor was the creative head of BTL, most of the successes of the company could be traced back to her. She was a hands-on manager, closely involved with all aspects of the serials– from the concept, to the script, the actors and the sets. She believed she had a knack for choosing the right faces for the right parts. Since she felt she understood audience preferences, she maintained full control over the development of serials. She paid a lot of attention to detail and monitored all aspects of BTL's serials for the first few episodes. After she was convinced that her creative team could manage on its own, she eased off. However, she still kept track of the ratings and responses. If there was a crisis, like a fall in ratings, she stepped in again. Ekta was constantly on the look out for new ideas for serials and claimed to source most of her stories from real life situations or people. She sourced the concept of KSBKBT from a short story she read in a magazine. BTL productions were lavishly presented and slickly marketed. Most its new serials could easily sail through on the basis of its past successes, but Ekta Kapoor ensured that nothing was left to chance. She advertised constantly to create visibility. In fact, she even made some of the characters in her serials praise other serials. For instance, some of the characters in the serials are shown discussing her other serials or finishing housework quickly to catch up with them. Her unique style of naming the serials (all names started with K and all the titles were structured in a strange manner) also drew the attention of viewers. She was once advised by an astrologer that the letter 'K' would be lucky for her.

As a result, she started naming all her serials with K. According to Ekta, ninety percent of her serials beginning with that letter have been successful, so she does not see the need to change the practice. On the human resources front, Ekta Kapoor seemed to be something of an autocrat. She yelled at her subordinates as she believed that if she did not shout, things would not get done. She was also completely indifferent to star status and expected all the actors in her serials to toe her line.

Erring or rebellious actors were replaced by others, or the character done away with in the serial to dispense with the actor. Analysts felt that Ekta Kapoor was able to succeed because of some of the shrewd business decisions she took. Firstly, she did not depend on any one channel, but catered to a wide range of channels. This reduced over dependence on one channel. Secondly, BTL diversified risk by distributing resources between commissioned and sponsored serials. This ensured a good mix of risk and returns. Thirdly, the cost of production was kept under control by shooting most of the serials in BTL's own studios.

In addition, the actors were also employed on a contractual basis which gave the producer more control over them. This contract system also helped BTL reduce costs. In 2001, Kapoor was selected by the Confederation of Indian Industries, (CII) to head the committee on entertainment. She also received a number of awards in the early 21st century. Some of the awards are: One of "Asia's 50 most Powerful Communicators," from Asiaweek magazine in 2001; Ernst and Young Entrepreneur of the Year in 2001; "Corporate Excellence" from Bharat Petroleum in 2002; and "Rajiv Gandhi Award" in 2002. The entrepreneurial style of Ekta Kapoor may smack of authoritarianism, but analysts felt her refusal to compromise on quality and her attention to detail contributed greatly to her success. Her perfectionism seemed to have helped make BTL one of the most powerful television software companies of the 2000s.

Kiran Mazumdar Shaw

"My vision is to grow into a global bio therapeutics company with very innovative and proprietary products and technologies."

She is India's first woman Brew Master and the founder director of the Biocon Group.7 India's first lady biotech entrepreneur, Kiran Mazumdar (Mazumdar) was born and brought up in Bangalore. She was educated in Bishop Cotton Girls School and Mount Carmel College in the same city. Mazumdar's childhood ambition was to be a doctor, but when she was unable to get admission in a medical college, she decided to study zoology. After graduation, she was encouraged by her father (who was a brew master) to pursue a career in the science of fermentation. She went to Ballarat College in Melbourne to study malting and brewing technology and qualified as a Brew Master. After returning to India, she worked with her father for a few years as a consultant to some breweries in Kolkata, Mumbai and Bangalore. She was on her way to join a brewery in Scotland when a chance meeting with the founder of Biocon Biochemicals (Ireland), Leslie Auchincloss, steered her into a career in business. She started Biocon India in 1978 in a joint venture with the Irish firm. The company was first set up in her garage in Bangalore and later shifted to a rented house in the suburbs of the city. Her Irish partners were willing to help her set up the company but she refused their help as she wanted to build the company totally on her own. In 1980, the company acquired 20 acres of land in Bangalore and shifted operations to the new location.

In the late 1970s, biotechnology was unheard of. As a result, it was not easy to obtain funds for the venture. Banks and financial institutions were wary of giving her loans as biotechnology was a new field and was therefore considered "high risk". Being a woman, and one with no business qualification at that, made things even more difficult. Mazumdar also faced problems recruiting people. People were reluctant to work for women entrepreneurs as they doubted their credibility. She soon overcame these problems through dedication and hard work. In 1999, the Biocon Group was formed with the merger of all the companies under Biocon, i.e. Biocon India Ltd (founded 1978), Biochemizymes (founded 1990), Syngene (founded 1994) Biocon Quest (founded 1996) and Helix (founded 1998). Later, in 2000, Clinigene was also incorporated into the Group. Mazumdar owned 70 percent of the stock of Biocon and 75 percent of Syngene (the contract research organisation). Clinigene was a fully family-owned company, operating in the area of clinical research. Syngene was started in the late 1990s, when Mazumdar heard from some foreign visitors about the opportunities in contract research. Clinigene was started in 2000 on the advice of a former business associate who felt that clinical research offered a lot of possibilities.

Commenting on Mazumdar's foresightedness, R.A Mashelkar, director-general of CSIR8 said, "Kiran Mazumdar has the ability to see an opportunity much before others." Mazumdar, however, did not take hasty decisions. She started a business slowly, first testing the waters and expanding only when she was sure of its potential. Syngene, for example was conceived in the 1990s but took off only in 1998. In 2001, it earned Rs 140 million, and in the first half of 2002, it made Rs 130 million. When Biocon first started working in 1978, it was a small-scale industry manufacturing industrial enzymes for packaged fruit juices. Over the years it evolved into a $ 60 billion global biotherapeutics10 business. By the early 2000s Biocon had 25 percent of the global market share for pectinases11 and had patents for 15 novel enzymes. Totally, the company manufactured and marketed 73 enzymes.

Biocon was the first Indian company to get Food and Drug Administration (FDA) approval for the manufacture of fermentation derived molecules for pharmaceutical purposes. The Group boasted of clients like Glaxo Smithkline, AstraZeneca and Bristol Myers Squibb. Mazumdar believed in encouraging an open and supportive culture at Biocon. The company had a flat organizational structure and anybody in the organization, from the gardeners to the presidents, had equal access to her. She said, "The moment you start building boundaries, you destroy open culture". She believed that motivation comes from empowerment, and consequently, she encouraged her employees to challenge themselves and solve their own problems.

In the initial years of the business, Mazumdar believed in employing more women than men in her company. But she realized that a large number of women eventually succumbed to societal or family pressures and stopped working. She therefore decided to recruit on the competency parameter alone. The ratio of women to men in Biocon was 1.5: 4 in 2002. A lot of key positions were occupied by women, but men were also well represented in the core team.

Biocon also set up a crèche, so that women employees could bring their small children to work. The company thus relieved them of at least one of the pressures they had to face. Biocon was very successful in retaining employees. Most of the core team had been there for 10 years or more.

Nirupa Bareja, the head of human resources, said, "I can't think of working for another company. It's either Biocon or nowhere." Biocon created a culture in which employees could grow and develop. This helped the company attract and retain the best talent in the country. Biocon also gave importance to customer relations. It did not simply sell the customer a product; it sold a product as well as a service. "We do not just provide the customer with a product.

We also provide information on the market, a strategy, a future," said Rakesh Bamzai, vice-president, marketing, Biocon. Mazumdar enjoyed art and regularly visited art galleries and exhibitions. In 2001 she released her first book, "Ale and Arty," a coffee table book about brewing beer. The book contained reprints of paintings by some of India's best artists, like Jatin Das, Gurudas Chenoy, T.M Aziz, etc. Mazumdar won a number of awards. Prominent among them were the Padmashri in 1989 and the Rotary Award for Best Model Employer.

She also won the M. Visweswariah Award in 2002 for her achievements as an industrialist and her contribution to society. Mazumdar also held positions in industry councils. She was Vice President of the Association of Women Entrepreneurs of Karnataka (AWAKE) and the chairperson of the Vision Group on Biotechnology in Karnataka, which was charged with formulating the state's Biotech policy. Under Mazumdar's leadership, Biocon grew from a small business in the garage of her house to becoming the largest biotech company in India. She was able to achieve this by attracting and retaining the best talent in the country. She said that she was able to achieve this success because of her belief in the field, her magnificent team of people who shared her passion and her determination, and her desire to succeed. Mazumdar wanted to make Biocon a global bio-therapeutics company which developed innovative and proprietary products and technologies. She believed that Biocon would achieve this position around 2005.

Shahnaz Husain

"I do not sell products. I sell an entire civilization in a jar."

Shahnaz Husain (Shahnaz) was another successful woman entrepreneur of India. She popularized herbal treatments for beauty and health problems. Her company, Shahnaz Husain Herbals, was the largest of its kind in the world and had a strong presence in over 100 countries, from the US to Asia. By 2002, the Shahnaz Husain Group had over 650 salons around the world, employing about 4200 people.

The net worth of the Group was $100 million. Shahnaz Husain was born into a royal Muslim family which originally came from Samarkand (in Pakistan) and later held important posts in the princely kingdoms of Bhopal and Hyderabad before India's independence. Shahnaz's father, Justice N.U Beg, was a progressive man who instilled in her a love for poetry and English literature. Shahnaz Husain received her schooling in an Irish convent. A western education coupled with a traditional family background gave Shahnaz Husain wide exposure and developed her into a well rounded personality.

She was married at the age of 15 and had a child by the next year. When her husband was working in Iran, Shahnaz Husain became interested in cosmetology. After she began her training, she realized that chemical cosmetics had a harmful effect on the human body. As a result, she turned her attention towards ayurveda, the ancient Indian system of medicine, which used natural substances and extracts to heal and improve the body. Subsequently, she trained extensively in cosmetic therapy for 10 years in some of the leading institutes of London, Paris, New York and Copenhagen. On her return to India in 1977 she set up her own salon at her house in Delhi with an initial investment of Rs 35000. Instead of offering chemical treatments like other salons, Shahnaz Husain's salon offered Ayurvedic treatments.

Shahnaz's custom made natural products for skin and hair problems quickly became successful. Shahnaz Husain pioneered the commercialization of ayurvedic cosmetics. Until she started her business, ayurveda was practiced in peoples' homes or by local ayurvedic doctors. The commercialization of ayurveda was relatively unknown in the 1970s when Shahnaz Husain entered the business. Shahnaz Husain capitalized on this deficiency. She identified ayurveda as a niche market and catered to it. Her products gained popularity in India, and her treatments were booked months in advance. Encouraged by her success in India, Shahnaz Husain started exploring avenues abroad. She was disturbed by the fact that India was not represented in any of the international beauty forums.

Determined to change the situation, she represented India for the first time in the CIDESCO beauty congress, 17 where she was appointed President for the day's proceedings. She used this opportunity to focus the world's attention on India and ayurveda. The turning point in her business came when she represented India at the Festival of India in 1980. Her team was given a counter in the perfumery section of Selfridges in London. She managed to sell her entire consignment in three days and also broke the store's record for cosmetics sales for the year. As a result, she was offered a permanent counter in Selfridges. Shahnaz Husain was also the first Asian whose products were retailed in the Galeries Lafayette in Paris and to be featured in the 18-foot shop window of the store.

Shahnaz Husain products were carried by many prestigious stores across the world, such as Harrods and Selfridges in London, the Galeries Lafayette in Paris, Bloomingdales in New York, the Seiyu chain in Japan, Sultan Stores in the Middle East and other exclusive outlets in the Middle East, Asia and Africa. Shahnaz Husain operated on the principle of natural care and cure. Her company formulated and marketed over 400 ayurvedic products for various health and beauty problems. Ayurvedic products became popular across the world because they were natural, well suited to the human skin, and were non toxic. Shahnaz Husain claimed that her products were completely pure and were formulated in strict accordance with ayurvedic principles.

They were environment friendly and were not tested on animals. All products went through strict quality control before they were marketed. Her products captured the imagination of the world with their promise of beauty in a natural and harmless way. Shahnaz Husain used natural ingredients like fruits, flowers, vegetables, herbs, honey, etc., which soothe and heal without causing any harm. The group had two R&D units and a herb and flower farm near Delhi. Strict quality control was exercised at every stage of product development, right from the raw material stage to the final product. This ensured that the final product lived up to the promise Shahnaz Husain made of quality and purity. Shahnaz Husain did not believe in advertising; instead, she relied entirely on word-of-mouth publicity for her products.

She believed that a satisfied customer was the best form of advertising. Before Shahnaz Husain entered the retail market, her clinics were the only outlets for her products. By the 1990s, the range and popularity of Shahnaz Husain's products had increased so much that her products were retailed in most of the big retail stores in India and abroad. She was able to achieve growth of this magnitude due to the quality of her products and the result oriented treatments she offered. She commented, "I have relied only on clientele feedback, based on clinical treatments and this is what has made the ranges truly unique and result oriented." In 1977, when she had set up a parlor at her home in New Delhi, she had put up a banner with her qualifications on it. Within days she was booked six months ahead.

She said, "I removed the banner and since then I have never advertised. I have let my products speak for themselves." By 2000, Shahnaz Husain had over 650 salons in 104 countries around the world. Using the franchising mode to expand in India and abroad, she built up a large network of over 600 franchisee and associate clinics around the world. All the franchisees were required to undergo training in specialized treatments at Shahnaz Husain's school of beauty therapy. After training, all franchisees obtained the right to use the Shahnaz Husain name and specialized treatments and were given a 30% profit margin on the sale of products.

Shahnaz Husain believed that an entrepreneur must have a dream and the commitment to pursue it. She believed that business was not simply about employing the right management principles. She said, "I have often gone beyond pure business dealings as such, because for me dua (blessings) is important." Shahnaz Husain believed that a true entrepreneur is a person who has independence of spirit: "One should be innovative, dynamic and willing to try every avenue towards success." She did not look on her work as a career. It was more like an obsession and the sole purpose of her existence. All her dreams revolved around her work and she applied herself to it with complete commitment. According to Shahnaz Husain, a desire to excel, hard work and relentless determination also go into making an entrepreneur.

She said, to succeed, one must never give up and never stop trying: "I always feel I have another mountain to climb and another frontier to cross. I never rest on my laurels." She puts in 18 hours of work and channelizes all her energy into her company. Her commitment and self confidence have made her company one of the most successful of its kind in the world.

Shri Mahila Griha Udyog Lijjat Papad (SMGULP)

"Our objective is to maximize employment opportunities for women through activities connected with village industries, while, at the same time, not sacrificing basic business principles and quality consciousness. We are a full-fledged commercial, self-reliant organization and not a charitable society. Any such benefits that occur are incidental to our business."

The entrepreneurial success of SMGULP23 is noteworthy. SMGULP was a cooperative system in which women over the age of 18 could become members. Starting humbly, with an initial capital of Rs 80, borrowed from a local money lender and social worker, SMGULP grew phenomenally. In 2002, it had a turnover of Rs 3 billion and exports worth Rs.100 million. It employed 42,000 people in 62 divisions all over the country.

SMGULP was the brain child of seven semi-literate Gujarati housewives, who started a venture to create a sustainable livelihood using the only skill they had- cooking. The seven women were Jaswantiben Jamnadas Popat, Parvatiben Ramdas Thodani, Ujamben Narandas Kundalia, Banuben. N. Tanna, Laguben Amritlar Gokani, Jayaben V. Vithalani, and one more lady whose name is not known. These women did not know what entrepreneurship was; neither did they envisage the proportions their small business venture would grow to.

All they wanted was to do something worthwhile with their time and help supplement their family income. In March 1959, this group of women borrowed Rs 80 from Chaganlal Karamsi Parekh, a member of the Servants of India Society and a social worker. With this capital, they started making papads and selling them to a merchant known to them.

Gradually the business grew and its membership increased. Within three months there were about 25 women making papads. Soon the women bought some equipment for the business, like utensils, cupboards, stoves, etc. During the first year, the women had to stop production during the rainy season as the rains would prevent the drying of the papads. The next year, they solved the problem by buying a cot and a stove.

The papads were kept on the cot and the stove below the cot so that the process of drying could take place in spite of the rains. By the end of the first six months, they were able to reward themselves with half a gram of gold each from the profit they had made. The group got considerable publicity through word-of-mouth and articles in vernacular newspapers. This publicity helped it increase its membership. By the second year of its formation, 100 to 150 women had joined the group, and by the end of the third year more than 300 women were rolling papads. In 1962, the name Lijjat was chosen by the group for its products. The organization was named Shri Mahila Griha Udyog Lijjat Papad. By 1962-63, its annual sales of papads touched Rs.0.18 million. In July 1966, SMGULP was registered as a society under the Societies Registration Act 1860. In September 1966, it was formally recognized as a unit belonging to the 'processing of cereals and pulses industry group' under the Khadi and Village Industries Act.

It was also recognized as a "village industry" by the Khadi and Village Industries Commission (KVIC).24 In 1966, SMGULP was granted a working capital of Rs. 0.8 million by KVIC and was allowed certain tax exemptions. It was also registered under the Bombay Public Trusts Act, 1950, as a Public Trust. In 1966, SMGULP evolved into a formal organization and the member sisters adopted the first written constitution. The logo chosen read, "Symbol of Women's Strength". Only women could become members; men could not become members of the organization and did not have any ownership rights. Men working in SMGULP provided only functional support.

The first branch of SMGULP was set up in Valod, Gujarat, in May 1968. Whenever a new branch was established, a few member-sisters from the established branches stayed there for a while (they took turns doing so) and trained the new member-sisters who had joined the new branch. Once the new member-sisters had learnt how to run the branch and monitor its activities, the branch functioned as an independent entity. In this manner, branches were established in all states. And the first branch that was set up in any particular state of India helped the other branches that were later opened in that state. The central office in Mumbai had the overall responsibility for the functioning of all the branches. SMGULP's branches and divisions were spread across fifteen states of India. Mumbai itself had 17 branches.

Among the various divisions were the Sales, Export, Advertising, Printing and Polypropylene divisions. As the number of branches and divisions increased, SMGULP's sales also grew by leaps and bounds. The organization soon diversified into other allied areas that seemed feasible for a cottage industry. In 1988, the group diversified into detergent production. The detergents were sold under the brand name SASA.

Later, soap cakes and liquid soaps were also manufactured under the same brand name. SMGULP's detergent manufacturing business expanded greatly over time. SMGULP emphasized equality. All the members were considered equal and were referred to as sisters. All kinds of work were also given equal importance; no work was considered inferior or superior to any other. The women were also given the freedom to choose the work they liked best; be it preparing the dough, rolling papads or packaging.

Quality was also emphasized and supervisors constantly checked for quality and weight against set standards. SMGULP was based on sound, commercial principles. Since the beginning, all the members were aware of the importance of running the institution as a business enterprise, keeping a constant vigil on every aspect of its working, and maintaining accounts properly. The main aim of SMGULP was to help members earn an honest income through legitimate means. It provided self-employment opportunities to women and helped inculcate in them a measure of self-confidence and self-reliance. Business was also done ethically.Care was taken to see that the products were priced reasonably, and whenever the cost of raw materials fell, the prices were also revised downwards. These revised prices were advertised in newspapers to ensure that the distributors did not overcharge.

Labor charges worked out to 20-25 percent of the consumer price, raw materials consumed 55-60 percent, sales and other administrative expenses accounted for the remaining 20 percent. This principle was followed for all its products, be it masalas or synthetic detergents. Products were marketed on an area wise basis. Each branch was individually responsible for marketing its products in the area allotted to it. SMGULP's wide network of dealers and the goodwill it enjoyed made the marketing of products easy.

No supplier was asked for credit and none was extended. The papads, produced everyday, were taken to SMGULP's depots. The distributors and exporters picked up their respective stock of products daily against immediate payment. To ensure consistent quality, the head office supplied the most important raw materials to all its branches. Apart from supplying the raw materials, the head office did not involve itself with the different branches. SMGULP's products were advertised in print (vernacular newspapers) and electronic media. The cooperative also sponsored some TV programs and gave gifts to winners of certain shows. The cost of advertising was borne by all the branches and divisions of SMGULP through an ingenious method. The money for advertisements was spent by the Polypropylene Division, which recovered the same by increasing the price of the bags that it supplied to all the branches and divisions of SMGULP throughout India.

Thus all of them shared the cost of advertisements in an equitable manner, according to their individual production capacity. SMGULP had a managing committee (which had the highest decision-making powers) consisting of 21 members, a president, a vice president, two secretaries and two treasurers. They were chosen by the sisters (from among the member-sisters) once every three years.

Any member-sister could become a managing committee member through a selection process. The members of each branch could elect a branch committee, consisting of eleven sisters. The managing committee could unilaterally terminate or appoint any member in the branch committee. Its decisions could even supersede those of the branch committee. The various branches situated all over the country were managed in a decentralized manner. The Sanchalikas or directors of the branches were selected by the members of the concerned branch every three years. They were responsible for managing the day-today-activities of a particular branch or division. They could be transferred to other branches also.

Meetings were also held at regular intervals on a branch, area and countrywide basis. Open meetings were also held at the head office regularly, to encourage participation by all members. As all the members were equal owners and shared profits equally at the end of the year, they were directly responsible for the profitable functioning of the branch they worked in. Mismanagement or loss due to negligence would lead to the dismissal of the concerned Sanchalika or other member-sisters from SMGULP. In one particular case where losses were reported due to a fall in quality standards, the member-sisters lowered their daily wages by Re. 1 per kilogram of papads, to compensate for the loss. When a particular branch performed well financially, the member-sisters increased their wages and also gave themselves additional incentives. Irene Almeida, spokesperson of SMGULP, said "The system is self sustaining. Each member works to improve efficiency and reduce wastage. They know that profits and losses have to be borne by them." SMGULP took part in several trade fairs and exhibitions held in various parts of India. This not only increased its sales but also made the brand name Lijjat famous. In addition, participation in such activities encouraged the numerous member-sisters to become active agents in the functioning of their institution, thus indirectly increasing their self-confidence. Many organizations in India took a leaf out of SMGULP's book tried to emulate its model of working. It seemed to be a good option for rural or semi-skilled women, who were not qualified for other types of jobs, as it provided them with a livelihood without demanding high skills and instilled in them a sense of self-worth and self-reliance.

Any member-sister could become a managing committee member through a selection process. The members of each branch could elect a branch committee, consisting of eleven sisters. The managing committee could unilaterally terminate or appoint any member in the branch committee. Its decisions could even supersede those of the branch committee. The various branches situated all over the country were managed in a decentralized manner. The Sanchalikas or directors of the branches were selected by the members of the concerned branch every three years. They were responsible for managing the day-today-activities of a particular branch or division. They could be transferred to other branches also.

Meetings were also held at regular intervals on a branch, area and countrywide basis. Open meetings were also held at the head office regularly, to encourage participation by all members. As all the members were equal owners and shared profits equally at the end of the year, they were directly responsible for the profitable functioning of the branch they worked in. Mismanagement or loss due to negligence would lead to the dismissal of the concerned Sanchalika or other member-sisters from SMGULP. In one particular case where losses were reported due to a fall in quality standards, the member-sisters lowered their daily wages by Re. 1 per kilogram of papads, to compensate for the loss. When a particular branch performed well financially, the member-sisters increased their wages and also gave themselves additional incentives.

Irene Almeida, spokesperson of SMGULP, said "The system is self sustaining. Each member works to improve efficiency and reduce wastage. They know that profits and losses have to be borne by them."25 SMGULP took part in several trade fairs and exhibitions held in various parts of India. This not only increased its sales but also made the brand name Lijjat famous. In addition, participation in such activities encouraged the numerous member-sisters to become active agents in the functioning of their institution, thus indirectly increasing their self-confidence. Many organizations in India took a leaf out of SMGULP's book tried to emulate its model of working. It seemed to be a good option for rural or semi-skilled women, who were not qualified for other types of jobs, as it provided them with a livelihood without demanding high skills and instilled in them a sense of self-worth and self-reliance.

Entrepreneurial Style

The entrepreneurial style of all these entrepreneurs was different. Ekta Kapoor was a complete hands-on manager. She exercised control over all aspects of the functioning of BTL and had the final word on everything. Her style of working was criticized by many, but there were others who feel that it was the main reason for her success. Ekta Kapoor was very young when she made her foray into television software.

She faced a lot of problems convincing people of the seriousness of her purpose. According to Ekta Kapoor, people did not take her seriously because they thought she was only working to pass the time. They also tried to take advantage of her inexperience by trying to force her to accept sub-standard scripts. In addition, they tried to exploit her by overcharging, because she had a wealthy father. Faced with these obstacles, analysts felt Ekta Kapoor did well to adopt a high-handed autocratic style. Had she not been assertive, people would have taken advantage of her and, consequently, she would not have been able to achieve what she did. Her assertiveness helped her overcome the problems created by her youth and inexperience.

Kiran Mazumdar had neither a business degree nor business experience, yet she successfully set up Biocon from scratch. She adopted a democratic leadership style. Kiran Mazumdar believed in creating an open atmosphere and a culture which encouraged risk taking. Such an environment is essential for research based organizations which thrive on innovative ideas. She recruited people only on the basis of competency, thus ensuring that she got the best talent. This approach to recruitment helped Biocon become the largest biotech company in India. Shahnaz Hussain, believed in flexibility in business. She said that she did not believe in rigid principles of management, and that she often went beyond pure management principles because 'dua' (blessings) was more important to her.

She did not advertise because she knew that her products spoke for themselves. Since she relied on her products for publicity, she had to ensure that they were of good quality. To maintain a high level of quality, all her products were put through strict quality control processes. Even the raw materials went through stringent quality tests before they were used.

By not advertising, she gave her products an aura of glamour and exclusiveness. Shahnaz felt that entrepreneurship was about dreaming and having the determination to achieve that dream. The women of SMGULP showed how women could overcome any number of barriers to establish a successful business. SMGULP was essentially a venture of and for semi-literate, unskilled women.

These women were able to create a successful business out of something as mundane as cooking. Despite being untrained, they were able to make their business a success because of their discipline and commitment. The ingenious methods adopted by the women of SMGULP (such as their method of sharing advertising expenses) demonstrated that business acumen was not the prerogative of those who held graduate degrees in business. Work at SMGULP proceeded smoothly, as there were set procedures for most of the important activities. All the women entrepreneurs discussed in this case were able to overcome odds to create successful business ventures in their respective fields. They also were an inspiration to a number of other women in India.

6

Reaction of Government Employee on Entrepreneurship

Given the fact that many developing countries will suffer serious gaps in the number of formal sector jobs available to those seeking employment for the foreseeable future, enterprise development will be the only employment alternative for many of the world's low-income youth. In other words, many youth are becoming entrepreneurs more out of need, than due to personal preference. This was a finding of a recent IDB study, which also found that even for those youth that prefer formal sector employment, Self-employment can later facilitate the transition to paid employment for youth. Nonetheless, youth face many disadvantages in trying to start a business. They tend to have limited access to capital and business networks, as well as knowledge of markets and opportunities. Business development services that are available are often not holistic or integrated. Several approaches have been applied to develop young people's entrepreneurial skills and to overcome these limitations. Excessive or over-complex red tape and bureaucracy provide a particular disincentive to young people starting a business and can put an unsustainable burden on their new businesses. There are a number of regulatory challenges to young entrepreneurs which include pricing policies, credit policies and import /export tariffs.

To Know better about what Government of India takes initiatives for entrepreneurs, what are the benefits that government support entrepreneurs? and How government plays an important role to encourege entrepreneurship? ....

Mr. Ravi Anand
(Chief Marketing Executive of SBI, Gwalior)

Mr. Ravi Anand, Chief marketing executive of SBI, Gwalior holds entrepreneurship in positive light. He talks of policies and schemes offered by Government of India as well as the problems blocking the growth of entrepreneurship. According to Mr. Anand there are many perks of entrepreneurship over government jobs. Government of India is helping young entrepreneurs through banks (State Bank of India) and to reap maximum benefit from such schemes.

Views of Entrepreneurship in Gwalior: Mr. Anand, views that entrepreneurship is becoming an important aspect of the Indian society, as more and more number of individuals are coming forward to start their own ventures due to limited number of Government jobs. From the point of view of a banker, Mr. Anand regards that there are lots of opportunities in entrepreneurship and role of banks in helping young entrepreneurs is important. In banking, also, there are many openings where entrepreneurs can link in. Banking is of two kinds service banking and retail banking. Although, there are no such hurdles as such, but he drew the attention towards the guidelines that are not clearly stated by the government due to which payments are not possible and the schemes of which people are unaware of. If proper awareness can be implemented then these hurdles can also be overcome. There are many policies government has introduced from time to time like SCTPI etc of which people are unaware of. Many schemes and subsidies from government are there for small to large Entrepreneurs of which people are yet unknown and should be made aware of.

Dr. Sunil Agrawal (M.B.B.S., M.D.)
(Chief Medical and Health Officer, Morena)

Dr. Sunil Agrawal knows the benefits of the govt. sector and he is also aware of the pros and cons of the entrepreneurship. According to him, it is the personal choice of the person combined with the circumstances that matter and enable him to make a decision.

Views of Entrepreneurship in Gwalior: Dr. Agrawal talked mainly about the medical and health sector, there is a huge scope for entrepreneurs in health sector as there is scarcity of good big hospitals in Gwalior like the ones in Delhi or other big cities.. But then in this field, education is also a limiting factor as only a qualified doctor can enter in this field. The other main hurdles are Unavailability of qualifies staff, Unavailability of high quality labs, Customer dissatisfaction: due to Gwalior being a small city, Government laws. . He also highlighted an important thing that at least in the health sector, govt. does not promote entrepreneurship at all. In fact through its various rules and regulations, which although are aimed at public welfare, it has an inhibitory effect on entrepreneurship.

Dr. R. Singhal, Proctor and Coordinator (Entrepreneurship and Development Cell, RTU, Kota)

Dr. R. Sighal views Entrepreneurship is a nice option as a career. It is better to start own business rather than depending on others. However due to lack of enough support in India people often come back and leave entrepreneurship. Many people have started their own business. But due to corruption in government organization they are discouraged.

Views of Entrepreneurship in Gwalior: In his view there is very less support from government in this field. Government organizations are corrupt and legal processes are too long and tedious. There is always lack of information in this field. To overcome this problem He suggests that there should be a separate window opened for supporting entrepreneurs. A course should be introduces at all levels in every college. If anybody wants to become an entrepreneur it should be like that government people should approach him and provide him the required support in this regard.

Mr. Jagdish Kumar, System Administrator ABV-Indian Institute of Information Technology & Management, Gwalior

Mr. Jagdish opinion was that entrepreneurship must be encouraged and it plays a vital role in country's overall development and employment generation. He shared his view that a man should have a clear demarcation between his aspirations and capabilities; one should take the path of entrepreneurship based on the inner confidence and capabilities. In his view jobs especially government bound the potential of a person and the true inner character of a man is never exploited to get the best out a man. Entrepreneurial path gives a new direction and way of life with limitless potential and limitless opportunities. Mr. Jagdish specially emphasized on the financial constant bounds in a job which directly affects the inner hunger of a person to strive for more. He said that a person with a good salary gets satisfied easily whereas an entrepreneur does not know what is there next waiting for him, it can be good it can be bad that keeps him on his toes to keep striving.

Views of Entrepreneurship in Gwalior: Mr. Jadish supported a view of a great entrepreneur of our time founder of Apple Computer Mr. Steve Jobs. He once said that a person *"should remain foolish and stay hungry"* to never let his inner flame to strive and achieve what he want out of life die. Mr. Jagdish made a clear cut point that nothing great can be achieved if a person's potential is constrained in a simple job. He implied that if one wants to achieve the best fruits out of life one should go for entrepreneurial path rather than just making himself bound in a job.

Mr. Ashok Khare (Officer NAREGA, Indore)

Mr. Ashok Khare views entrepreneurship is a good thing if you have the new idea and family support. In your own business we can use our resources by doing hard work and having potential. He said that in government job there is very less growth, and you will be promoted until you are aged, may be you can end with CEO if you are the best.

Views of Entrepreneurship in Gwalior: In his view, Gwalior is a growing city; if you have a new idea then it is the best opportunity to start your own venture here. He said that before starting your own venture you have to see that whatever you are going to start is acceptable in Gwalior or not!. The main problem was to get financial support. The government procedure for getting loans is a big problem here. After that procedure of getting registered your company is very difficult here. Entrepreneurship is a good thing and young generations like us should be encouraged. He believes that more and more people will start their venture then employment will increase and it will help to growth in your region and of course nation's also. He also said that government is also starting various plans in which government is providing loans for very poor people so that they can start their own business of shoes, clothes shop and many more. Government is starting various plans in which peoples are learning that how to start our own venture and what is the procedure, from where they can get loans.

Mr. Ravindra Prasad
(Senior Branch Manager BOI IIITM Branch)

Mr. Ravindra Prasad is seeing entrepreneurship as a good future for young generation and Entrepreneurship is important to make a country developed but to maintain the internal discipline and to run the System in a well mannered way government is important. According to him for a developing country like India, one need to promote entrepreneurship as it creates more jobs and helps in the overall improvement of the country. Since it solves the problem of today's generation (Generation Y) both in the private and the public sectors entrepreneurial activity on a large scale based on a sensitive and innovative attitude guided by a broad concept of welfare is needed even more than before, because we have got limited government opening and our population is increasing very rapidly so for becoming self independent one has to start his own venture.

Views of Entrepreneurship in Gwalior: In business people are independent .But it is not secure but the government provides lot many facilities to their employees but it also promote the business and entrepreneurship such as it gives the loan to start the business "business loan". He believes that people don't want to take risks in their life while they know that they will be independent and can earn more money still they don't want to take risk.

Raksha Bundela
(Computer Operator NREGA Gwalior)

He was not aware of the term entrepreneur but after explaining them he understood and said yes this is obviously better than doing job under someone and being dependent on others. This gives them job security and independence and government also helps in financing small scale business such as starting a computer centre, Battery Farming etc.He was not aware of problems to entrepreneurs in Gwalior but he told due to corruption the person who demands for loan to start a small scale business had to try hard to get the loan and he receives small fraction of money only.

Views of Entrepreneurship in Gwalior: In his view Entrepreneurship is risky business he himself did not wants to take risk.They said they are happy with their life and though having one's own business will make them independent but they didn't want to take risk and they also had financial problems. Government employees do not strive to achieve or do something good in life. They are happy with their life and though government helps in funding their small scale business but it's very tough for them to get those funds due to corruption at so many levels.

Mr. Santosh Kumar Aharwal
(DEO, Head Office MGNREGS Bhopal)

Mr. Santosh Kumar views Entrepreneurship as a way to become independent or it is the need of the hour .He is ongoing a training of MANREGS and is being actively involved in implement government's plans for providing self employment to rural people. He elaborated the changes occurred in village level due to self employment. Many people are employed in brick making, pickles making, vegetable marts etc. In his view availability of jobs with respect to the demand is very less, so it's not possible for everyone to get the job of their liking so a greater focus towards self employment.

Views of Entrepreneurship in Gwalior: He views Gwalior as a potential place for entrepreneurship. As it is a tourist place an entrepreneur can get more outside interactions and hence can use it to enhance his/her business. He cited that the response from people of Gwalior in Rural Self Employment programs run by government is very encouraging. The climatic condition of Gwalior is not suited for many agriculture based industries so for village people it's important to focus on self employment. The most important problem is its climatic condition and slow pace of development. The schemes initiated by government are still out of the reach of many villagers. Lack of good education at village level a well as city is one of the major hindrance to entrepreneurship.

M. Sasidhar (Director)
District Industries Centre (Hyderabad)

Mr. Sasidhar believes that entrepreneurship is definitely necessary in our country with loads of opportunities and one can clearly see that every rural area in this country has the scope to become a developed place and this can only be achieved by Entrepreneurs. Young generation really has the potential in themselves and they can achieve their goals by a strong determination and dedicated hard work. New students have to take up things independently, become innovative and can always take the challenge and win. According to him Mr. Narayana Murthy, from Infosys should be the role model for every entrepreneur who had started the company with very few people like 3 or 4 employees and also with a very minimum financial support and now it has become one of the largest IT services firms in our country.

Views of Entrepreneurship in Gwalior: Gwalior is not that well developed as compared to other metros like New Delhi or Hyderabad. It is slowly improving in fields of infrastructure and services as one can see the new malls and all telecommunications coming fast into the city. The local transport facilities also improved with the upcoming of city buses which wasn't there before last year. Still there's a lot to improve and there is huge scope for development. The government can also help by suggesting new ideas and also by supporting young entrepreneurs. People are reluctant to start bigger businesses and that is the reason why this city didn't develop as an industrial area. The reason for this may also be lack of relevant facilities like close raw materials and water facilities. The only reason for people not choosing to set up a business could be the high amount of risk involved and also due to lack of sufficient capital and motivation and this city still remains under developed.

R.K. Agarwal J.T.O.
(Junior Telecom Officer), Sanchar Bhawan
(BSNL) City Centre, Gwalior

Entrepreneurs not only help in increasing the growth of economy but also creating job opportunities for many other people of society. There are different ways that governments are trying to spur entrepreneurial activity. Each approach has its own costs and benefits, whether it's a direct subsidy, a loan guarantee program, or a venture capital model where the government is a direct investor.

Views of Entrepreneurship in Gwalior: The most important problem in Gwalior is its climatic condition and slow pace of development. The schemes initiated by government are still out of the reach of many villagers. Lack of good education at village level as well as city is one of the major hindrances to entrepreneurship. The solution is to ensure that schemes enacted for providing self employment should be corruption free and should be accessible to a large mass of the villagers.

Mr. Krishna Kishore
(Life Insurance Cooperation, Hyderabad)

Mr. Krishna Kishore views Entrepreneurship as an Act of creating own employment by launching new ventures based on an innovative idea, Act which transforms business equipment to useful goods and it also includes social and political forms of entrepreneur activity. The steps Government should take in India is to provide one stop services that provide assistance to the entrepreneurs to expand their business and schools that provide business skills and many more...

Views of Entrepreneurship in Gwalior: In his view the scope of entrepreneurship in Gwalior is more as it is a less developed city and in terms of area it is very big. As it is developing in recent years any innovative idea can be launched and the success rate is very high. Innovative idea should be launched based upon the economic, social, political factors in Gwalior to become a success in the society. The hurdle is that economic background of most of the people is not as good as in other cities. So the act of entrepreneurship is added with mush risk. To develop entrepreneurship government should provide some basic financial help to launch an innovative venture. Entrepreneurship is something which develops the economic status of the country. Government should target young entrepreneurs in the country by providing financial help and encouraging innovative ideas.

Mr. Ajay Kumar Roy (Senior Production Management) Lecturer: IHM, Gwalior (Institute of Hotel Management)

Mr. Ajay Kumar believes that Entrepreneurship is necessary for India due to two reasons one government jobs are less in numbers and second thing is that person who works in the industry gain experience about work but if they have skills and capabilities they can start their own business for creating jobs for others. Present government is starting many plans to self business for the young generation and they are providing loan for it on less interest. Short term courses are also conducted to increase their business skills.

Views of Entrepreneurship in Gwalior: Gwalior is good growing city of India; there are many fields to be developed (like malls and restaurant etc) in this city so entrepreneurship is good way to the youth to earn money. Gwalior is connected with road ways, railways and airways to the country so transportation problem is not here. Present government is starting many plans to self business for the young generation and they are providing loan for it on less interest. Short term courses are also conducted to increase their business skills. In spite of highly favorable environment for entrepreneurship in Gwalior, it still has some challenges like economic challenge, social challenge, and MP

Govt. support to initiate any new venture. Water supply is not good because water level is too low.

S.H.N Babu
(Assistant Manager) SBI, Macharla Branch (A.P)

Entrepreneurship is good one and helps in individual growth (as per profit and personality development) and results in employing people and helps in economic growth of the country. He explained about various schemes of SBI like SME loan schemes and various subsidies employed by the government in order to encourage Entrepreneurship. Thinking of establishing a business with an innovative and feasible idea is not self sufficient but we must also find the target public to it. He seems to be in favor of encouraging Entrepreneurship.

Views of Entrepreneurship in Gwalior: In his view In Gwalior, The scope of becoming successful entrepreneurs is as high as it is in the stage of development considering all the current emerging trends. Movie theatres, City malls etc are some of the examples that can be established in a city like Gwalior. Although, there is lot of scope for current emerging trends, most of the public are middleclass and they are not interested in these trends. Due to extreme climatic conditions, less number of upper-class, pollution and the neatness (cleanliness) of the city etc, public are hesitating to get settled in Gwalior.

Mr. Rampal Singh Kushwah
(Assistant in T&P Cell) ABV-Indian Institute of Information Technology and Management, Gwalior

Mr. Rampal has optimistic reaction about entrepreneurship. He himself wants to be an entrepreneur. He believes that entrepreneurship success has no limit that is the place where we can really examine our potential. In entrepreneurship you have no foundation, no constraint on income, no limit on work hour. One saying is proved here "As much as you sow, so shall you get."

Views of Entrepreneurship in Gwalior: In his view Gwalior is not much exposed about entrepreneurship, as the people still thinks that success and experience in business comes from previous generation. They are very poor in risk taking capability. They believe on the business legacy. In Gwalior the main problem is about lack of motivation, support of society and family members. They don't have much example after who see they can stand with their idea in front of challenges. The other hurdles are lack of financial support by government bodies and no education and training program for entrepreneurs.

Mr. Kamal Kishor Sharma (Section Engineer) Railway Ticket Employee, Gwalior

Mr. Kamal views towards Entrepreneurship are totally positive and he views Entrepreneurship is a field where one can show his own strength and gain the growth according to his own hard work. Mr. Kamal says that few years earlier there is no any support provided by government but these days things has changed. Now government provides big amount of loans for establishing own business & also they provide infrastructural support for nationwide growth of Entrepreneurship. So today's young generation should must try for Entrepreneurship because in this, one can achieve unlimited success and growth as compare to a traditional government job.

Views about Entrepreneurship in Gwalior: In Gwalior Entrepreneurship is carried by push factor, only those who do not get the job or they don't have anything to feed their family are Entrepreneur. Push factor Entrepreneurship are very less, they are lacking the awareness. There is no environment present for Gwalior people to encourage Entrepreneurship. In colleges they don't study about Entrepreneurship and they leave the thought because they don't know how to start, what is our first step. Mr. Sharma says that few years earlier there is no any support provided by government but these days things has changed. Now government provides big amount of loans for establishing own business & railways also got scholarship where you will get 5000/- per month. So today's young generation should try for Entrepreneurship because in this, one can achieve his life goal, his idols and the growth he wanted for himself.

Mr. Arvind Sehgal (Manager), Speed Post Center, Railway Station, Gwalior

Since population is increasing day by day and government is not able to provide employment to all so it's very appreciative if anyone want to start its own business. This will result in not only his growth but also in the nation's growth. According to him you will be independent and use your full potential which is not in the case of government job.

View of Entrepreneurship in Gwalior: In his view Gwalior is a potential place for entrepreneurship. Since Gwalior is not much developed city so there are a large number of sectors in which people can set up their own ventures. The most important problem is slow rate of development in Gwalior mainly in rural part of the city. Mr. Arvind government is giving more emphasis on professional education. Also now a days government is helping entrepreneur in variety of ways by giving bank loans at low interest rate and providing subsidy.

Mr. B.S. Srivatsav DEO (Data Entry Officer) NREGA

Mr. B.S. Srivatsav views entrepreneurship is necessary in present time since the scope of earning in Indian market is rapidly increasing .It gives more job satisfaction and makes the life more challenging. In olden days people thought government job as security but now a day's u can earn far more better and lead your life as you need to Mr. B.S. Srivatsav holds entrepreneurship in positive light. He talked of policies and schemes offered by Government of India as well as the problems blocking the growth of entrepreneurship. At the end of the interview I came to know of how entrepreneur is far better than government one .I also got knowhow of how Government is helping young entrepreneurs through loans, training, subsidies and how to reap maximum benefit from such schemes.

Views about Entrepreneurship in Gwalior: In his view Gwalior has a lot of opportunities as it is developing city but Gwalior is not much exposed about entrepreneurship, as the people still thinks that success and experience in business comes from previous generation. They are very poor in risk taking capability. They believe on the business legacy. The main problem Gwalior is facing is in terms of man power regarding technical assistance. He feels that it's very difficult to in source from other place since Gwalior is not developed city. And the other problem is about lack of motivation, support of society and family members. The other hurdles are lack of financial support by government bodies and no education and training program for entrepreneurs. There are many policies government has introduced from time to time like loans.

Dr. Ritu Tiwari (Associate Professor) ABV-Indian Institute of Technology and Management, Gwalior (M.P)

Entrepreneurship is very much necessary if a person wants to grow and reach to very high level. Since the awareness of the entrepreneurship is less hence the first step is to increase the level of awareness among the people. The awareness can be increased only if they see other people surrounding them becoming a good entrepreneurship and a successful entrepreneurship.

Views of Entrepreneurship in Gwalior: Gwalior is a little less developed city hence the level of the awareness must be increased so as to promote the entrepreneurship. People are very reluctant in changing and hence there are very less possibilities of people in Gwalior becoming good entrepreneurs. The positive effects and advantages of being the entrepreneurs should be shown. To overcome this problem, measures should be taken to Promote and make awareness of entrepreneurship as much as possible.

7

Change Management

Introduction

Change management is a structured approach to shifting/ transitioning individuals, teams, and organizations from a current state to a desired future state. It is an organizational process aimed at empowering employees to accept and embrace changes in their current business environment. In project management, change management refers to a project management process where changes to a project are formally introduced and approved.

Here are some rules for effective management of change. Managing organizational change will be more successful if you apply these simple principles. Achieving personal change will be more successful too if you use the same approach where relevant. Change management entails thoughtful planning and sensitive implementation, and above all, consultation with, and involvement of, the people affected by the changes. If you force change on people normally problems arise. Change must be realistic, achievable and measurable. These aspects are especially relevant to managing personal change. Before starting organizational change, ask yourself: What do we want to achieve with this change, why, and how will we know that the change has been achieved? Who is affected by this change, and how will they react to it? How much of this change can we achieve ourselves, and what parts of the change do we need help with? These aspects also relate strongly to the management of personal as well as organizational change.

Do not 'sell' change to people as a way of accelerating 'agreement' and implementation. 'Selling' change to people is not a sustainable strategy for success, unless your aim is to be bitten on the bum at some time in the future when you least expect it. When people listen to a management high-up 'selling' them a change, decent diligent folk will generally smile and appear to accede, but quietly to themselves, they're thinking, "No bloody chance mate, if you think I'm standing for that load of old bollocks you've another think coming..." (And that's just the amenable types - the other more recalcitrant types will be well on the way to making their own particular transition from gamekeepers to poachers.)

Instead, change needs to be understood and managed in a way that people can cope effectively with it. Change can be unsettling, so the manager logically needs to be a settling influence.

Check that people affected by the change agree with, or at least understand, the need for change, and have a chance to decide how the change will be managed, and to be involved in the planning and implementation of the change. Use face-to-face communications to handle sensitive aspects of organizational change management. Encourage your managers to communicate face-to-face with their people too if they are helping you manage an organizational change. Email and written notices are extremely weak at conveying and developing understanding.

If you think that you need to make a change quickly, probe the reasons - is the urgency real? Will the effects of agreeing a more sensible time-frame really be more disastrous than presiding over a disastrous change? Quick change prevents proper consultation and involvement, which leads to difficulties that take time to resolve.

For complex changes, refer to the process of project management, and ensure that you augment this with consultative communications to agree and gain support for the reasons for the change. Involving and informing people also creates opportunities for others to participate in planning and implementing the changes, which lightens your burden, spreads the organizational load, and creates a sense of ownership and familiarity among the people affected.

For organizational change that entails new actions, objectives and processes for a group or team of people, use workshops to achieve understanding, involvement, plans, measurable aims, actions and commitment. Encourage your management team to use workshops with their people too if they are helping you to manage the change.

You should even apply these principles to very tough change like making people redundant, closures and integrating merged or acquired organizations. Bad news needs even more careful management than routine change. Hiding behind memos and middle managers will make matters worse. Consulting with people, and helping them to understand does not weaken your position - it strengthens it. Leaders who fail to consult and involve their people in managing bad news are perceived as weak and lacking in integrity. Treat people with humanity and respect and they will reciprocate.

Be mindful that the chief insecurity of most staff is change itself. Senior managers and directors responsible for managing organizational change do not, as a rule, fear change - they generally thrive on it. So remember that your people do not relish change, they find it deeply disturbing and threatening. Your people's fear of change is as great as your own fear of failure.

Responsibility for Managing Change

The employee does not have a responsibility to manage change-the employee's responsibility is no other than to do their best, which is different for every person and depends on a wide variety of factors (health, maturity, stability, experience, personality, motivation, etc). Responsibility for managing change is with management and executives of the organisation - they must manage the change in a way that employees can cope with it. The manager has a responsibility to facilitate and enable change, and all that is implied within that statement, especially to understand the situation from an objective standpoint (to 'step back', and be non-judgemental), and then to help people understand reasons, aims, and ways of responding positively according to employees' own situations and capabilities. Increasingly the manager's role is to interpret, communicate and enable - not to instruct and impose, which nobody really responds to well.

Change Must Involve the People - Change Must Not be Imposed Upon the People

Be wary of expressions like 'mindset change', and 'changing people's mindsets' or 'changing attitudes', because this language often indicates a tendency towards imposed or enforced change (theory x), and it implies strongly that the organization believes that its people currently have the 'wrong' mindset, which is never, ever, the case. If people are not approaching their tasks or the organization effectively, then the organization has the wrong mindset, not the people. Change such as new structures, policies, targets, acquisitions, disposals, re-locations, etc., all create new systems and environments, which need to be explained to people as early as possible, so that people's involvement in validating and refining the changes themselves can be obtained.

Whenever an organization imposes new things on people there will be difficulties. Participation, involvement and open, early, full communication are the important factors. Staff surveys are a helpful way to repair damage and mistrust among staff-provided you allow people to complete them anonymously, and provided you publish and act on the findings.

Management training, empathy and facilitative capability are priority areas - managers are crucial to the change process-they must enable and facilitate, not merely convey and implement policy from above, which does not work. You cannot impose change-people and teams need to be empowered to find their own solutions and responses, with facilitation and support from managers, and tolerance and compassion from the leaders and executives. Management and leadership style and behavior are more important than clever process and policy. Employees need to be able to trust the organization.

The leader must agree and work with these ideas, or change is likely to be very painful, and the best people will be lost in the process.

Models of Change Management

John P Kotter's 'Eight Steps to Successful Change'

American John P Kotter (b 1947) is a Harvard Business School professor and leading thinker and author on organizational change management. Kotter's highly regarded books 'Leading Change' (1995) and the follow-up 'The Heart Of Change' (2002) describe a helpful model for understanding and managing change. Each stage acknowledges a key principle identified by Kotter relating to people's response and approach to change, in which people see, feel and then change.

Kotter's eight step change model can be summarized as:

1. *Increase Urgency*- inspire people to move, make objectives real and relevant.
2. *Build the Guiding Team*- get the right people in place with the right emotional commitment, and the right mix of skills and levels.
3. *Get the Vision Right*- get the team to establish a simple vision and strategy, focus on emotional and creative aspects necessary to drive service and efficiency.
4. *Communicate for Buy-in*- Involve as many people as possible, communicate the essentials, simply, and to appeal and respond to people's needs. De-clutter communications-make technology work for you rather than against.
5. *Empower Action*- Remove obstacles, enable constructive feedback and lots of support from leaders-reward and recognize progress and achievements.
6. *Create Short-term Wins*- Set aims that are easy to achieve-in bite-size chunks. Manageable numbers of

initiatives. Finish current stages before starting new ones.

7. *Don't let up*- Foster and encourage determination and persistence-ongoing change-encourage ongoing progress reporting-highlight achieved and future milestones.
8. *Make Change Stick*- Reinforce the value of successful change via recruitment, promotion, new change leaders. Weave change into culture.

Lewin's Change Management Model

Understanding the Three Stages of Change

Change is a common thread that runs through all businesses regardless of size, industry and age. Our world is changing fast and, as such, organizations must change quickly too. Organizations that handle change well thrive, whilst those that do not may struggle to survive.

The concept of "change management" is a familiar one in most businesses today. But, how businesses manage change (and how successful they are at it) varies enormously depending on the nature of the business, the change and the people involved. And a key part of this depends on how far people within it understand the change process.

One of the cornerstone models for understanding organizational change was developed by Kurt Lewin back in the 1950s, and still holds true today. His model is known as Unfreeze - Change - Refreeze, refers to the three-stage process of change he describes. Lewin, a physicist as well as social scientist, explained organizational change using the analogy of changing the shape of a block of ice.

Understanding Lewin's Model

If you have a large cube of ice, but realize that what you want is a cone of ice, what do you do? First you must melt the ice to make it amenable to change (unfreeze). Then you must mold the iced water into the shape you want (change). Finally, you must solidify the new shape (refreeze).

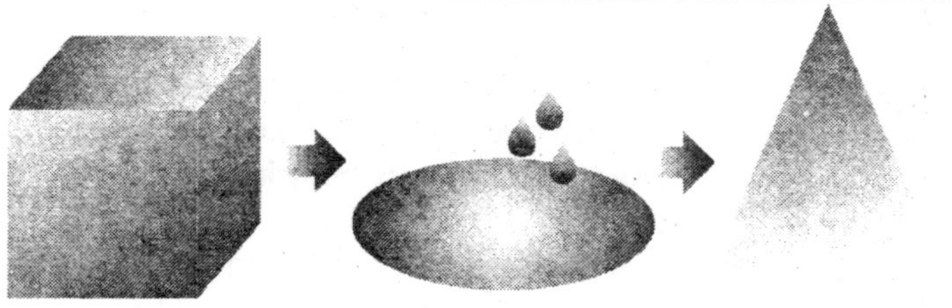

Source: Lewin's Model

By looking at change as process with distinct stages, you can prepare yourself for what is coming and make a plan to manage the transition - looking before you leap, so to speak. All too often, people go into change blindly, causing much unnecessary turmoil and chaos.

To begin any successful change process, you must first start by understanding why the change must take place. As Lewin put it, "Motivation for change must be generated before change can occur. One must be helped to re-examine many cherished assumptions about oneself and one's relations to others." This is the unfreezing stage from which change begins.

Unfreeze

This first stage of change involves preparing the organization to accept that change is necessary, which involves break down the existing status quo before you can build up a new way of operating.

Key to this is developing a compelling message showing why the existing way of doing things cannot continue. This is easiest to frame when you can point to declining sales figures, poor financial results, worrying customer satisfaction surveys, or suchlike: These show that things have to change in a way that everyone can understand.

To prepare the organization successfully, you need to start at its core - you need to challenge the beliefs, values, attitudes, and behaviors that currently define it. Using the analogy of a building, you must examine and be prepared to change the existing foundations as they might not support add-on storeys; unless this is done, the whole building may risk collapse.

This first part of the change process is usually the most difficult and stressful. When you start cutting down the "way things are done", you put everyone and everything off balance. You may evoke strong reactions in people, and that's exactly what needs to done.

By forcing the organization to re-examine its core, you effectively create a (controlled) crisis, which in turn can build a strong motivation to seek out a new equilibrium. Without this motivation, you won't get the buy-in and participation necessary to effect any meaningful change.

Change

After the uncertainty created in the unfreeze stage, the change stage is where people begin to resolve their uncertainty and look for new ways to do things. People start to believe and act in ways that support the new direction.

The transition from unfreeze to change does not happen overnight: People take time to embrace the new direction and participate proactively in the change. A related change model, the *Change Curve,* focuses on the specific issue of personal transitions in a changing environment and is useful for understanding this specific aspect in more detail.

In order to accept the change and contribute to making the change successful, people need to understand how the changes will benefit them. Not everyone will fall in line just because the change is necessary and will benefit the company. This is a common assumption and pitfall that should be avoided.

Tip

Unfortunately, some people will genuinely be harmed by change, particularly those who benefit strongly from the status quo. Others may take a long time to recognize the benefits that change brings. You need to foresee and manage these situations.

Time and communication are the two keys to success for the changes to occur. People need time to understand the changes and they also need to feel highly connected to the organization throughout the transition period. When you are managing change, this can require a great deal of time and effort and hands-on management is usually the best approach.

Refreeze

When the changes are taking shape and people have embraced the new ways of working, the organization is ready to refreeze. The outward signs of the refreeze are a stable organization chart, consistent job descriptions, and so on. The refreeze stage also needs to help people and the organization internalize or institutionalize the changes. This means making sure that the changes are used all the time; and that they are incorporated into everyday business. With a new sense of stability, employees feel confident and comfortable with the new ways of working.

The rationale for creating a new sense of stability in our every changing world is often questioned. Even though change is a constant in many organizations, this refreezing stage is still important. Without it, employees get caught in a transition trap where they aren't sure how things should be done, so nothing ever gets done to full capacity. In the absence of a new frozen state, it is very difficult to tackle the next change initiative effectively. How do you go about convincing people that something needs changing if you haven't allowed the most recent changes to sink in? Change will be perceived as change for change's sake, and the motivation required to implement new changes simply won't be there.

As part of the Refreezing process, make sure that you celebrate the success of the change - this helps people to find closure, thanks them for enduring a painful time, and helps them believe that future change will be successful.

Practical Steps for Using the Framework

Unfreeze

Determine What Needs to Change

- Survey the organization to understand the current state.
- Understand why change has to take place.

Ensure there is Strong Support from Upper Management

- Use *Stakeholder Analysis* and *Stakeholder Management* to identify and win the support of key people within the organization.
- Frame the issue as one of organization-wide importance.

Create the Need for Change

- Create a compelling message as to why change has to occur.
- Use your vision and strategy as supporting evidence.
- Communicate the vision in terms of the change required.
- Emphasize the "why".

Manage and Understand the Doubts and Concerns

- Remain open to employee concerns and address in terms of the need to change.

Change

Communicate Often

- Do so throughout the planning and implementation of the changes.
- Describe the benefits.
- Explain exactly the how the changes will effect everyone.
- Prepare everyone for what is coming.

Dispel Rumors

- Answer questions openly and honestly.
- Deal with problems immediately.
- Relate the need for change back to operational necessities.

Empower Action

- Provide lots of opportunity for employee involvement.
- Have line managers provide day-to-day direction.

Involve People in the Process

- Generate short-term wins to reinforce the change.
- Negotiate with external stakeholders as necessary (such as employee organizations).

Refreeze

Anchor the Changes into the Culture

- Identity what supports the change.
- Identify barriers to sustaining change.

Develop Ways to Sustain the Change

- Ensure leadership support.
- Create a reward system.
- Establish feedback systems.
- Adapt the organizational structure as necessary.

Provide Support and Training

- Keep everyone informed and supported.

Celebrate Success!

Key Points

Lewin's change model is a simple and easy-to-understand framework for managing change.

By recognizing these three distinct stages of change, you can plan to implement the change required. You start by creating the motivation to change (unfreeze). You move through the change process by promoting effective communications and empowering people to embrace new ways of working (change). And the process ends when you return the organization to a sense of stability (refreeze), which is so necessary for creating the confidence from which to embark on the next, inevitable change.

Strategies for Overcoming Resistance to Organizational Change

It is human nature to resist what we see as different. Change requires that we work to learn a new set of rules, when the old rules may have suited us just fine. In reality, neither our personal nor professional lives will always be aligned with what we perceive to be comfortable. In other words, we are not the center of universe and the world does not revolve around our comfort levels. Circumstances outside of our control will occur that force us to adapt to new policies, new systems, and new sets of laws. In the very best situations our participation will be valued and our opinions will be sought giving us the opportunity to create the means that justify the end.

Individuals demonstrate their commitment to change through their deeds and actions. Strong managers solicit staff participation to build buy-in and to make sure that the affects of the proposed changes are vetted to avoid system breakdowns. Non-management employees can demonstrate their buy-in by educating themselves about the process, seeking ways to build consensus, giving and receiving feedback, and communicating their concerns to peers and management constructively.

Many theories attempt to explain why employees resist change even when it is obvious that change is necessary for an organization's survival. Resistance to change can be averted via:

- *Commitment:* From the CEO to the janitor, every employee must be committed to the change plan. That commitment begins at the top; hence the organization's leadership must be especially attuned to successful implementation. One naysayer on the leadership team can ruin the entire process.
- *A Change Mandate:* Change can not be a choice. With gentle respect it must be made clear that change is not an option, it is a requirement.
- *Input:* Anyone who will be affected by the impending changes must be given the opportunity to voice his or her opinion in a respectful and collegial setting.
- *Accountability:* Every person affected by the change program must be held responsible for implementing his or her individual change activity. Not meeting that responsibility must carry consequences.
- *Rewards and Celebration:* Successful implementation should be acknowledged via compensation and/or recognition. The organization as a whole should commemorate the successful implementation of the change program as well.

- *Evaluation:* Examining the success of the implementation at planned intervals is a strategic decision designed to gauge success over time and make corrections for unanticipated consequences.

Overlooking any one of the items above reduces the chance of successfully implementing a change program.

When change occurs, the relationship ("personal compact") between employers and employees suffer. This "personal compact" has three prongs - formal, social, and psychological.

- *The Formal Compact:* Captures basic tasks and performance requirements as defined by company documents such as job descriptions, employment contracts, and performance agreements.
- *The Psychological compact:* Incorporates feelings such as trust and dependence between employee and employer, which is the foundation of an employee's personal commitment to individual and company objectives.
- *The Social Compact:* Includes employees' perceptions about the culture of the organization and their chances for success.

Change destabilizes the foundation upon which the employer/employee relationship ("personal compact") is built. It is this uncomfortable shift in organizational dynamics (social, formal and psychological) that causes resistance to change, not simply the launch of new ideas or different ways of conducting business.

Once the change program is announced, many employees will employ tactics to protect themselves, their turf, and ultimately their place in the organization.

- *Argumentative:* Some employees will aggressively challenge the necessity for change. This is a time waster, which prevents critical objectives from being met. Every person who facilitates the change process must work diligently to build consensus. The employee must be assured that every idea is worthy of consideration. Should an exchange devolve into broad proclamations such as, "I just don't like it", "This will never work", or "This is a waste of time" the speaker must be challenged. Simply ask the speaker to explain why he or she feels the way they do and ask for three or four suggestions for making the process work.

- *Avoidance:* Some managers and members of the leadership team will avoid change by subtlety refusing to commit to the process. Often these leaders will sabotage the change effort by being unavailable for meetings, denying resources, or withholding feedback. "The leadership" is a particularly difficult foe, because change efforts often require the use of resources managed by the leadership, such as time and money. Without these resources change efforts are likely to fail. Accountability with consequences is the primary means for assuring leadership participation.
- *Distraction:* Many employees and organizational leaders search for personal or professional diversions during the change process that will ultimately hinder the effort. A distracted individual can undermine the change effort by not being present physically or mentally when his or her critical input is needed. Not being mindful of change creates an unnecessarily difficult experience for every member of the team. Such carelessness calls to mind the wasted energy expended when one runs against the wind. Change efforts provide an opportunity for every one affected to secure a new place in the organization or make a decision to seek a better fit elsewhere.

Top Ten Reasons People Resist Change

The Risk of Change is Seen as Greater than the Risk of Standing Still

Making a change requires a kind of leap of faith: you decide to move in the direction of the unknown on the promise that something will be better for you. But you have no proof.

Taking that leap of faith is risky, and people will only take active steps toward the unknown if they genuinely believe- and perhaps more importantly, feel – that the risks of standing still are greater than those of moving forward in a new direction. Making a change is all about managing risk. If you are making the case for change, be sure to set out in stark, truthful terms why you believe the risk situation favors change. Use numbers whenever you can, because we in the West pay attention to numbers. At the very least, they get our attention, and then when the rational mind is engaged, the emotional mind (which is typically most decisive) can begin to grapple with the prospect of change. But if you only sell your idea of change based on idealistic, unseen promises of reward, you won't be nearly as effective in moving people to action. The power of the human fight-or-flight response can be activated to fight for change, but that begins with the perception of risk.

People Feel Connected to Other People Who are Identified with the Old

We are a social species. We become and like to remains connected to those we know, those who have taught us, those with whom we are familiar – even at times to our own detriment. Loyalty certainly helped our ancestors hunt antelope and defend against the aggressions of hostile tribes, and so we are hard wired, I believe, to form emotional bonds of loyalty, generally speaking. If you ask people in an organization to do things in a new way, as rational as that new way may seem to you, you will be setting yourself up against all that hard wiring, all those emotional connections to those who taught your audience the old way - and that's not trivial. At the very least, as you craft your change message, you should make statements that honor the work and contributions of those who brought such success to the organization in the past, because on a very human but seldom articulated level, your audience will feel asked to betray their former mentors (whether those people remain in the organization or not). A little good diplomacy at the outset can stave off a lot of resistance.

People have No Role Models for the New Activity

Never underestimate the power of observational learning. If you see yourself as a change agent, you probably are something of a dreamer, someone who uses the imagination to create new possibilities that do not currently exist. Well, most people don't operate that way. It's great to be a visionary, but communicating a vision is not enough. Get some people on board with your idea, so that you or they can demonstrate how the new way can work. Operationally, this can mean setting up effective pilot programs that model a change and work out the kinks before taking your innovation "on the road." For most people, seeing is believing. Less rhetoric and more demonstration can go a long way toward overcoming resistance, changing people's objections from the "It can't be done!" variety to the "How can we get it done?" category.

People Fear They Lack the Competence to Change

This is a fear people will seldom admit. But sometimes, change in organizations necessitates changes in skills, and some people will feel that they won't be able to make the transition very well. They don't think they, as individuals, can do it. The hard part is that some of them may be right. But in many cases, their fears will be unfounded, and that's why part of moving people toward change requires you to be an effective motivator. Even more, a successful change campaign includes effective new training programs, typically staged from the broad to the specific. By this I mean that initial events should be town-hall type information events, presenting the rationale and plan for change, specifying the next steps, outlining future communications channels for questions, etc., and specifying how people will learn the specifics of what will be required of them, from whom, and when. Then, training programs must be implemented and evaluated over time. In this way, you can minimize the initial fear of a lack of personal competence for change by showing how people will be brought to competence throughout the change process. Then you have to deliver.

People Feel Overloaded and Overwhelmed

Fatigue can really kill a change effort, for an individual or for an organization. If, for example, you believe you should quit smoking, but you've got ten projects going and four kids to keep up with, it can be easy to put off your personal health improvement project (until your first heart attack or cancer scare, when suddenly the risks of standing still seem greater than the risks of change!). When you're introducing a change effort, be aware of fatigue as a factor in keeping people from moving forward, even if they are telling you they believe in the wisdom of your idea. If an organization has been through a lot of upheaval, people may resist change just because they are tired and overwhelmed, perhaps at precisely the time when more radical change is most needed! That's when you need to do two things: re-emphasize the risk scenario that forms the rationale for change (as in my cancer scare example), and also be very generous and continuously attentive with praise, and with understanding for people's complaints, throughout the change process. When you reemphasize the risk scenario, you're activating people's fears, the basic fight-or-flight response we all possess. But that's not enough, and fear can produce its own fatigue. You've got to motivate and praise accomplishments as well, and be patient enough to let people vent (without getting too caught up in attending to unproductive negativity).

People Have A Healthy Skepticism and Want to be Sure New Ideas are Sound

It's important to remember that few worthwhile changes are conceived in their final, best form at the outset. Healthy skeptics perform an important social function: to vet the change idea or process so that it can be improved upon along the road to becoming reality. So listen to your skeptics, and pay attention, because some percentage of what they have to say will prompt genuine improvements to your change idea (even if some of the criticism you will hear will be based more on fear and anger than substance).

People Fear Hidden Agendas Among Would-Be Reformers

Let's face it, reformers can be a motley lot. Not all are to be trusted. Perhaps even more frightening, some of the worst atrocities modern history has known were begun by earnest people who really believed they knew what was best for everyone else. Reformers, as a group, share a blemished past . . . And so, you can hardly blame those you might seek to move toward change for mistrusting your motives, or for thinking you have another agenda to follow shortly. If you seek to promote change in an organization, not only can you expect to encounter resentment for upsetting the established order and for thinking you know better than everyone else, but you may also be suspected of wanted to increase your own power, or even eliminate potential opposition through later stages of change.

I saw this in a recent change management project for which I consulted, when management faced a lingering and inextinguishable suspicion in some quarters that the whole affair was a prelude to far-reaching layoffs. It was not the case, but no amount of reason or reassurance sufficed to quell the fears of some people. What's the solution? Well, you'd better be interested in change for the right reasons, and not for personal or factional advantage, if you want to minimize and overcome resistance. And you'd better be as open with information and communication as you possibly can be, without reacting unduly to accusations and provocations, in order to show your good faith, and your genuine interest in the greater good of the organization. And if your change project will imply reductions in workforce, then be open about that and create an orderly process for outplacement and in-house retraining. Avoid the drip-drip-drip of bad news coming out in stages, or through indirect communication or rumor. Get as much information out there as fast as you can and create a process to allow everyone to move on and stay focused on the change effort.

People Feel the Proposed Change Threatens their Notions of Themselves

Sometimes change on the job gets right to a person's sense of identity. When a factory worker begins to do less with her hands and more with the monitoring of automated instruments, she may lose her sense of herself as a craftsperson, and may genuinely feel that the very things that attracted her to the work in the first place have been lost. I saw this among many medical people and psychologists during my graduate training, as the structures of medical reimbursement in this country changed in favor of the insurance companies, HMO's and managed care organizations. Medical professionals felt they had less say in the treatment of their patients, and felt answerable to less well trained people in the insurance companies to approve treatments the doctors felt were necessary. And so, the doctors felt they had lost control of their profession, and lost the ability to do what they thought best for patients.

My point is not to take sides in that argument, but to point out how change can get right to a person's sense of identity, the sense of self as a professional. As a result, people may feel that the intrinsic rewards that brought them to a particular line of work will be lost with the change. And in some cases, they may be absolutely right. The only answer is to help people see and understand the new rewards that may come with a new work process, or to see how their own underlying sense of mission and values can still be realized under the new way of operating. When resistance springs from these identity-related roots, it is deep and powerful, and to minimize its force, change leaders must be able to understand it and then address it, acknowledging that change does have costs, but also, (hopefully) larger benefits.

People Anticipate A Loss of Status or Quality of Life

Real change reshuffles the deck a bit. Reshuffling the deck can bring winners . . . and losers. Some people, most likely, will gain in status, job security, quality of life, etc. with the proposed change, and some will likely lose a bit. Change does not have to be a zero sum game, and change can (and should) bring more advantage to more people than disadvantage. But we all live in the real world, and let's face it – if there were no obstacles (read: people and their interests) aligned against change, then special efforts to promote change would be unnecessary.

Some people will, in part, be aligned against change because they will clearly, and in some cases correctly, view the change as being contrary to their interests. There are various strategies for minimizing this, and for dealing with steadfast obstacles to change in the form of people and their interests, but the short answer for dealing with this problem is to do what you can to present the inevitability of the change given the risk landscape, and offer to help people to adjust. Having said that, I've never seen a real organizational change effort that did not result in some people choosing to leave the organization, and sometimes that's best for all concerned. When the organization changes, it won't be to everyone's liking, and in that case, it's best for everyone to be adult about it and move on.

People Genuinely Believe that the Proposed Change is a Bad Idea

I'll never forget what a supervisor of mine said to be, during the year after I had graduated from college, secure as I was in the knowledge of my well earned, pedigreed wisdom at age twenty-two. We were in a meeting, and I made the comment, in response to some piece of information, "Oh, I didn't know that!" Ricky, my boss, looked at me sideways, and commented dryly, "Things you don't know . . . fill libraries." The truth is, sometimes someone's (even – gasp! – my) idea of change is just not a good idea. Sometimes people are not being recalcitrant, or afraid, or muddle-headed, or nasty, or foolish when they resist. They just see that we're wrong. And even if we're not all wrong, but only half wrong, or even if we're right, it's important not to ignore when people have genuine, rational reservations or objections.

Not all resistance is about emotion, in spite of this list I've assembled here. To win people's commitment for change, you must engage them on both a rational level and an emotional level. I've emphasized the emotional side of the equation for this list because I find, in my experience, that this is the area would-be change agents understand least well. But I'm also mindful that a failure to listen to and respond to people's rational objections and beliefs is ultimately disrespectful to them, and to assume arrogantly that we innovative, change agent types really do know best. A word to the wise: we're just as fallible as anyone.

Change Management Principles

1. At all times involve and agree support from people within system (system = environment, processes, culture, relationships, behaviours, etc., whether personal or organisational).
2. Understand where you/the organisation is at the moment.
3. Understand where you want to be, when, why, and what the measures will be for having got there.
4. Plan development towards above No.3 in appropriate achievable measurable stages.
5. Communicate, involve, enable and facilitate involvement from people, as early and openly and as fully as is possible.

Ideas on Illustrating Change Management Issues

When people are confronted with the need or opportunity to change, especially when it's 'enforced', as they see it, by the organization, they can become emotional. So can the managers who try to manage the change. Diffusing the emotional feelings, taking a step back, encouraging objectivity, are important to enabling sensible and constructive dialogue. To this end, managers and trainers can find it helpful to use analogies to assist themselves and other staff to look at change in a more detached way.

On this site there are several illustrations which can be used for this purpose, depending on the type of change faced, and the aspect that is to be addressed. Here are a few examples, useful for team meetings, presentations, one-to-one counselling or self-reminder, particularly to help empathise with others facing change:

On the Stories section look at 'Murphy's Plough' (negative thinking = obstacle to change) and 'We've always done it that way' (not questioning need for change). Both good aids for understanding and explaining why people - all of us - find it difficult to change assumptions, conditioned thinking, habit, routine, etc.

Job Reorganization, Task Analysis, Job Transfer Due to IT Development or Outsourcing Etc.

First see the modern principles which underpin successful change. It's not always easy or perhaps even possible to consider matters at such depth, but try to if you can, or try to persuade others above in their ivory towers to think about the fundamental integrity of the situation, instead of short-term profit, or satisfying greedy shareholders.

There are various approaches to task analysis and job reorganization, whether prompted by outsourcing or IT development. Generally change process of this sort is pragmatic, and it's difficult to identify transferable processes, templates, etc. Examples of projects don't generally find their way into the public domain, although the likelihood is increasing of government project pdf's becoming available on the web as this sort of information is increasingly required to be available to the public. IT vendor case studies and trade journals of the IT and outsourcing sectors can also provide indicators of best practice or transferable processes. There are some useful software tools now available, which are helpful, especially if the change involves a high level of complexity and a large scale.

As a broad guide when managing this sort of change, these aspects are important for the process:

- Really understand and clarify mutual expectations about the level of detail and cost that the project requires. Sometimes it's possible to see it what you need on a table napkin. The organisational context, and other strategic drivers, personalities and politics are often more significant influences than the task analysis.

- If you are a consultant or project manager, agree expectations on a pragmatic basis. Agree the templates and systems to be used and the the level of report data required for the decisions to be made.
- Assume that the situation can be improved - it generally can be, so while it's essential to capture all activities based on current jobs, many of these can be absorbed, superseded, updated, etc., when you begin to look at the ideal situation ('blank sheet of paper') possibilities, so;
- A new overview analysis enables fresh unencumbered look at the whole, which suggests new and better ways of doing things. A flip chart and a few creative minds are the main pre-requisites. It makes a great workshop session and is good for creating ownership and buy-in for major change. It's a good process also to cascade down to departments to bring out ideas for improved processes and new ways of doing things.
- In terms of capturing all current processes and inputs, the individual job analysis templates need to enable jobs to be broken down into sub-tasks, and elements within sub-tasks.
- This is a tricky one, and not practicable in certain X-Theory cultures, nevertheless, be aware of the high probability of upsetting people whose jobs are threatened by change and try to develop a way of anticipating and reducing damaging fall-out. Treat people at risk with the respect they deserve and avoid keeping them in the dark - involve threatened people wherever possible so they can see what's happening and why. If possible encourage the executive team to take the same humane approach, and try to establish counselling and support resources if none exist already.

- Analyses are more helpful if they identify critical vs essential task elements - this will help you to help the decision-makers to be more pragmatic (not least because by applying pressure to some of the 'essential' elements will reveal them to be habitual dispensable or traditional replaceable elements).
- Flow diagrams identify subtask linkage (inter and intra), variation and chronology.
- Behaviour needs identifying aside from processes.
- Standards, performance tolerance, % reliability, etc., should be indicated in task analysis as applicable to the sub-task or activity concerned.

Business Development Driven Change

Business development potentially includes everything involved with the quality of the business or the organization. Business development planning first requires establishing the business development aims, and then formulating a business development strategy, which would comprise some or all of the following methods of development.

- sales development
- new product development
- new market development
- business organization, shape, structure and processes development (eg, outsourcing, e-business, etc)
- tools, equipment, plant, logistics and supply-chain development
- people, management and communications (capabilities and training) development
- strategic partnerships and distribution routes development
- international development
- acquisitions and disposals

Generally business development is partly scientific, and partly subjective, based on the feelings and wishes of the business owners or CEO. There are so many ways to develop a business which achieve growth and improvement, and rarely is just one of these a single best solution. Business development is what some people call a 'black art', ie., difficult to analyse, and difficult to apply a replicable process.

Fast Changing Environments

Planning, implementing and managing change in a fast-changing environment is increasingly the situation in which most organizations now work.

Dynamic environments such as these require dynamic processes, people, systems and culture, especially for managing change successfully, notably effectively optimising organizational response to market opportunities and threats.

Key Elements for Success

- Plan long-term broadly - a sound strategic vision, not a specific detailed plan (the latter is impossible to predict reliably). Detailed five years plans are out of date two weeks after they are written. Focus on detail for establishing and measuring delivery of immediate actions, not medium-to-long-term plans.
- Establish forums and communicating methods to enable immediate review and decision-making. Participation of interested people is essential. This enables their input to be gained, their approval and commitment to be secured, and automatically takes care of communicating the actions and expectations.
- Empower people to make decisions at a local operating level-delegate responsibility and power as much as possible (or at least encourage people to make recommendations which can be quickly approved).
- Remove (as far as is possible) from strategic change and approval processes and teams (or circumvent) any ultra-cautious, ultra-autocratic or compulsively-interfering executives. Autocracy and interference are the biggest obstacles to establishing a successful and sustainable dynamic culture and capability.

- Encourage, enable and develop capable people to be active in other areas of the organization via 'virtual teams' and 'matrix management'.
- Scrutinise and optimise ICT (information and communications technology) systems to enable effective information management and key activity team-working.
- Use workshops as a vehicle to review priorities, agree broad medium-to-long-term vision and aims, and to agree short term action plans and implementation method and accountabilities.
- Adjust recruitment, training and development to accelerate the development of people who contribute positively to a culture of empowered dynamism.

Change Management Principles

Adopting a principled approach that displays integrity and engenders openness and trust will see your change program through the hard times. Our consultancy promotes five key principles of successful change management. Adopting these principles in both spirit and practice will enhance significantly your chances of success. These principles are:

Sponsorship: The change program has the visible support of key decision-makers throughout the organization and resources are committed to the program.·

Planning: Planning is conducted methodically before program implementation and committed to writing. Plans are agreed with major stakeholders and objectives, resources, roles and risks are clarified.

Measurement: Program objectives are stated in measurable terms and program progress is monitored and communicated to major stakeholders.·EngagementStakeholders are engaged in genuine two-way dialogue in an atmosphere of openness, mutual respect and trust.

Support Structures: Program implementers and change recipients are given the resources and supporting systems they require during and after change implementation.

Change Management Process—A Structured Approach

Adopting a principled approach is great, but how do you apply these change management principles in practice? Business Performance Pty Ltd has developed an easy to understand and structured approach to implementing change in your organization. We call our unique way of planning and delivering real organizational benefits the CHANGE Approach

This approach consists of six phases that successful change programs progress through.

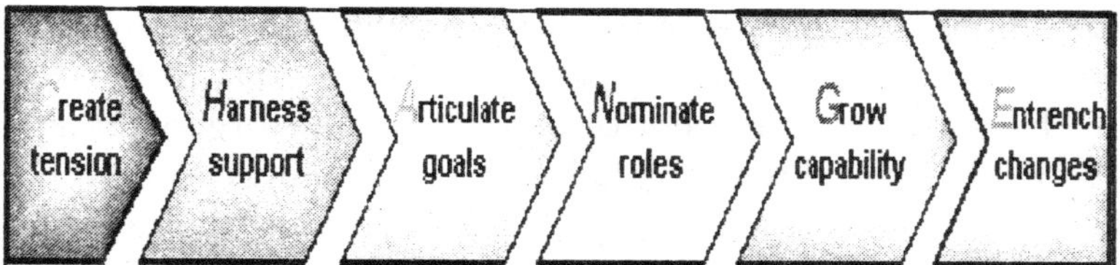

Source: Managing Change in the Workplace by Leslie Allan.

Figure 1: Change Management Process

Create Tension: Articulate why change needs to happen and why it needs to happen within the planned timeframe.

Harness Support: Get on board the key decision-makers, resource holders and those impacted by the change.

Articulate Goals: Define in specific and measurable terms the desired organizational outcomes.

Nominate Roles: Assign responsibility to specific individuals for the various tasks and outcomes.Grow capabilityBuild organizational systems and people competencies necessary for affecting the change.Entrench changesInstitutionalize the change to make it "the way we do things around here".

Key Areas for Managing Change

Whatever your change program, one key area requiring your attention is the identification and management of change stakeholders. A stakeholder is any person with an interest in the change process or the outcome of the proposed change. Stakeholders bring with them an amalgam of competing interests and often act to further their own power, influence and survival. The added difficulty for change managers rests in the fact that such political maneuvering is often in the guise of impartial and rational argument. Who are your major stakeholders? How will you get them on board and retain their support throughout the life of your change program?

Another essential activity often neglected by failed changed initiatives is the setting of clearly defined and measurable objectives. Goal setting done well engages stakeholders and commits them to the program. Other benefits include focusing effort to where it is important and providing a yardstick for measuring program success. Are your goals fuzzy and hard to put a finger on, or are they SMART goals? Do they link to the strategic objectives of the organization and do they have widespread and genuine support across the organization?

People, and only people, can make your organizational change happen. Programs fail where roles and tasks are not agreed and clarified. In organizations with a low performance culture, many employees and managers will expend considerable effort in hiding from responsibility. What are the key roles and responsibilities for bringing about the change in your area? For any change initiative, we have identified four key change roles: Change Driver, Change Implementer, Change Enabler and Change Recipient. Who are the people that occupy each role in your change program? Have the right people been selected for the right roles?

Whatever your change initiative, most likely the above-mentioned roles will not be working in isolation. More and more, results can only be achieved through people working in collaboration - in teams. Are your teams of the optimal size - not too small and not too big? Have you got the right team leader? Do they have the necessary technical and interpersonal skills? One reason why teams are much more productive than individuals working in isolation is that members may leverage off each other's strengths and compensate for each other's weaknesses. Do your teams have the right balance of natural working styles? At times, teams get stuck. What is your strategy in moving stuck teams forward?

Training is an indispensable tool for skilling teams and bedding in change. Many organizations, however, fail to benefit from the resources spent on training. Soon after the training is completed, employees continue to cling on to the old way of doing things. How successfully are you using training in your organizational change program? Do you have a well-articulated training plan? Does the training focus on behavior change or simply on content? Have you planned for back in the workplace support? Do your managers actively support the training?

No matter how good your training, some employees, customers and suppliers will resist the change. Unless you have a well-thought out strategy for dealing with resistance, resisters will wear your program down till it grinds to a halt. Are your resisters out in the open or do they work from the underground? The stated reasons for resisting may simply be a smokescreen. Have you uncovered the real reasons for resistance to your program? How have you helped people work through the psychological process of change? What is your strategy for overcoming resistance to change?

Areas of Change Request Management Process

The Five Critical Change Management Process Areas

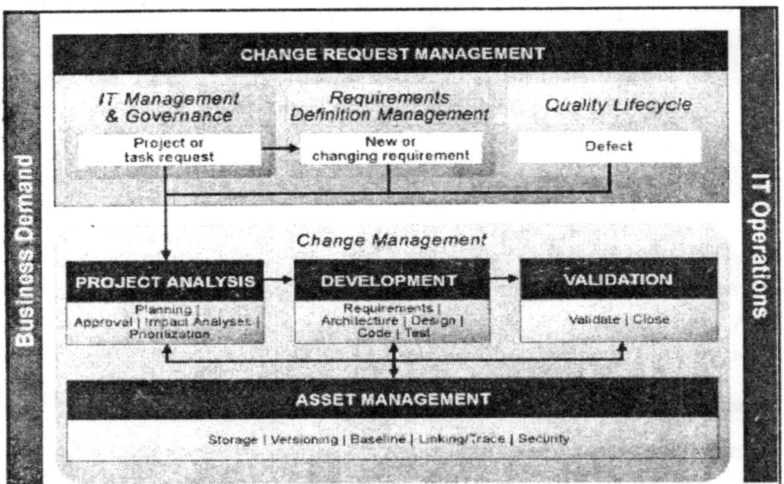

Source: www.Borland.com

Figure 2: Change Management Process

Change Request Management

To predictably respond to ever-present change, Borland helps organizations mature their existing demand management process by:

- Defining unique categories of requests appropriate for an organization
- Developing standard forms for collecting the information needed for evaluation and policies for using them
- Deploying specific Borland technology to manage the entire request lifecycle—from information collection through an approval process.

Borland helps organization orchestrate all incoming requests, including project demand, requirements changes, or defects. With the Borland Software Change Management Solution, IT is able to consistently and efficiently respond to change.

Project Analysis

To choose which efforts are likely to have the greatest benefit, Borland helps organizations mature their existing project analysis process by:

- Developing project planning processes that reflect best practices for impact analysis, estimation and prioritization
- Helping develop clear repeatable guidelines for selecting changes to pursue

With the Borland Software Change Management Solution, organizations can gain clear visibility into project status, so they can respond in a timely manner when project costs or business requirements change or when defects are encountered.

Development

To manage Development where distributed, heterogeneous IT environments are essential, Borland helps organizations mature and optimize their existing development process, whether they are agile-based, RUP-centric or waterfall, through:

- Implementing best practices tailored to the organization
- Educating teams on their chosen methodologies
- Using

With the Borland Software Change Management Solution, organizations can support all development needs through a robust and flexible platform for coordinating and managing the entire software development process, promoting team communication and collaboration through centralized control of all project assets.

Validation

To ensure completeness of the end product in meeting the requests, Borland helps organizations mature their existing software change management process by:

- Defining and implementing a review process
- Improving consistency and quality through automated workflows supported by Borland® StarTeam™ technology
- Defining and implementing a process for approval of completed change packages

With the Borland Software Change Management Solution, organizations improve build reliability, application quality and overall predictability.

Management

To eliminate chaos, Borland helps organizations mature their existing software change management process by:

- Establishing version control of all project assets
- Defining a standard process for managing requests, defects, and tasks
- Enabling better control of project scope and task commitments through effective workflow
- Improving project communication and decision tracking

- Increasing reliable project planning
- Defining procedures for evaluation and acceptance among stakeholders–in some cases establishing a Change Control Board

Change management encompasses all changes in technology, systems, applications, management, processes, as well as roles and responsibilities of people. A change could be anything from doing a task in a different way to developing a venture. Although change management takes a structured, phased approach, it should also be able to respond to urgent changes immediately, thus minimizing the interruption. In addition, it should be able to satisfy minor or standard changes with minimal administrative efforts.

However, change management without its application has the minimum utility in an enterprise simply due to the volume of changes involved. The goal of change management is to ensure that all changes are deployed successfully into all the functional areas of enterprise in the least disruptive manner. Applying change management including the development of business cases makes the change management process more proactive, predictable and it guides the reader to arrive at an effective decision. Taking a decision, while interacting with the business environment can be tracked easily with change management, thereby reducing management complexity.

Case No.1 IIMs Good at Surprises: Giving Goosebumps to Coaching Institutes

It was April and amid the hot weather Mr. Paritosh Garg, Central Indian Regional Head of Career Launcher, hung the phone at 3:30 pm after having a word with Chairman Satya Narayan R, and the pounds of sweat increased on his forehead. It was an intense atmosphere in his office and the reason was the decision taken by IIMs to conduct CAT in an online format. His worries were concerned with the very fact that CAT had always been on paper right from its genesis and with this kind of idea proposed by IIMs, Career Launcher had to make rapid and radical changes in all aspects so as to match the aspirants' expectations.

Career Launcher is Asia's leading education service provider with presence in over 130 locations across India, Middle East and the United States. It provides test-prep education to enable school and college students gain admission to professional courses especially MBA. It is also actively involved in the field of mainstream education, mainly through its growing network of play schools and secondary schools. It describes its core values as Risk Taking, Openness, Honesty and Commitment to customers Ownership and Innovation. CL as it is lovingly called has always been at the leading edge of implementing technology in education delivery. Several groups at CL are working on building knowledge repositories to help academic staff and students to have better access to educational resources. But this surprise from IIMs has compelled top management team to think of the changes that have to be made in their processes, structure and portfolio.

Marketing Executive (Gwalior), Ashutosh was called by Paritosh in his office and was informed that they have to rush immediately to attend an urgent meeting scheduled by the top management team of Career Launcher, the very next day in New Delhi. Motive of the meeting was clear; discussions would be encouraged to face this new challenge and what all changes have to be done so as to not loose the market share and also maintaining the continued existence of Career Launcher.

While they were on their way to Delhi, both discussed about the specific problem areas and issues that Career Launcher has to look upon. They were more afraid because Career Launcher in central region achieved great amount of revenue in 2008 for an on paper test for CAT. They also threw out their competitors: IMS, Career Forum and PT in Gwalior by applying innovative strategies. Paritosh Garg, who is recognized for his innovative ideas and risk taking abilities never bothered about investing in resources until and unless they generate something fruitful for students. Career Launcher, since its inception in Gwalior in 2002, has focused on two important aspects: Services and Faculties. This got them a competitive edge over other players. Ashutosh said, "*The two pillars will surely get affected because of the online pattern of CAT examination. Present study material, correspondence courses and test series will become irrelevant owing to the new paper structure that will be adopted by CAT."* Paritosh added, *"That calls for a change in Orientation and Pedagogy. Students will now seek for online availability of study material and other services."* Agreeing to that, Ashutosh wondered how Career Launcher would adapt itself to the situation and said *"All tests have to be conducted online; study material has to be uploaded on internet which is already flooded with competitors providing similar services for GRE and GMAT examinations. Now providing CAT material online will become their main source of income. The importance of infrastructure that we built, in accordance with the classroom preparation schema, will not be significant now. Moreover the cost incurred by these online companies will only be the cost of material they are uploading on internet and for us the infrastructure we have will be a baggage of cost load. Already we have reduced our fees to half for all our students in this month so as to cut out the competition and we did succeed in that but now this investment-appealing challenge in front of us is threatening the financial solidity of Gwalior center."* Paritosh in order to cool down Ashutosh, said, *"Online form of this paper could also be an opportunity to us. So think positive and be positive."*

They finally reached, Head Office Career Launcher, New Delhi and took rest for an hour and headed for the meeting. Satya Narayan R commenced the meeting with a tensed smile on his face and said *"Technology, a blessing for all seems to act disastrous for us. CAT going online would have given goose bumps to all of you. I called this meeting so that we can come up with the solutions for the specific issues we all have in our minds."* Rajesh Dua, Western regional head, said *"Our institution's USP is our services and faculties on which our students trust. But CAT going online will reduce the importance of faculty as well as our paper material and they will shift to material available with websites like pagalguy.com, minglebox.com, and total gudhha.com etc. because of the lower costs."* Prashant Chandra, Southern Regional Head, said *"We are short of seven months from CAT'09 and we have to accommodate many changes that I see as a herculean task to carry out and therefore we will need a strong technical support."* Technical head, New Delhi, Sanjay replied *"I think technologically we are sound and our Planning Department, on the basis of online CAT rumors in the month of February, has utilized the software that we are using for LST (Law Test Prep) program and converted previous 2-3 year CAT papers in online format with the help of that software. Also, some of the class tests have been transformed into Test Gyms in online interactive format. That I think gives us an edge over our competitors."* Paritosh says *"But we would need solid infrastructure to conduct those tests, as in a proper computer lab, which could give students a proper feel of the online environment."* Financial head, CL, immediately interrupts and says *"We already have cut down the fees to half for each student and investments at this moment can be risky because we also don't know about the future existence of online examination. It can be a once in a blue moon thing for IIMs."* Ashutosh says, *"We are soon going to see decreased significance of faculty and paper based study material of CL and that's why we can create a solid technical infrastructure like setting up labs which can be our USP. Initial investments will be high but then we will also save at extra faculty costs and paper costs."*

Mr. Satya Narayan pondered over a new thought given by Paritosh and Ashutosh and said *"Visionary work done by our planning department is worth an appreciation and will definitely back us up on this issue. The idea presented to set up computer labs at each center is commendable but it also poses a risk of getting the huge investment into a ditch, if IIMs again come back to a paper format of conducting CAT. So, within 10 days I need to know a concrete answer to this problem and then we can implement the idea."*

He calls off the meeting but then everyone doubted the risk of IIMs returning back to paper pattern.

Questions

1. Had you been in Mr. Satya Narayan's shoes, what decision you would have taken given the huge amount of financial risk involved? Give reasons to support your answer.
2. If you as the chairman of CL agree to the new pedagogy proposed by Paritosh and Ashutosh how will you propose to manage the laying off of the faculty throughout the country? What USP do you propose for CL after the change and how do you propose to popularize it.

3. What other methods of revenue generation do you suggest to the chairman as the Marketing Executive (Gwalior) in order to recover the huge investment made to adopt the new technology?
4. Why did everyone doubt the 'risk' of IIMs returning to paper based format after all these investments made to tackle changes? Logically support your answer.

Case No. 2. Majestic City Mall: Does Recession Really Need a Change?

Mr. Ramesh Pandey, the marketing director of Majestic City Mall in Gwalior has been called for an immediate meeting at the head office located in Raipur to discuss about the revenue model with the respective board members. Mr.Ramesh Pandey is a person with good leadership skills which can be seen by the encouragement he gives to his subordinates to come up with new innovations. He has been working in the organization from the day it started which makes him a big asset for the organization.

Promoted by Majestic City Group and developed by same, MAJESTIC CITY MALL has become a popular hangout of Gwalior right from the time it came into operation in July 2008. Exquisitely designed with a built up area of 214000 sq. ft. The art of this mall magnifies the shopping experience on a truly grand scale. With well-known brands like Big Bazar, McDonalds, Reebok, Levis, Café Coffee Day it is catering to needs of all age groups and attracting a constant flow of consumer traffic by providing them with a wide range of choices and convenience. Majestic Mall being the only mall in Gwalior enjoys monopoly in its field. To attract the youngsters it has Discotheque, Ambiance Arena (Gaming zone) and Fun Cinemas. The Mall has more than 150 outlets consisting of kiosks, showrooms, bazaars and restaurants in sizes ranging from 80sq. feet to 30,000 sq. feet.

The mall is located at the heart of the city and hence it attracts a crowd of approx. 20,000 during weekends and 12,000 during weekdays. This prime location adds a competitive edge to the mall compared to any new entrants. During festival season the crowd increases up to 30,000 per day. The employee strength is about 150 including 30 administrative staff. The mall has been governed in a structural hierarchy. From the period of inauguration it was collecting fixed rentals from the outlets, 95% of the stalls in the mall were occupied by November 2008. During November 2008 when the financial status of Majestic City Mall's outlets was affected due to recession, the sales of the outlets in the mall declined. The owners of the outlets were overburdened by the fixed rents levied, due to which they proposed revenue sharing model. The mall administration has changed its income policy from fixed rental for 4 best selling and trust worthy shops as they being the top brands around the world.

In addition to rents, Parking Area of the mall serves as an additional source of revenue. The parking fee which varies between 2 wheelers and 4 wheelers is charged on per vehicle basis. Mr. Ramesh Pandey, said "the mall administration is planning to charge parking fee on time basis but fearing resistance from visitors it could not implement this". To further boost the sales of the shops under revenue sharing model, the marketing director proposed an idea of reimbursing the parking fees for purchase of over Rs 700 from those shops.

After witnessing this mode of revenue structure, the other outlets with less brand value are also proposing for revenue sharing model. These local brands are doing good sales because of their intensive advertisements. But, as they are not trust worthy and the administration is not sure about their future growth, they are in situation of dilemma whether to accept their proposal for revenue sharing. As per the marketing director, this reluctance in accepting their proposal is due to the disadvantages of revenue sharing model, they are:

- No guarantee that these shop owners will/not reveal the correct figures to the administration.
- The fluctuating past sales figures makes Mr. Ramesh Pandey to doubt about the consistency of rent.
- These shop owners might feel very much relaxed (they will pay only when they earn).

But, this has its own advantages as it develops a sense of belongingness between shop owners and the organization. This also builds a long term relationship which gives a sense of security for both the parties.

Questions

1. Should Ramesh Pandey go for revenue sharing model or stick to fixed rentals for the low value-branded shops?
2. If you are in the place of Mr. Ramesh pandey, which one do you prefer, a fixed parking rental or rental based on timing.
3. Since this mall enjoys monopoly in the city., would you like suggest any strategies to increase the revenue of Majestic City mall?

Case Study No.3. Transforming Tatkraft Transformers for New Era

15th Oct. 2010, is a big day for all of us here at Tatkraft Ltd., as there is an important board meeting scheduled with the agenda of merger with a conglomerate in the sector which will take the combined entity to the top 25 position amongst the electrical equipment manufacturing companies. Before going into further details let me introduce myself. I am Prashant Roy, working as a Production Manager in the Ahmednagar plant of Tatkraft Ltd. For the mentioned big day I am required to submit a brief summary on the current status of the company and practices we are following to remain competitive in the market.

Tatkraft Limited is a pioneering leader in the management and application of electrical energy. Today it is India's leading private sector enterprise, extensively engaged in designing, manufacturing and marketing high technology electrical products and services related to power generation, transmission and distribution, as well as executing turnkey projects. The Company has posted a net profit of Rs 1421.70 million and total Income of Rs 13576.90 million for the quarter ended June 30, 2010.

Tatkraft's Street Light Automation Solution jointly developed by Tatkraft Global R&D Centre and the Lighting

Division of Tatkraft has won the CII's (Confederation of Indian Industry) prestigious National Award for Excellence in Innovative Energy Saving Product for the Year 2010.

Indian Power Industry

The demand of power in India is enormous and is growing steadily. The vast Indian power market, today offers one of the highest growth opportunities for private developers.

The power sector in India is dominated by the government. The State and Central Government sectors account for 58% and 32% of the generation capacity respectively while the private sector accounts for about 10%. The private sector has a small but growing presence in distribution and is making an entry into transmission. Power Sector mainly through budgetary support and external borrowings, was opened to private sector in 1991.

Major private players in Indian power industry are Tatkraft, Crompton Greaves, ABB, Havells India, Techno Electric, HBL Power, Bharat Bijlee, Honda Siel, Emco, Numeric Powe and Easun Reyrl.

Tatkraft Transformers- An Overview

The *Tatkraft* Ltd., was established in India in the year 1927 with its headquarters in Mumbai. Presently, the company is offering wide range of products such as power & industrial transformers, HT circuit breakers, LT & HT motors, DC motors, traction motors, alternators/generators, railway signaling equipments, lighting products, fans, pumps and public switching, transmission and access products. In addition to offering broad range of products, the company undertakes turnkey projects from concept to commissioning. Apart from this, Tatkraft exports its products to more than 60 countries worldwide, which includes the emerging South-East Asian and Latin American markets. Tatkraft's products are approved by all leading Indian consultants such as Engineers India Ltd., TATA Consulting Engineers, M.N.Dastur, Davy Power Gas, NTPC, Power Grid, Desein Consultants, Development Consultants Ltd., Humphreys and Glasgow, Fitchner Consultants, PDIL.

Challenges

The Quarter of July-September, 2008 was a watershed period for the entire industrial sector in India. During this quarter, the prices of major raw materials went up by as much as 28%.

Electrical equipment is a volatile business and requires serious responses to such kind of market volatility. Issues in these conditions that electrical equipment manufacturers need to deal in order to stay competitive in the Indian market are, increasing material cost, entrance from foreign manufacturer, material shortage, stringent specification and ability to become one stop center service provider.

Our Company was quickly able to sniff a latent opportunity generated because of the events triggered by the Global melt down. The need of the hour was to be nimble, be aware of the dynamic changing scenario and act proactively to stay ahead. The Economic crisis led to the shrinkage of spending across the Globe, in general and in India particularly, especially on electrical goods and services. This led to pressure on sale of capacities across all industries/ segments.

Our Company realized that this was an opportunity to significantly streamline the Production Capacity. Accordingly, when the other major players were cutting down their Production and deferring their Projects, our Company, on the other hand, embarked on an ambitious program for integrated production system. Our Company ramped up its Plant capacity to higher levels and also implemented 7-day working resulting in a significant improvement in the Production capacity.

The Initiatives in Material Management

Material costs constituting around 55-60 % of the total cost, it became imperative for the company to introduce a host of innovative practices in the area of materials management. These initiatives need to be in consonance with the nature of global electronics business characterized by high rate of obsolescence, falling prices, high quality inputs and global sourcing.

Supplier Communication

It was ensured that the requirements of the customers of Tatkraft Transformers are clearly communicated to the suppliers, thus making the latter jointly responsible for ensuring customer satisfaction. This is done through constant touch with the suppliers to indicate the priorities through written and verbal means and by hosting vendor meets Vendor Development and Quality Assurance.

The suppliers were continuously provided all the support during product development and engineering, prototype testing, evaluation, qualification and guidance in the implementation of ISO 9000 Quality Management system and other industry standards and practices. Emphasis was on prevention rather than detection and correction. Suppliers are encouraged to imbibe the culture of 'Ownership of Quality.

Inventory Control

The scheduling of placement of orders and receipt of materials was streamlined to ensure efficient inventory management covering such requirements as timely availability of material, minimization of waste and surplus etc.

Negotiations and Payments

Suppliers are involved right from the tender stage to offer the most competitive terms to the customers in terms of quality, cost and delivery. Mutually beneficial payment terms are negotiated and strictly adhered to.

Implementation of IT

All the processes involved in Integrated Materials Management are fully computerized for speedy disposal of material requisitions, resulting in substantial reductions in lead times across various operations.

The Results

These simple initiatives were implemented effectively resulting in incredible results that culminated in the historic turnaround of the company that brought wide recognition and Improved financial position of the company.

Future Plans

The multi-disciplinary competencies and capabilities of Tatkraft Ltd coupled with the Strategic Sectors it has chosen, is bound to give the company a competitive advantage to succeed in the national market but explore avenues in the international market. Most of its products have been identified for export promotion and the brilliant performance .While all the processes under materials management are fully computerized, plans are underway to install a fully IT enabled Supply Chain Management including e-procurement. The company is fully aware of the competitive global environment surrounding it and is focusing continuously on enhancing its technology base and enriching its skill base to strengthen its status as a valued national asset.

Questions

1. What are the causes and consequences of the behavior, events or situation described in the case?
2. Identify and draw on particular Change Management theories to analyze this case.
3. Why did the company decided to go on for an extensive expansion plan for the company in such an environment when other companies were curbing their operations.
4. What are the key trends in this case? What are the positive and negative factors in this case?
5. Make recommendations or suggest some better solutions to the problems encountered.

Case Study No.4 Crisp Corner and Its ever-increasing Expansion Spree...

Introduction

"Dad, can we not give our city-mates a taste of more for less?" enquired Mr. Samir Olyai one fine day. "Of course son, but we have been sweating it out for two decades now to make it a possibility. Alas! We are tied up by the shortage of time and management." The very statement laid the foundation of a revolutionary thought process at least for a city like Gwalior where a local chain hardly meant reality. With budgets going hay while, all credits to the recent price hikes in almost every commodity essential for daily lives, even a thought of extravagance immediately provokes a step back. "Oh God, we are all so stuck up in this world of ever-increasing inflation," said a commoner surveyed by Crisp Corner. Junior Olyai found the reason and made a vision that he will tap this need which looked to be augmented then and convert it to quench everybody's thirsts. No wonder, today Crisp Corner, is the largest bakery chain in the northern region of Madhya Pradesh. At present, the stores have penetrated in every nook and corner of the historical city of Gwalior. In spite of the fact that the organization stepped its foot in the field of snacks in the mid 1980's, there lay only a single outlet even twenty years post its establishment. It was just about three years ago when the management pondered into what it would take to be in the league of expansion. The very idea knew no bounds which can be exemplified by the fact that Crisp Corner so heavily concentrated in spreading its arms that it even lacked market analysis before opening new outlets and launching new products.

Background

It must be acknowledged that this did not happen overnight. When the founders of Crisp Corner Ms Tina and Mr. Sunil Olyai started the venture in the mid 1980's, they had no choice but to put it only as a secondary business. The reason for the same which had even continued for years thereafter was that they were grossly engaged in their school. Many-a-times the frustration of running it, set back Mr. Sunil Olyai to limits. "How am I to manage it all alone?" said Mr. Olyai not once but whenever he got to know that he can do much better. And all this while, there was one person who knew he could make a difference. Crisp Corner was struggling with limited number of products and was offering the same taste because it had no direction and its operations were left in the hands of contractors and that would just fetch a negligible amount.

It was then that their son, Sameer Olyai, came for his vacation from Australia. He used to sit idle at home having merely to do nothing except to go to their school with the family but that was useless. Then his interest for his bakery outlet developed. He implemented various changes and strategies to help it flourish. Now it is a subsidiary of Balfour's India Foods Pvt. Ltd. The products available now in stores- puffs, patties, buns with various fillings, burgers, pizzas, pastries, rolls, cakes, etc.

It was not possible to open an outlet in all the places so the concept of "Spicy Express"-Crisp Corner vehicles, was introduced. At present there are 12 outlets and 15 expresses.

Sameer wants to take the taste of Crisp Corner out of Gwalior. By the end of October 2010, 3 outlets would start functioning in Agra. "As the generation today is health conscious we would be providing them with the multi grain healthy bread by the end of 2011. Balfour's India Foods Pvt. Ltd. is going to set up a bread production unit in Indore next year" says Sameer.

Issues

Various outlets do not do well in sales as compared to others and the products sold at these outlets are least cost products because the locality nearby these outlets comprises of the lower middle income groups.

The organization is not distinctly segregated according to the broader functions. At present there are various managers in the organization- factory, production, distribution, outlet, purchase, development, account's head. Each one is responsible for their domain but does not have independence to make decisions. These domains can be reduced under various functions as purchase and outlet can be clubbed under operations, so on and so forth. The marketing department is almost missing and this may be one of the factors leading to the partial failure of the new products.

Opportunities

As the plans are to expand the operations to Agra, Jhansi and Bhopal can also nearby cities to look forward for. It could even look for starting a fast food restaurant and could club the existing items in the menu of the restaurant so that consumers could come and enjoy for a while. As the clientele is generally the youth so the concept would be loved. It can also start up their joints in the campuses as the products are economical and would be affordable snack for the day.

Questions

Is the expansion scheme as taken by Crisp Corner plausible in the near future?

How would setting various departments help the company do better or vice versa? Make a comparison with the current organization protocol.

Do you predict conflict between father and son Olyai in course of further expansion? If yes, what is the best subsequent course of action?

Case No.5. Out with the Old, In with the New.... The Career Xent's Way!

Career Xent Pvt. Ltd. is a leading and renowned coaching house in Gwalior. The institute excels in providing quality guidance and training to aspirants of different professional competitions like CAT, GRE, MAT, etc. Presently the institute offers different courses including classroom teaching, crash courses, study at home, test series and many more options. Although factors like day-by-day increase in the number of career conscious youth with varying expectations, increasing number of colleges, easy and cheaper availability of funds for higher education provide great business opportunities, they have also posed threats from time to time due to lucrative returns on investments. Thus, to be in business in such rapidly changing environment, the institute has come a long way in 7 years- evolving through various phases and adapting to the changing requirements of the aspirants, and successfully established a brand in the market.

The institute was started in year 2002 with 240 students and provided preparatory courses for premium MBA entrances like CAT and MAT. The booming economic scenario led to an increase in the number of MBA aspirants in middle tier cities like Gwalior, resulting in a conducive environment for the institute to grow. The assertion can be supported by the fact that in just one year, the number of students in institute rose to 400 in 2003.The institute recognized the three prime needs of the hour- need to expand, need to structure and need to organize. It went ahead to open a centres at Kurukshetra in 2003 and at Jhansi and Jabalpur in 2004.The revenues scaled up from 25-26 lacs in 2002 to 1 crore by 2004. Though financially things were going well, the centres at Jhansi and Kurukshetra had to be closed down owing to some other circumstances.

The next target for the organization was expansion and structuring of the organization with an eye on future. This called for reinvesting but it faced a lack of sufficient reserves. In order to facilitate revenues for expansion, they concentrated on policies, notably - introducing other MBA-preparation programs and outsourcing GK development material by entering into an alliance with Career Pacer (GK being a unique strength for them).

The booming markets for MAT were tapped by the organization by developing a product for Career Pacer, which assured them a recurring loyalty of 30lacs/annum from the same. By 2007, they had become the largest business partner of Career Pacer and generated revenue of 2 crores.

The institute aimed for further expansion but owing to manpower crisis, it failed to do the desired. Therefore, they moved on to NCR and in January 2008, they opened a new centre at Greater Noida and did a phenomenal business.

Tables turned in 2009 when recession had an impact on all B-schools and TIME made simultaneous attack in all its three markets. Career Xent responded by increasing advertising efforts which helped to retain some numbers. To get better results, they decided to cut down the prices of its courses and also started exploring opportunities for growth outside MBA like CLAT, which was expanding at that time. Another significant change was CAT going online which prompted the institute to set up a computer lab and adapting to the changed format. They resorted to organizing B-school fairs to create other sources of income as the market was static.

By 2010, things had become really bad. Monthly losses were now touching 30 lacs and 60% of revenues were draining to cover those losses. To ensure customers, they had to cut down the fees by 50% and the team size was reduced to 15 employees with bare minimum salaries(in contrast to a team size of 35 in 2008). So the question now was of survival instead of expansion.

Towards the latter half of 2010, things started looking up. The competition was decimated. The expenses were reduced by cutting manpower costs and resorting to direct marketing approaches rather than media. The institute is now looking for better opportunities to cash in on aptitude training. The possible avenues appear in shape of Civil Services preparation and CLAT.

Career Xent has come a long way, facing tumultuous times and battling challenges that came its way. Its motto of prioritizing customer service and reacting to the first available piece of information helped it achieve success in a very dynamic environment. Keen focus on future, proactive responses and strong goodwill also added to it. The management has provided ample opportunities for growth to its employees and shared its vision with exemplary leadership. Thus, Career Xent has created success for itself by kicking out the old and bringing in the new idea as and when change demanded it.

Questions

1. List the key characteristics of the organization that helped it manage the changes.
2. Identify the major forces of change the organization encountered.
3. Why, in your opinion, was the organization able to score above its competitors?
4. Can you chalk out the different strategies the organization undertook over the given period of time?

Case No.6 J. B. Mangharam Pvt. Ltd.

J. B. Mangharam Pvt. Ltd. is a very old factory; it was established in 1951 under the name of J. B. Mangharam & Company with the objective of manufacturing biscuits & confectionary products. The company was restructured in 1969 & 1977, after the death of Seth J. B. Mangharam. In 1983, the company started manufacturing biscuits for Britannia Industry Limited. Originally the production started with Marigold & Bourbon varieties of biscuits. To meet the increasing volume of production targets and customer satisfaction, the company went into an expansion plan in 1994 and the operation shifted to balding with state of art technology in biscuit manufacturing. The old hybrid oven were replaced by LDO (Light Diesel Oil) fired oven & LPG fired ovens. This center is still well known for its quality and consistency in performance and is bench marked for many activities.

In 1996, Jim Jam production was started and JBM is the National Centre for this variety. Beside these Britannia 50-50 and Britannia Milk-Bikis are the two other varieties which are being manufactured in the industry. The infrastructure of the unit allows the production of only premium quality biscuits at JBM.

J.B. Mangharam is a contract packer of Britannia. Britannia has 100% equity of J. B. Mangharam. J. B. Mangharam is a subsidiary of Britannia and it does the job work for Britannia. Britannia provides all the raw material, packing material to J. B. Mangharam whether it is engineering material or ingredients like Maida, sugar, Chemical, Oil, Ghee or Packing Papers etc. J. B. Mangharam converts it into finished goods and gives it to Britannia; J. B. Mangharam cannot sell any of its Biscuits. Britannia has this right while J. B. Mangharam has to work out the order of Britannia. The staff of the department is from J. B. Mangharam and material provider is Britannia.

Soon when more number of competitors started targeting the biscuit segment, Britannia decided to take an ISO 9001 certification and put a financial burden on JBM which had to undergo the same. The key problems here were the cost of training, documentation machinery and quality work force.

With more market forces coming into the play and increased customer and government concern towards health, quality has become an essential element in the industry.

Due to its vast experience in the industry, the unit was able to achieve highest orders of biscuits it produces and is one of the favorite sons of Britannia out of its 83 manufacturing plants.

JBM has been producing biscuits profitably from its inception. The key worry is the continuously rising cost of production. The factory is located at a prime location in Gwalior city rather than in industrial areas. This cuts down a number of advantages of the firm. The firm therefore has higher safety standard (so is the cost), expensive electricity, water and disposal charges and greater taxes imposed by local government.

The biscuit industry is continuously shrinking. Now the market is full of substitute products like chips and '*Kurkure*' which is forcing Britannia to continuously experiment with its variety of products. JBM has thus automatically become a victim of uncertainty. The products it is producing today, may not be in existence tomorrow. If in future, Britannia launches new type of products which JBM is not able to produce, the unit will shut down.

The firm's problem of higher running cost has also become a key concern now. One of the senior executive suggested that the firm can purchase new machinery which can help in waste reduction and can cut down some labor cost too. But with the quality standards required by Britannia the machinery purchase would definitely leave JBM with heavy interest payments to the loan providers for a decade ahead. Another old member of the management suggested that JBM should search for more scope under present infrastructure. Searching for another client may damage the relations with Britannia, but can prove vital for future survival. Expansion to other markets like chips, cakes etc. are also there but are presently out of the reach keeping in view the firm's financial capabilities.

With all these things already disturbing JBM's management, Britannia has recently adopted ISO 22000 which has increased the running cost of the firm by Lakh 3 to Lakh 5 per annum; the heavy initial investment is a plus.

One of the major competitors of J B Mangharam, Rudrapur plant has recently won much higher orders for the parent company. The bid of Rudrapur plant was much less than that of JBM. Rudrapur is situated in an industrial area and has lesser running expenditure and thus can afford a lower bid. The incident has given a nice shock to JBM management, as heavy orders were the key compensator for lower profit margin.The management of JBM is in serious talks to find out a solution. They are worried about present profit and future viability both. What do you think JBM should do?

- Should JBM buy the new machine to reduce its operating cost? Will it be a sensible investment considering the future market perspective?
- Should JBM enhance its infrastructure so that is can produce greater variety of biscuits?
- Should the firm try for more clients?
- Should JBM looks for new market dimensions? Does the location of the firm have any advantage for the firm?

Case No7. Soaring Saffron Insulations

Saffron Insulations is an entrepreneurial venture of Mr. Sunil Shrivastava which came into shape in the year 2008. This was a bold decision, as Mr. Shrivastava was settled in Thailand in a Multinational company called "Metrod Industries Limited" producing transformers. He is a mechanical engineering graduate passed out in 1992 from MITS, Gwalior and had been working with Crompton Greaves (CG) from 1992-2004. He had served CG up to a level Head-Maintenance department and carries vast technical and professional experience with him. He is a firm believer of learning and delivering best with hard work. He always envisage a dream of starting his own enterprise, therefore inception of saffron Solution is like dream comes true.

Saffron insulation as a special type of industry has got very rich experience in manufacturing insulations for Transformer, Fabrication and Engineering services. It has got combination of young and experienced team to carry out all the operations with latest technologies and quality requirements. The plant is designed and manufactured with latest technology and state of art facilities. It has a Turnover of US$ 0.75-1 Million (or Rs. 3-4 Crore Approx.). Major Markets include Indian Subcontinent, East/Middle Africa, East Europe, Central America, South America, South East Asia and North America.

The Problem

The company started its operation as a vendor for transformer insulation requirements for Crompton Greaves and was solely dependent on it. Since there were other vendors also (Like Kapoor Insulation Pvt Ltd) established in the market for long time, it was hard for the company to work with very lean margins specified by the company. The problem further worsened when company officials quoted very low job rates just for the sake of getting orders. Sustaining with this kind of business scenario was very hard for the company. Therefore Mr. Shrivastava critically examines the case and found there were mainly two kinds of Job-Work. One was relatively simple which involve relatively less labor and resources and other was Complex job-work which involves heavy labor and resources. It was also observed that KIPL was not having expertise of processing complex job- work. Therefore he scheduled a meeting with CG officials and manage to explain them with intricacies involved in complex job-work and how competent they are in doing such things efficiently. With his polished professionalism he succeeded in getting revised rates for Complex Job work.

Secondly sustenance on the basis of single company doesn't seem to be having long term profitability to the company. They followed the strategy of diversification for its growth. In 2008 when the company started, there was only one product that is transformer insulations. The company had few workers who were selected and trained by Mr. Sunil Shrivastav personally for this work. The only client they had was Crompton Greaves (CG).

Saffron Insulation has survived and overcome this challenge by diversifying its products, increasing its client base and at the same time cutting its cost of production. Mr. Sunil's experience in the industry and his technical skills played an important role in the success of the company in this endeavor. Most of the machines for the new products were manufactured in-house by the workers under the supervision of Mr. Sunil. He himself took the responsibility of training the same workers for the manufacturing of new products on new machines. Thus, cost of purchasing new machines and employing new labors was reduced to a considerable extent. It was because of the friendly and humble nature of Mr. Sunil that he was able to develop a strong relationship with the suppliers and the clients. Currently they have extended their reach other cities of India and are also exporting their products to other countries like East/Middle Africa, East Europe, Central America, South America, South East Asia and North America.

Product Diversification

Mr. Sunil realized that, their existing capacity can be utilized to produce other products as well, therefore they explored new opportunities. Currently they have diversified in-to maintenance and machine manufacturing, beeding and packaging material for solar panels. Out of these, major source of revenue is maintenance and machine manufacturing. The client base has also expanded to include Areva (Baroda) and Amko (Thane, Mumbai).

Improved HR Practices

In order to increase productivity and generate desired profits, the company felt the need to make some changes in its HR practices. Earlier the workers were paid on a monthly basis but this has been changed and now the workers are paid on a piece rate basis. This measure has motivated the workers to remain focused and achieve their target in time. Other motivating factor for the workers is the company's culture which focuses on delegating responsibility and accountability to them for their work.

In future the company is planning to start a new plant for the fabrication of tanks for transformers.

Questions

1. What further improvements do you recommend can be brought about in the company?
2. What are the HR practices followed by the company.
3. What do you think are the environmental challenges faced by the company?
4. What is the nature of change deployed in the company since inception?

Conclusion

Driving conclusion as a result of change management is not a very simple task. There are many things to take into consideration that will lead to the gradual creation of conclusions that transpired during the change process. There are the people, policies, processes, technology, and culture as key ingredients that determine how change management can directly impact the organization. A wide range of change management practices have been carried out in the business organization with varying degrees of success as well as the diversity of conditions. However, firms need to recognize that the change management initiatives have to be designed for specific contexts and environments.

8

Advice to Web Entrepreneurs

There are tens of millions of small enterprises, including micro-enterprises, in developing countries (DCs). More than 90% of all firms in DCs are micro- and small enterprises (MSEs), and these typically contribute 80-90% of all employment. They are also significant in wealth creation, making up perhaps around a quarter of gross domestic product and often contributing to exports as well.

In an increasingly competitive and globalised world, MSEs need to compete more effectively in order to further boost domestic economic activity and contribute toward increasing export earnings. MSEs will also continue to play an important role in increasing employment and incomes and thus contribute to poverty reduction on a sustainable basis.

eCommerce is emerging as a new way of helping business enterprises to compete in the market and thus contributing to economic success. eCommerce can help deliver economic growth, increased business opportunities, enhanced competitiveness and better access to markets. At present, though most small enterprises lack the knowledge of how investment in eCommerce could benefit their businesses and help them develop that competitive edge. This is at a time when the opportunities for small enterprises to adopt eCommerce are growing due to improved access to the technical and communication infrastructure.Thisbook will help you to understand more about eCommerce and what eCommerce has to offer your business.

What is eCommerce?

eCommerce involves the sale or purchase of goods and services over computer networks by businesses, individuals, governments or other organisations. eCommerce builds on traditional commerce by adding the flexibility and speed offered by electronic communications. This can facilitate improvement in operations leading to substantial cost savings as well as increased competitiveness and efficiency through the redesign of traditional business methods.

eCommerce is the application of current and emerging information and communication technologies (ICTs) to conduct business. These include existing technologies like landline telephone and fax, but the ICTs offering most scope for small businesses are mobile phones, electronic mail and other Internet-based services.

However, *eCommerce* is not just about using new technologies. eCommerce can also help support profitable business relationships and assist you to more effectively manage and run your business enterprise. This will involve creating more effective external interactions with customers, clients, collaborators and suppliers, but it can also mean improving internal business efficiency and even the emergence of new products and services.

eCommerce may involve selling directly from businesses-to-consumers (*B2C eCommerce*). For example, a number of craft producers and tourism enterprises have already found some success dealing directly with customers.

eCommerce can also be conducted directly between businesses (*B2B eCommerce*). This is by far the most common type of eCommerce at present. B2B activity includes portals that operate as electronic marketplaces or as auction sites. Benefits of eMarketplaces can include reduced costs, better research and quicker transactions for buyers. Rewards for sellers include improved customer service levels and cheaper exposure to customers. There is also business-to-government activity (*B2G eCommerce*) that refers to the growth in supply of goods and services for online government procurement–potentially a large growth area in developing countries.

How eCommerce Can Helps to Improve Your Business?

eCommerce can provide substantial benefits for your business via improved efficiencies and raised revenues. It can enable new ways of working to emerge as your business faces the future and embraces the new economy. eCommerce enables you to gain access to better quality information, and thus empowers you to take informed decisions about your business. Most importantly, eCommerce can give your enterprise a competitive advantage. It can help strengthen your market position and open up new business opportunities with the potential to improve profits. Benefits of eCommerce can arise in the following ways:

Cost Reduction Benefits

- *Reduced Travel Costs:* by using a mobile phone, email and other ICTs to substitute for journeys.
- *Reduced Cost of Materials:* more information means better choice of suppliers and more competitive prices.
- *Reduced Marketing and Distribution Costs:* for example, publishing a brochure online can reach an unlimited number of potential export customers and allow regular update.
- *Reduced Sales Costs:* the Internet provides unprecedented opportunities for businesses to reduce the costs of trade locally and, even more, across borders.
- *More Efficient Supply Chain Management:* can eliminate the need for middlemen leading to lower transaction costs (including marketing, sales, transaction processing), reduced overhead, and reduced inventory and labour costs.
- *Improved Internal Functions:* cutting down on meetings, improving the exchange of critical knowledge, eliminating red tape, and streamlining communications.

Market Benefits

- *Greater Reach:* a web presence can allow you to reach out to customers far beyond your immediate location.

- *More Brand Awareness:* offering new avenues of promotion for products and services.
- *Improved Customer Service:* providing more responsive order taking and after-sales service to customers; this, in turn, can lead to increased customer loyalty.
- *Increased Market Awareness:* you can become more aware of competition within your market and more aware of market changes, which can lead to product/service innovation or quality improvement.

Other Competitiveness Benefits

Increased Efficiency: eCommerce not only reduces costs but it can also increase the speed of transactions; both buying and selling.

- *Continuous Trading:* suppliers and customers, if they wish, can access a 24-hour/7-day sales service - particularly important when trading through time zones.
- *Specialisation:* eCommerce can help you to focus your activities - making it easier to build relationships with other enterprises and communicate your needs to support agencies.

Many of these benefits can be gained through relatively modest investments in new technology and systems. Greater benefits may accrue as the enterprise moves up the eCommerce adoption ladder (see Section B1). It is important to realise, however, that the benefits outlined are not exclusively tied to eCommerce. For example, market benefits may be achieved more effectively through better business networking and the building of personal business relationships, rather than through use of the Internet. This emphasises the importance of adopting an approach towards eCommerce that puts business objectives first, rather than believing that technology alone can deliver the benefits described above.

eCommerce Pitfalls

There are great potential benefits but there are also pitfalls of going into eCommerce. They are the financial costs, the business 'opportunity costs' and the dangers of failure. These are detailed below:

- eCommerce will bring extra costs as well as potential cost savings. The start-up costs (initial investment in a computer/network connection, etc) will be high and there will be additional running costs (see Advice Sheet 9).
- eCommerce activity will need to run in parallel with existing business methods. For example, you will need to continue to produce paper-based marketing material (brochures, stationery, leaflets, etc) as well as building up your web presence. This will duplicate some activities adding to overall costs.
- eCommerce may divert attention away from more important offline activities. It is important that online and offline efforts are not in competition with each other within a business. In fact, for most MSEs, offline activities (such as face-to-face meetings and personal networking) will remain far more important than online communication.
- An eCommerce venture may well fail completely like any new business venture. This highlights the importance for small businesses of not throwing all their eggs into the eCommerce basket.

However, there are also risks of ignoring eCommerce! Technology and innovation can bring positive changes to your business - which can improve the way you do business in the future. The risks of not effectively embracing technology may be felt throughout your business in years to come. For example:

- Having no website, or a badly designed or marketed website, may put your business at a disadvantage as compared with your competitors, particularly if you are an exporter or a tourism business.
- Unsuitable or inadequate technology can mean that your enterprise is without the communications systems that it needs to compete efficiently.

- Increasingly, enterprises that lack a customer and sales database may find it difficult to carry out the regular and effective direct marketing and communication that competitor's conduct, and which customers expect.

What You Need to Do for eCommerce?

The basic requirements to get started are as follows:

- A computer.
- A landline telephone.
- A Modem. This device converts digital information from computers into electronic signals that can be transmitted over telephone lines.
- *Internet Browser Software.* This usually comes installed already but make sure when purchasing your computer you ask if it has this software.
- *The Services of an Internet Service Provider (ISP).* These provide you with access to the Internet.
- *An Email Addresses* in order that local, regional, and especially, international customers can communicate with you.

See the Advice Sheets later in this handbook for more details of all these requirements. Remember that you do not have to own all of these yourself - you could access them via a telecentre or Internet café, or you could share ownership with other entrepreneurs. You can also make a start on eCommerce just using a mobile phone.

But Don't Forget - personal face-to-face contact is still the most important method of business communication - particularly with your customers. There are still many effective ways to build your business communications that don't involve modern technology, such as:

- *Building a Good Reputation* for your business. This will help to spread information about your business through word-of-mouth.
- *A Professional Image* will help to promote your business. The use of a printed business card, a

letterhead and a logo, or signboard outside your business premises will help in this respect.

- *Advertising* your business. The use of printed leaflets, posters, cards in shops or adverts in local/national papers will reach a wide customer base.

The use of eCommerce technologies will help you build on these good business practices: for example, using the Internet (or a mobile phone) to promote your business; to take or give orders; or to communicate with your customers at a cheap rate via email.

Small Enterprise on the Road To eCommerce

This section outlines the 'steps to eCommerce' describing the differing stages of eCommerce development that you may find in a small enterprise. It does this through a model and then presentation of six real-life case studies of small enterprises using eCommerce. The case studies show how enterprises are benefiting from eCommerce, as well as some of the pitfalls. Which step of the eCommerce ladder are you on? Read through the case studies. You may identify an enterprise that is at a similar stage to your own.

Moving Up The eCommerce Ladder

The 'steps' model can help you understand the different types of eCommerce business applications you may encounter. It may also help you to identify the type of assistance you may require.

Step1. Starting Out: Simple Messaging Using Mobile Communications

Currently 'wireless' communications–including short messaging services (SMS)–provide a cheap and widely available option for enterprises. Mobile phones offer a number of key advantages over fixed line communications for small businesses–such as instant communications with customers and suppliers, even when on the move. They also provide greater connectivity and network coverage than landlines–users can be instantly connected by text messages and mobile chat–a powerful marketing and advertising tool.

Step2. Getting Online: Email Messaging

You can send or receive emails from a computer terminal either located on your business premises or via a facilitator (such as an Internet café or telecentre). Email is a cheap, quick and reliable way to exchange business information with customers, suppliers, and business contacts that are also connected to email. A variety of information can be sent - not just messages, but documents, photographs, drawings, or any other computer data file (see Advice Sheet 2 for more information on email).

Step3. Web Publishing

Web publishing can be used to make enterprise information available- by using an online brochure, for example. Its simplest form may consist of a 3-4 page website giving a basic business profile, some information about products and services, and contact information - physical and postal address, telephone and fax, and email contact. In a more advanced form it may include an online catalogue - an online version of a conventional catalogue that can be easily updated. Even a simple web presence offers the ability to access a wide - potentially global - market with 24/7 accessibility. (See Advice Sheet 4 for more information on creating websites.)

Step4. Web Interacting

Web interaction will allow customers (for example) more scope to browse through images, descriptions and specifications relating to your products and services. It may allow them to submit email enquiry forms, to order online, to use online services or to use a shopping cart facility and order confirmation – that could be paid for and fulfilled (delivered) offline. Interaction over the web can improve customer service and response to customer queries.

Step5. Web Transacting

This can be termed as having a full eCommerce capability that covers the whole transaction process from the placing of an order to online payment for goods and services via secure networks. For B2C eCommerce this will involve making use of secure credit card payment systems, and for B2B eCommerce will involve payment through secure banking systems.

Step6. Web Integration

eCommerce may also take on a wider role within a business through web integration. Web integration provides an electronic platform that links customer-facing processes such as sales and marketing (the "front office") with internal processes such as accounts, inventory control and purchasing (the "back office"). This is often called eBusiness or the business may be described as becoming fully "e-enabled". eBusiness links internal systems with external networks (customers, suppliers and collaborators) via the Internet. Integrating systems can make it easier and cheaper to do business, and it can encourage customer loyalty and repeat business.

Case Study 1: Sedu Welding and Fabrication–eCommerce Step 1

Overview: A micro-enterprise run by a single entrepreneur producing fabricated metal products - windows, doorframes and beds - with two employees, and a turnover of about US$300-600 per year. The enterprise sells to local markets and serves many sectors including the construction sector, supplying windows and doorframes, and rural schools and hospitals supplying beds. The enterprise mainly sells to individual consumers and schools.

ICT Resources: The enterprise has a mobile phone which cost the owner US$80 and requires a monthly fee of at least US$4 of airtime to operate on the network. This enterprise has no financial support and depends solely on income generated and savings.

eCommerce Benefits

- The use of a mobile phone has greatly improved business by enabling constant access to customers, even when the entrepreneur is away from his business site.
- Both customers and suppliers can be contacted giving an immediate response and direct communication that has tremendously cut down transport costs and given access to a wider market.
- The phone has helped him forge a personal relationship with clients for repeat orders.
- Suppliers can also be readily contacted.
- The enterprise has built use of the phone into its marketing strategy by distributing the phone number whenever possible via business cards and displaying it on finished products.

eCommerce Challenges: The phone itself does not bring challenges. As to further eCommerce steps, the business owner regards other ICTs (such as computers) as too expensive to use. Besides he does not know how to use them. He prefers to spend his resources on a cell phone as he could not risk being without one in his business.

eCommerce Support: The enterprise has not received any support except in the sense that the mobile network provider delivers the infrastructure required for the phone.

Lessons Learned: The phone should be available for use at all times of the day. Hence, it is advisable to join networks that do not charge a service fee. It is important, therefore, to compare the packages that phone companies are offering in order to minimise costs and select a service that will meet your needs. Unfortunately he lost most of the numbers of his customers and contacts when his mobile phone was stolen – this reinforces the importance of keeping back-up records also.

Case Study 2: Mukono Women's AIDS Task Force–eCommerce Step 2

Overview: MWATF is a self-help enterprise producing tree seedlings, vegetables and metallic stoves, employing sixty women, with a turnover of US$3,600. It serves the home market only. The vegetables are perishable so they only harvest when they can be sure of the market.

ICT Resources: The enterprise has no direct access to ICTs but uses a community telecentre that is located 2km away from their premises. They regularly use the telecentre landline phone that charges them US$0.25 per minute. They also use the email service to correspond and communicate with agencies in at home and abroad. They usually use the email services twice a week (costing US$0.025 per minute). Since the connections are slow it can take up to twenty minutes to complete their communication.

eCommerce Benefits:

- The telephone service is used to ascertain the market for their produce before they harvest or take their produce to market.
- The phone has saved both time and money, giving rise to better prices.
- Via email, they have been able to establish contacts with a number of new organisations and individuals who have subsequently offered assistance.

eCommerce Challenges: The computer currently provided at the telecentre are too few–just two for the whole local community–and also too slow. Slow transmission speeds also mean high costs for access.

eCommerce Support: MWATF has received support from the telecentre which has offered computer training to the staff and some members at a subsided rate. They have also assisted with training of the staff, and demonstrated how the Internet can be used to search for information. The telecentre also passes on messages to MWATF. Hence the telecentre is an important point of contact for the organization.

Lessons Learned: When using the telecentre users are encouraged to have letters typed beforehand and then just copied to send. This costs less compared with composing a letter online. It is also important to use the telephone effectively to find out about the market or the prices before setting off to market - this is especially valuable if the market is far from the locality. The enterprise intends to install a phone at their premises that can be used by its members at a cheaper rate.

Case Study 3: Adam Sons–eCommerce Step 3

Overview: The business makes machinery used in plantations such as machinery for processing coffee. They have nine employees, and recent annual turnover was US$126,000. Their main market is the home district but 5% of turnover comes from exports - they have been exporting machinery for five years.

ICT Resources: They have five landline phones and three mobile phones. In addition, there is a single personal computer (PC) operating in the business for email, Web and other purposes. The PC has a UPS back-up system. Adam Sons also has created its own website.

eCommerce Benefits

- They have attracted prospective clientele and enthusiastic persons who have browsed through their website to get information regarding their coffee machinery units.
- They have received a number of visitors by ensuring that the site is listed on some main Web search engines.
- They have also found benefits as users of the Web; for example in finding information they needed about gasoline-powered generators.
- Email has been useful in saving costs when contacting external clients or suppliers; some orders are also received via email.

eCommerce Challenges

- Climatic conditions in their location can cause problems, including some unreliability of telecommunications.

- The high charges for airtime when using mobile phones.
- Problems upgrading website to obtain details of interested/prospective customers.

eCommerce Support: They have received no direct support, but the entrepreneur was motivated to make a website by a friend based in the US who said that this would help enhance the scope of the business.

Lessons Learned

The entrepreneur states *"Advertising in newspapers turns out to be expensive but if we have a website, we can just put the URL of the website in the newspaper–which saves a lot of space/money. Interested parties can log on to the net and find information about our business. Thus it should be on the agenda of every entrepreneur to have a website".* He also stated that customers are more enthusiastic about reputable companies and having a website gives weight to a company's reputation. They plan to upgrade the website in order to add more transactional functionality to it, like a chat facility to allow one-to-one interaction with clients. They recommend seeking out a good network connection that offers attractive and less expensive packages. The entrepreneur would like to see government agencies supporting a website specifically for/about small enterprises, including a product catalogue displaying images with easy ways to order the products.

Case Study 4: Star Café–eCommerce Step 4

Overview: This enterprise roasts, blends and packages coffee products and has 15 employees. The customer base is large since coffee is widely sold locally, including in rural areas. The enterprise supplies businesses, traders, supermarkets, restaurants, shops, and offices, with the local market making up 99% of turnover. The enterprise is planning to target the export market, and sees its eCommerce base as an important foundation for this.

ICT Resources: The enterprise has access to two computers with Internet access that was acquired in 2001/2002. It also has a fax and phones (both landline and mobile). The company has set up its own website that provides details of the products it offers.

eCommerce Benefits

- 70% of the supermarkets and hotels that the enterprise supplies have email (though most other local customers tend to use the telephone to place orders). Email is a key tool to create or strengthen personalised relationships with major clients through faster communication links.
- Star Café has become better known and many new business contacts have been made through its website and email.
- The website has already demonstrated that it is a cost effective way to reach out to the export market. They estimate the costs for a network connection and designing and hosting the website to be about US$2500 per year.
- The enterprise also uses email for most business correspondence – this has proved to be a more efficient and cost-effective way of communication than non-ICT-based means.

eCommerce Challenges

- Service breakdowns and slow dial-up Internet connections.
- High investment costs for the ICTs.
- Lack of sufficient know-how related to use of ICTs and their future development.
- Logistical requirements for the delivery of physical goods in order to fulfil electronic orders.

eCommerce Support: The enterprise has not received any support in the area of eCommerce. The company had its own in-house strategies to finance these ideas. The general manager indicated that once the benefits seem to justify the costs then an idea is considered.

Lessons Learned: Enterprises should apply cost/benefit analysis and determine if they really need the technology. Requirements need to be specified carefully and enterprises should shop around for different ways of solving problems in a cost effective manner.

Case Study 5: Kamal Bells–Elements of eCommerce Step 5

Overview: The business has 40 employees and was established in 1983. They manufacture machine and pressed metal components. Their customers are 100% home market but some export products containing their components are used in the motor industry. Their main customers are large motor engineering companies, and recent annual turnover was almost US$400,000.

ICT Resources: The Company has four phones (two Landline and two mobile) and three personal computers, one with an Internet connection. They make use of standard accounting software and a customised system for billing and invoicing. They use email but have no company website. However, they are able to transact online by make use of websites owned by suppliers or customers.

eCommerce Benefits

- Access to a mobile phone is very useful to the CEO who is always on the move.
- Email has made communication much faster and easier
- They have registered with an export portal website through which they have received a lot of information from various similar units and clients from all over the world.
- They have saved time and money by completing transactions online. For example, from one major customer they received order details via email. They then used the customer website to fill in all necessary details about the order, enabling it to be processed electronically. All further correspondence was conducted via email so that the entire transaction was completed online.

eCommerce Challenges

- Slow access speeds due to limited ICT infrastructure
- Lack of training in ICTs.
- Need to integrate basic business processes such as inventory and product lists with web-based tools.

eCommerce Support: The business has received support in the use of email and other aspects of eCommerce from one of their main clients, who are already experienced in using eCommerce.

Lessons Learned: There is a need for a continuous upgrading of technology. However, along with technology it is important the human element is retained in the unit; like the business owner says *"each employee in my unit is treated like a family member, and we discuss various problems together"*. Hence, too, the human element must also remain in dealings with suppliers and customers. Location is also important: they have benefited from being located alongside heavy ICT-using enterprises.

Case Study 6: Project ToeHold–Getting to eCommerce Step 6

Overview: ToeHold manufactures and markets traditional leather slippers and sandals. These are manufactured by artisans of a local marginalised community Established in 1999; it is run on a cooperative basis with eight full-time employees. ToeHold's customers are mainly shoe shops and boutiques in Australia, Japan, Italy and other countries.

ICT Resources: The Company has three computers at its head office and one in the manufacturing centre. ToeHold communicates with its customers and its own manufacturing unit via email. Its website contains a catalogue of its products and customers are able to browse and purchase its products via the integrated shopping cart application.

eCommerce Benefits

- Workers in the villages are able to speak to their head offices via mobile telephony. Decisions get taken faster and more cheaply, removing the need for travel. Decisions also get communicated down the line more quickly and cheaply.
- Requests are received via email and company representatives follow up with a quotation. Clients also use email to send in suggestions, alterations and photographic evidence of damage/faults in products that might need

replacement. This helps ToeHold improve the quality of their product design.

- Orders are received via the website that would otherwise be very unlikely to come: ToeHold's export ambitions would have been very difficult to fulfil without eCommerce.
- A management information system keeps track of customers and predicts their buying patterns. This helps the enterprise to optimise their leather and accessories purchases and keep inventory levels low.

eCommerce Challenges: Power supply remains erratic in the villages, which can sometimes undermine use of email. Internet connectivity is also limited in rural areas and finding trained staff is difficult. ToeHold is also concerned about retaining the intellectual property rights of its original designs– showcasing these designs on the web means they could be copied by others.

eCommerce Support: A local ISP offered a free template-based shopping cart application. Donor agencies have also provided ToeHold with computers and software at subsidised costs.

Lessons Learned: A digital camera is useful as images of new products or test designs can be edited and uploaded quickly onto a website, and images are an important element of web-based sales. ToeHold has trained staff members in the use of computers and they can now manage most communication via email. The artisans come from a poorer section of society and their literacy levels are low. This has so far prevented them from being part of the eCommerce process. ToeHold is trying to bring their levels to a basic standard so they may take a more substantial role in using ICTs, but this requires a concerted effort. The firm sees creation of a more sophisticated website as valuable for future sales; for example enabling buyers to create their own footwear designs or colour combinations.

Are You Ready For Web-Based eCommerce?

Before making a decision about what type of eCommerce to adopt – and whether you are ready for web-based eCommerce– you should ensure that:

- You have clearly defined your business goals and strategies.
- You intend to use eCommerce in creative ways to improve existing business tools and capabilities.
- You are able to successfully balance you existing offline commerce activities and new online eCommerce activities.
- You have a realistic and achievable plan for realising genuine benefits.

Planning for eCommerce involves setting achievable business goals, developing business strategies to achieve those goals, and making use of practical business tools. Table 1 can help you to identify your business goals and help you to consider potential strategies and practical tools to achieve those goals.

eCommerce technologies can help bring improvement to all of the business tool examples listed in Table 1 particularly those that involve better communications–using email or mobile phones, for example.

It will also be important that you are able to prioritise your actions in order that you can use eCommerce to produce benefits in the areas that are most important to your business. For example, if your main strategy is to build repeat orders then efficient and effective communications with your existing local customers will be paramount. Here, effective use of mobile communications rather than web-based eCommerce should probably be prioritised, so that you can always be in touch with all your customers and they can also leave messages for you.

How to Analyse Your Enterprise

The use of web-based eCommerce is likely to affect all aspects of your business. Therefore, it is very important for you to analyse all aspects of your business before you make any decisions regarding eCommerce. Go through the following sets of questions and note down some responses that apply to your business. Then read the comments alongside the questions to gain some feedback.

Table1
Business Goals and Strategies

Possible Business Goals	*Business Strategies You Could Adopt*	*Business Tools You Could Use*
Increase revenue from existing customers	Build repeat orders. Develop customer loyalty.	Increased advertising and promotion. Better communication. Better customer service.
Locate new customers in existing or new markets	Expand domestic markets. Explore export markets.	Better market information. Attendance at trade shows. Better cross-border business networking.
Diversify products and services	Development of new products or services.	Market research. Use of consultants and/or technical assistance.
Increase competitiveness through product/service innovation	Undertake product or process improvements. Technology upgrading. New production or service technology.	Branding. Improved design and packaging. Standards compliance. Employee involvement.
Increase competitiveness through cost reduction	Internal/external business efficiency improvements.	Better purchasing. Workforce/resource planning. Training and skills development.

First, You Should Consider Your Market

- Are your main competitors marketing or selling similar products or services over the Internet?
- Do your main customers or suppliers have access to the Internet or are they seeking to use eCommerce?

Feedback: If you answered predominantly 'Yes' then you need to consider whether you are ahead, on a par, or behind in comparison with your competitors, customers and suppliers, in using the Internet and eCommerce. If you answered predominantly 'No' then web-based eCommerce may not be a priority for you.

... and then your Proximity to the Market

- Where are your main customers and suppliers located?
- Where are your business premises located?

Feedback: If your customers or suppliers are located overseas, and you are located in a well-connected urban area, then you have high potential for web-based eCommerce. If your customers or suppliers are located in-country and you are located in a rural area, then you may want to consider using a mobile phone or gaining access to a telecentre to use email.

... what about the Products and Services you Offer

- Do your products or services have broad or specialised (niche) market appeal?
- Are your products or services suitable for marketing or selling over the Internet?
- Can your products or services be delivered electronically?

Feedback: More specialised products or services are more suited to Internet marketing or selling. Conversely, if your products or services are serving saturated markets where there are large numbers of competitors then your potential for web-based eCommerce may be lower. If you are unsure about the suitability of your products then you need to do some additional market research.

... *pay Special Attention to your Existing Customers*

- Are your customers 'other businesses' or 'final consumers'?
- Are your business customer's small or large enterprises or organisations?
- Are your customers operating in sectors that have high or low potential for eCommerce?
- If you sell to final consumers, do they tend to have high disposable incomes or low?

Feedback: If your customers are large or medium-scale businesses operating in high potential sectors or if they are consumers with high disposable incomes then you have high potential for eCommerce. If your customers are low-income consumers or small and medium-scale enterprises operating in low potential sectors then you may have lower potential for eCommerce. If you are unsure then you need to do some additional market research concerning your customers.

... *next Consider your Business*

- Is your enterprise new or well established?
- How many employees does your enterprise have?
- Is your enterprise growing, contracting or reasonably stable?
- What was the turnover of your enterprise in the last financial year?

Feedback: The size and the growth-rate of your enterprise are not as important as your market, your products and the nature of your customers for determining your potential. However, if you have larger well-established businesses then you are more likely to have greater available resources for investment in web-based eCommerce. On the other hand, if you have a greater number of employees then climbing the steps to eCommerce may present greater challenges in terms of transforming skills and attitudes across your workforce. Smaller enterprises employing two-five persons may find it easier to adapt, although it is likely that available resources will be lower.

... *your Access to ICTs*

- Do you currently have access to email or the Internet on your business premises or via a third party?
- Does your enterprise currently have a website?
- Are your internal IT systems networked?
- To what extent are your business processes (customer database, accounts, invoicing, purchasing, etc.) computerised?

Feedback: If you are already a computer/email or Internet user and those facilities are accessible on your business premises, you have greater potential to climb the steps to eCommerce. If you have yet to deploy ICTs within your enterprise then you need to consider carefully the issues covered in this handbook and decide what type of ICTs would be most beneficial.

... *your ICT and Business Skills*

- Are you an ICT enthusiast and do you have ICT skills?
- Are your employees familiar with ICTs and what is their level of ICT skills?
- Do you have ICT support available 'in-house' or do you depend upon external maintenance and development of your ICTs?

Feedback: Enthusiasm (commitment and leadership) is probably the most important skill you can bring to any eCommerce initiative. It will also be necessary to develop the technical and business skills to successfully implement the technology and the innovations that will lead to new ways of doing business. If you already have ICT skills and experience this will greatly increase your potential for eCommerce. However, good business skills - the ability to recognise how new technology can be used both wisely and cost effectively - are likely to be more important than your technical skills

... *your Business Environment*

- Are local telecommunication services provided to suit eCommerce?

- How advanced is your nation regarding the legal, regulatory and banking requirements for eCommerce e.g., secure payments?
- To what extent can transport and delivery systems meet the needs of potential eCommerce customers?

Feedback: The ability of your enterprise to climb the steps to eCommerce will depend not only upon your own skills, but also upon the level of support, and the constraints, that exist locally. An increased level of awareness of these 'e-readiness' issues will help you understand the constraints under which your enterprise is likely to be operating.

... and Finally Your Finances

- How financially stable is your business?
- What investment resources do you have available?
- Are you aware of the total likely financial cost (investment + recurrent costs) of eCommerce?
- Have you weighed the costs against the benefits?

Feedback: It is necessary that you have access to financial resources to make your initial investment, but you also need to be able to generate sufficient revenue to sustain your eCommerce activities in the years ahead. A lot will depend on your business continuing to thrive and grow. It is important that eCommerce can contribute to growth of revenue (and profits) whilst not imposing a heavy burden on your cash flow or threatening your financial stability. Ideally, the financial benefits will need to exceed the financial costs significantly.

After analysing your own situation, you may decide not to adopt web-based eCommerce and instead concentrate on other aspects of business development or make better use of cheaper communication technologies - such as mobile phones - or you may decide to make use of facilities provided by others (Internet cafés or telecentres) rather than invest your own resources in new ICTs.

Careful analysis of the factors outlined will help you understand your own strengths and weaknesses for eCommerce. If you do consider web-based eCommerce to be an essential part of your business plan, then take a step-by-step approach that avoids the pitfalls. You can take note of the following tips.

Ten Tips for eCommerce

Tip 1: A sound and stable commercial proposition is a crucial first step. Getting carried away by all the eCommerce hype could cause a loss of control over the eCommerce venture.

Tip 2: Your target market should shape your business planning. Remember, your eCommerce plans cannot be separated from your business plans. As with business plans, then: a) you should ensure that staff, customers and suppliers have their say, and b) your available resources will also influence your plan - make sure the costs can be justified by the benefits.

Tip 3: Flexibility all through the venture is very important for the venture to meet with success. Which means you simply cannot keep waiting for technology to catch up. The venture has to be treated as an on-going process.

Tip 4: Often, the whole venture is controlled by an IT specialist, not sales people. Once a website goes live, the marketing team is of utmost importance. That's when the public will flood the site and no amount of software technology will come in handy. So an excellent rapport with the marketing and sales team sets apart a successful eCommerce venture.

Tip 5: Vendors will only deliver the exact technology or application you want when you properly communicate it to them. A lack of understanding between the user and vendor can cause huge losses in investment and a flagging morale at the end of the day. A thorough knowledge of the technology you need and effective communication with your vendors could avoid big headaches.

Tip 6: Considering the outsourcing option is quite natural and necessary at times, so always know what you need to outsource. Gauge your in-house talent to see if you meet the requirement. There are plenty of cases of companies, without the adequate know-how, having approached consultants who vanish when they're in need of ongoing support (when the project goes live). Staying in control is absolutely necessary.

Ideally, the IT people should handle the outsourcing contracts and not the business department.

Tip 7: Never underestimate the scale on which your site has to operate. The losses will be Herculean if a site that cannot support customers comes to a grinding halt. In spite of knowing the importance of a scalable system, many eCommerce ventures are not prepared for a, say, 100% traffic increase. eBusiness sites need to scale rapidly in order to respond to the changes in market and an increasing number of hits.

Tip 8: Get as much advice on technical architecture as possible before you go live. Keep a tab on your expenses as most of the times the budget seems to be exhausted much before a certain level of functionality is even reached. It should not occur that the business platforms are up and running while the IT development side has staggered into the background. Business on the Internet may seem extremely easy to begin but after that it is very difficult to continue if the necessary technology is absent.

Tip 9: More than half of all eBusiness ideas fail to break even. A thorough understanding of the key business issues is very important, as is a good relationship between those responsible for technology and those responsible for finance. IT staff need to use the language of the business as eCommerce makes links between IT and business closer than ever. The approach towards an eBusiness solution should not be like that towards a project. A good planning approach and sound methodologies should do the trick.

Tip 10: Many eBusinesses forget planning about security measures from the initial cycle. This is a grave mistake. Most companies bring in the security issue in the end, more as a panic response, after they have experienced a mishap. There are a number of things that affect security at the infrastructure level itself. So getting things to the right places at the right time from the start is important.

What Kind of eCommerce?

For those who want to get into eCommerce, the following chart is a guide to which of the eCommerce steps would be most appropriate.

Table 2
Steps for eCommerce–What Kind of eCommerce?

Steps to eCommerce	*Market Drivers*	*Benefits*	*Costs*	*Overall Impact*
Step 6: Web Integration	Requirements of main customers and suppliers.	Merging online and offline processes. Reductions in operating costs. Better relationships with customers and suppliers.	Financial costs of investment in technology, systems and services are very high.	Very high costs,but potential high benefits.
Step 5: Web Transacting	Primarily driven by requirements of Customers.	Speed and convenience, but only a requirement if offline transactions not processed effectively.	High costs of investment in necessary systems and secure network requirements.	Relatively lowBenefits, but high costs.
Step 4: Web Interacting	Requirements of customers suppliers,collaborators andSupport agencies.	Better business communications. Better marketing. Better knowledge of market and customers.	Moderate costs of investment in web-based technologies and network access.	Relatively high benefits with relatively moderate costs.
Step 3: Web Publishing	Requirements of Customers and the marketplace.	Better marketing. Better branding. Easily updated, Well presented materials.	Moderate investment costs.	Moderate benefits and relatively moderate costs.
Step 2: Email Messaging	Requirements of customers, suppliers, collaborator support agencies and employees.	Considerably improved business Communications.	Moderate investment costs.	High benefits and moderate costs.
Step1: Simple Messaging	Requirements of customers suppliers, collaborators support agencies and employees.	Considerably improved business Communications.	Low investment costs.	Potentially high benefits and relatively low costs.

eCommerce Facilitators

A wide range of facilitating organisations can offer you different types of eCommerce support. This support may range from business advice to web development or market access. Different facilitators can play different roles depending on your eCommerce requirements.

When seeking out eCommerce assistance you should try to choose a facilitating organisation that is actively involved with your target market and in tune with your business requirements - as well as your technical requirements.

For MSEs in developing countries, facilitating organisations fall into several categories. As follows:

Sector-Based Agents/Brokers & Resellers

These offer web-based marketing activities and tend to be commission-based. They are able to accept and place orders and they are skilled at information brokering, logistics and supply chain management. They may also offer Internet transactions and electronic banking.

eCommerce Trading Hubs or Portals

These are also commission-based but offer solely web-based marketing activities. They are able to accept and place orders, and will be more likely to offer Internet transactions and electronic banking.

Industry Organisations & Business Associations

These are usually membership-based (requiring payment of subscriptions). They probably will not have detailed expertise in eCommerce, but can often provide market coordination and information brokering services.

Fair Trade Organisations

They provide market outlets based on fair trade principles. Most offer web-based services and marketing, and some offer a full transaction-based eCommerce service.

NGOs/Business Support Organisations (including Telecentres)

They are the Providers of advice, training and some marketing assistance. They are not likely to have specific expertise in eCommerce, but may be able to offer advice and assistance.

ISPs/IT Consultants

They can offer access to networks, web development services and possibly eCommerce advice and strategy planning.

As summarised in Table 3, you should consider the strengths and weaknesses of any organisation that you consider for support – whether or not the organisation can meet your own needs – particularly for fee-paying services.

eCommerce Best Practice Guides

The guides provided in this section provide direct advice on practical issues that may arise when your implement eCommerce in your enterprise.

Advice Sheet 1: Getting Connected and Making a Start

Getting Connected: Connecting to Internet is an fairly simple process. You will need *a computer:* new personal computers might range in price from around US$300 to around US$1500 depending upon the type of computer, the software installed, where one buys the computer and the warranty given. Some computing outlets in developing countries also sell second hand-reconditioned computers that could range in price between US$100 and US$300.

Computers can often be purchased using hire purchase (paying by instalments). Deferred payment and discounts for cash are available. Some charitable organisations and NGOs offer computers as gifts to schools and enterprises that cannot afford the purchase price.

You will also need *a telephone line and a modem.* A computer you buy may or may not have a modem fitted. Thus you should always ask whether this is available. You will also need Internet browser software which may well have been

Table 3
eCommerce Facilitators–Strengths and Weaknesses

FacilitatingOrganisation	*Possible Strengths*	*Possible Weaknesses*
Sector-Based Agents/Brokers	Good market proximity, Market experience and knowledge. Market access.	Tend to create dependency relationships with suppliers and tie in producers to sole purchasing agreements.Likely low returns.
Resellers	Quick route to market. More flexibility for producers in the market.	Less security in the market. Price sensitive. Only purchase and resell.
eCommerce Trading Hubs or Portals	Wider market access.	Lack of personal market relationships and contacts.
Industry Organisations	Able to advocate on behalf of producers.	Limited access to market. Lack of market proximity.
Fair Trade Organisations	Assistance with quality control and product/service development. Special assistance to women producers. Better returns.	Tend to lose market share to commercial importers or agents. Narrow market that might be seasonal (high demand at Xmas, for example).
NGOs and Business Support Organisations	Possible sources of finance or subsidy. Local access to resources.	May have little market access, knowledge or proximity.
ISPs IT Consultants	Able to offer local technical support	May have technical expertise, but probably little knowledge of the market within which you are operating.

preloaded into your computer when you purchased it, but make sure when purchasing your computer you ask if it has this software.

Finally you will need to link your computer with a local *Internet Service Provider (ISP)* that will provide you with access to the Internet (and may also provide email, web space, etc). There are numerous ISPs in most developing countries mostly located in and around urban centres. Most ISPs provide 24-hour access through a dedicated dial-up number and will charge a monthly fee. Make sure you shop around for an ISP.

Starting to Use the Internet

- Take a course or make use of (recent) guides.
- Start using email to communicate and check your email every day.
- Investigate local business websites and websites of companies in your business sector
- Use web search facilities and investigate any business portals that cater for your business sector.

If you do not have your own computer and connection, make use of *Internet Cafés.* Most of these are located in cities or towns where any individual, who cannot afford to own a PC, but needs to use the Internet, can have access. Typical charges will be less than US$1 per hour. More details concerning the possible costs associated with developing web-based eCommerce are contained in Advice Sheet 9.

Advice Sheet 2: Using Electronic Mail (Email)

Electronic mail (email) is the exchange of messages between computers offering considerable advantages over letter-post and, increasingly, over fax communication.

It provides the cheapest, quickest and most reliable way to exchange business information with customers, suppliers, etc. who are also connected to email.

Emailing requires a computer with Internet access. Furthermore you need some client email software such as Microsoft Outlook or Lotus Notes. The easiest way to use email is to go to a website that offers free email facilities, such as Yahoo or Hotmail. Emails arrive almost instantly via the Internet. You can send 'attachments' with your email – these may be computer files of any kind (documents, photos, sound-clips, or even video clips).

Some advantages of email for business are:

- It allows a variety of information to be sent – not just messages, but also other types of computer data file including formal business correspondence and brochures.
- Messages can easily be recorded, to keep a record of correspondence.
- Messages can easily be organised, e.g., by building up an address book.
- Messages can be protected from outside view.
- Messages can easily be sent to multiple recipients (such as all of your customers).
- Services can be accessed by the entrepreneur whilst on the move and away from the office.

The main barriers to using email at present are:

- The investment costs (the total cost of computer/ modem ownership).
- The running costs (network access).
- The relatively few businesses in developing countries able to send and receive emails (although the number is growing rapidly).

In order to use email, enterprises need access to an Internet-linked computer. As described in Advice Sheet 1, owning this is somewhat costly but email services can also be accessed from shared facilities such as Internet cafés and telecentres.

If you are an exporter or you are regularly communicating with email-linked Customers, suppliers and other business contacts within the region or worldwide (such as in the tourist sector), then email is by far the cheapest and quickest means of communication. It will increasingly be an essential tool for your export business.

Advice Sheet 3: eCommerce Skills

When adopting eCommerce, basic business skills remain unchanged–what we might call the *business fundamentals.* They can be summarised as follows:

- A well-thought-out business plan and marketing plan.
- The ability to make yourself known and network effectively.
- The capacity to produce the right product/service at the right price in the right place at the right time.
- Knowledge of your customers and the ability to meet their expectations.
- The ability to pay your bills and get paid on time.
- The capacity to be flexible yet also plans for the future.

eCommerce can help to support these fundamental skills; for example, by capturing customer information and making it easier to segment your market or market directly to your customers possibly using email or web-based methods. eCommerce will also open up your business to *new skills and ideas* including the following:

Database Management: You can collect information on website visitors - usually customers or potential customers. Information can be used to target marketing efforts and improve customer service as well as forecast future trends in customer behaviour.

Improving Business Processes: This is a way of analysing the different tasks within an enterprise to identify better ways of achieving greater efficiencies. Restructuring your business whilst making use of eCommerce may assist your long-term survival and growth.

Knowledge Management: More effective management of information and knowledge within your business can bring benefits. eCommerce will help you to improve your skills in this area.

The Internet will also help you do *web-based market research.* By conducting investigation into market trends and customer requirements, enterprises can develop innovative strategies to compete. The Internet can be used to learn more about customers, industries, products and services, and market trends. As just noted, you can also collect information from the people who visit your website, helping you to plan for the future.

The Internet also has specific resources that will assist market research in relation to product development, business planning, eBusiness development and marketing. These can be accessed via a number of the websites listed in Section E2. For those further up along the eCommerce steps, the Internet may also help you with more advanced skills such as *Enterprise Resource Planning (ERP)* and *Materials Requirements Planning (MRP)*. Both use ICTs to automate core business functions. MRP is similar to ERP but is substantially cheaper to install and is more suitable for MSEs. It requires computerisation of many aspects of the business including accounts, inventory, and purchasing. Benefits focus on reduced inventory costs, better stock control, ordering and order fulfilment.

Advice Sheet 4: Web Development

Websites can be static or dynamic. Dynamic websites create pages in response to visitor requests. For example, the amazon.com website builds its pages according to the types of books that interest specific visitors from information stored in a database - a database-driven website. A simple static website can be designed using HTML code instructions plus image files such as JPEGs or GIFs. It will typically link a home page to other pages containing information on the enterprise (see diagram). The website may include a shopping cart where customers can purchase products online with their credit card or where offline payment methods are outlined. To create a dynamic information-driven website, a database is integrated into the site and information can be displayed when someone requests it. The advantage is that the database can be updated and changed regularly. The database serving the website may consist of client information, such as account details and sales history and can be stored on standard software packages such as Microsoft Access.

Updating your Website: To update a dynamic website you have three options:

- Agree an annual fee with your web developer for a set number of changes.
- Make the required changes you – requiring specific skills.
- Build an update facility into your website design.

The preferred (and cheapest) option is for an employee– using a username and password – to be able to add, modify or delete information on the website using the web browser.

Basic Web Design Tips

- Pages must display or download quickly. If your website downloads too slowly the customer may give up and try a competitor's website.
- Images (photographs and graphics) need more time to download than text, so use a small number of images, repeat the same few illustrations or logo throughout the site, or install a button on the web page, to allow the customer to access a text-only version.
- Short paragraphs and sentences are the norm when writing for the web.
- Customers need to locate information easily. Visitors to websites tend to scan pages rather than read the entire text, so signpost the information with clear headings.
- Information on the site needs to be organised and easy to find. Links and buttons, which take the visitor to different places on the site, should be labelled. Most important items should be accessible with minimal clicking.
- Some buttons need to be on all pages, such as: Home, Sitemap, Contact us and Search. Important information should be easily navigable.
- Websites also require tailoring for your customers. Customers want to buy products that are described in their own language, priced in their local currency, and supported by people they can communicate with.

Advice Sheet 5: Online Promotion

The Internet provides an additional (and complementary) means of marketing your products and building your enterprise profile. You should consider use of the Internet alongside other media like telephone (such as a help line), radio, and print. A website will not provide a solution to all your marketing problems but it may become as necessary as other forms of media - particularly if your competitors also have websites.

To be effective, websites need to attract the right customers. A high proportion of people who visit a website find it through a search engine or directory. These services present important marketing opportunities. Search engines generate lists of URLs (web addresses) in response to particular queries entered by the potential customer. The sites most likely to be visited are those at the top of the list. Web pages, therefore, need to be designed so that they are located high on lists produced in response to relevant keywords. Your web presence can particularly assist in the following two ways:

Branding: Customers tend to stick with tried and trusted brands rather than risk buying an unknown brand. An online brand will be an extension of your offline brand. Your website needs to integrate your brand into the customer experience of visiting the site. The brand (e.g., amazon.com) should be associated with an easy to use website that offers high value in terms of information and services, has a trustworthy reputation, and is visually appealing.

Personalisation: Customer information (names, addresses and registration details) can be used to track preferences and tailor the contents of your website to suit individual tastes. For example, your site can suggest products that a particular customer might be interested in; based on his or her purchasing history or the pages they have already viewed.

The most useful methods of direct promotion to customers are:

Email Marketing: Email is likely to be the most cost effective way to market your business. You should add a signature file to all emails. This is the same as using headed paper or attaching a business card. Most email software enables this to be done easily.

Testimonials: These are genuine comments that satisfied customers have made about your products or services. Effective use of testimonials builds credibility and makes customers feel more secure – especially for online purchasing. Effective testimonials will be unedited, genuine, freely given, used with the author's permission and accompanied by the author's name and location.

Other online marketing methods include:

- *Viral Marketing*– using your email contact list to spread your details through your contacts lists–by giving an incentive to pass on the message.
- *Banner Ads*– adverts that appear on web pages.
- *Reciprocal Links*– links to other sites that provide an easy way for a customer to travel from a related site to your website, and vice versa.

Advice Sheet 6: Networking and Communities on the Internet

By networking we mean connecting computers in order to share information. A network allows a small enterprise to share hardware (printer or a phone line) and software (an accounts package or email). The network may be extended internally to include local offices through an *intranet* or externally to key customers and suppliers forming an *extranet.*

Networking a small enterprise would involve linking PCs, printers, fax machine, scanners and phone connections. A common language or protocol known as TCP/IP allows computers, software and other hardware devices to communicate with each other. (SMTP and POP–commonly used for transmitting and receiving emails – are part of the TCP/IP protocol). These protocols allow different systems to share data and communicate with each other regardless of the type of operating system or computer used.

For larger networks you will need networking software such as Microsoft NT or Novell NetWare. This software will set up one of your PCs to act as the main server that will hold the enterprise database and act as the central point sending (to a printer, for example) and receiving data/information.

Key Benefits of Networking

- Information is shared quickly and efficiently.
- Hardware devices (e.g., printers) are better utilised by sharing with other colleagues.
- Access to information such as stock and accounts can be obtained any time of day from any location.
- Suppliers and customers can be included in the network and efficiencies achieved as a result.
- Communication within the enterprise improves overall.

Better communication can also be facilitated through networking over the Internet and web. For example, *online communities* can open up interaction between enterprises and customers and boost other marketing efforts. Networking avenues include:

eNewsletters: They allow enterprises to send regular, targeted stories and messages to people who have invited them to do so – a form of advertising.

Email Discussion Forums: People can subscribe and then send emails that will be automatically forwarded to all other subscribers. People seeking information can post emails to the forum, and those who are able to give advice reply. These are good for accessing technical advice and for stimulating new ideas.

Bulletin Boards: These allow subscribers' emails to be posted in a central location. Unlike email discussion forums, subscribers do not receive any emails; they have to visit the bulletin board to see what people are saying. These can be used in online auctions and for accessing invitations to tender.

Advice Sheet 7: Contracting Out Web Services

The decision whether to buy external web services or to develop your website in-house will depend partly upon budgetary constraints. As well as the necessary financial resources (see Advice Sheet 9) you should also make sure that you have the experience and know-how to do the job and a clear understanding of your business goals and strategy.

When involving an outside firm or individual, it will be necessary to inform them of your requirements. This will also provide a useful checklist for future reference when the project is up and running. Also, pay attention to the back-up service on offer, together with contractual terms and conditions of your potential website developer.

The core ingredient for any website is content. The presentation and content should be worked out between you and your developer - taking into account the needs of your customers. The developer should have a clear understanding of your requirements. You could use the following checklist for to provide the necessary information for a website developer:

- A description of the business sector and a short outline concerning any important issues specific to your industry.
- Clarity on how important the Internet will be to the enterprise's future.
- The objectives for the site. These should be concise and realistic.
- The target audience for the site.
- Who is going to develop the content?
- Will a writer/content editor be required to develop and structure content?
- What will the customer to be able to do on the site? Will the website facilitate online transactions, reply forms, search queries, etc?
- Will your enterprise require mailing lists and bulletin boards?
- What will be the time frame for construction of the website?
- How will web content be updated?

You will also need to consider who is going to host the site - *website hosting.* A web host provides the necessary hardware and software to store your website and allows access via telephone or other connections. All websites require hosting that typically includes: a one-off fee to a hosting company plus an annual subscription and (if required) credit card authorisation costs. These payments may be dependent on the expected number of visitors (traffic) to the site. When choosing a host, reliability is as important as speed. Downtime–time when your website is not accessible due to maintenance or some system failure of the host - can be expensive for a small enterprise.

Some website design companies offer turnkey solutions - *all-in-one packages.* These are useful for enterprises with no ICT background. They eliminate the need to find specialists supplying different Internet services. There are increasingly low cost or in some cases free packaged software solutions on offer.

Advice Sheet 8: Order Fulfilment and Logistics

Order or service delivery tends to be an area of weakness for many eCommerce ventures - depending, as it does, on the existing transport and supply infrastructure (the 'bricks' rather than the 'clicks'). Poor delivery damages customer loyalty and the enterprise reputation if not handled well. eCommerce therefore needs good logistics: getting the correct goods to the right place at the right time, in the right condition with the minimum of cost.

Some products or services are delivered more easily than others. Books, CDs, etc are often bought online because they are easy to ship through the post or via couriers.

When a customer buys online they tend to expect a better standard of service. To try to plan a good standard for your order fulfilment, ask yourself the following questions:

- How are you going to distribute the goods or services to your customer?
- What are the delivery options and their associated costs?

- How can you improve your response and delivery times?
- How dependent are you on the ability of others in your supply chain to respond to customer needs?
- Do you have a strategy for customer dissatisfaction or returns?
- Are you aware of your own limitations and those of your supply chain?

The use of the Internet will be more important if you are conducting B2B eCommerce. As trade between businesses increasingly moves online, so the processes and services that support this trade, such as logistics and document management also move online. Involvement in B2B eCommerce can help small enterprises maximise both internal and external efficiencies (e.g., filling excess transport capacity). Electronic networks may also open up new ways of managing the supply chain (e.g., cutting down on paperwork and speeding up communications), allowing streamlining of business operations, reducing costs and improving efficiency.

Some Tips for Improved Order Fulfilment:

Keep the Customer Informed– probably via email. This is vitally important and may include: confirming the sale, the expected delivery date and follow-ups to check delivery has been completed. Effective communication will help establish a relationship of trust with your customers. With eCommerce, many of these functions can be automated using off-the-shelf software.

Establish Personal Contact by telephone or in person if local. This is especially important when customers have problems or complaints. If you have a telephone number for customers to call, this should provide human interaction rather than recorded messages.

Advice Sheet 9: Costs of Web-Based eCommerce

The basic cost components (outlined in Advice Sheet 1) for web-based eCommerce include a computer (PC or similar), an internal/external modem plus an Internet connection via a landline: A suitable computer should include the necessary software packages that may be off-the-shelf or free software options.

Typically, an *Internet connection* can be achieved in a number of ways:

Most popular are dial-up Internet services (recommended for light users) using normal telephone lines through an ISP via a modem. The modem is usually internally placed in the computer. Your local landline provider will charge for every minute you are connected. There is also an annual charge for dial-up Internet services - perhaps US$ 20-30 per month. In addition a set up fee of, say, US$25-50 may be charged, especially for those clients without internal modems.

In some areas it is also possible to connect to broadband. Broadband offers high-speed, 24-hour Internet access and does not block your telephone lines during use. This comes at a high cost, though the cost is falling quite fast. Typical costs might be US$300 annually for the lowest bandwidth (64kbps) up to US$2500 and more per year for the high bandwidths (1 Mbps and above). In addition an installation fee of anywhere from US$100-200 may be charged.

Other Options and Additional Costs

For enterprises that cannot afford their own computer and dial-up connection, cost saving options includes a monthly/annual membership with a local Internet café/telecentre.

Additional costs for web development may include: website domain registration (registration of the name of your website), hosting and design, and search engine subscriptions. For full eCommerce, other costs may include shopping cart facilities and databases used to store and manipulate customer or sales information. Registration of a domain (which can often be done via overseas domain registration sites) might cost US$20-30 per year. Hosting and maintaining the website will depend on the complexity of the website. A simple website requires at least 15-50 megabytes (MB) of storage capacity, and could cost between US$60 and US$200 per year.

Website design costs vary enormously, but a typical price could beUS$5-10 per page for a simple website with few graphics. The cost of a full website could range from US$50 to US$1000 for a relatively simple website. However, the price is not fixed – it depends on the designer and complexity of the site required. Thus to have a website up and running might require an initial cost of anywhere between US$100 and US$1000 with hosting, maintenance and other subsequent costs likewise between US$100 and US$1000 per year. Updating costs should be taken into account at the design and development stage. It is possible either to train a staff member to look after the website or to sign a contract with the web development company.

Advice Sheet 10: Some Legal/Regulatory Issues

The Internet presents new legal/regulatory challenges. The global nature of electronic communications requires a global view of the legal implications. Legal issues and risks will become more severe as you climb the eCommerce ladder. A marketing type website will offer fewer challenges than a fully interactive eCommerce portal. Of critical importance is the location and nature of the target audience and the laws that are likely to apply in the user's country.

Some of the key issues are specified below. These will need investigating further in relation to specific local requirements and concerns.

Terms and Conditions of Use: These should be legally incorporated into the relationship between the website and the user. Electronic contracts have legal validity. Acceptance of a contract should be recorded in an acceptable manner giving the time and date of each customer's acceptance (payment, of course, may be made offline in the usual manner). It is possible for users to 'click' acceptance of terms and conditions of use when they enter a website or make a purchase.

Intellectual Property Rights (IPRs): The ease with which electronic content can be copied and reproduced raises issues about who owns material on a website. You may need to clarify this – particularly when using outside developers or all-in-one packages.

Hyper Linking: This encourages users to move to and from other websites. In all cases the consent of a third party website owner should be obtained, or it may be possible to examine the terms and conditions of the other site you wish to link to in order to find out what their policy on hyper linking is.

Data Protection: A database of customers, subscribers or members constitutes a significant enterprise asset that should be protected. In the absence of a framework of law covering these issues, it is up to the enterprise to ensure that its own data is protected.

Consumer Protection: There is a growing body of law that offers protection to consumers in their day-to-day transactions and requires the disclosure of certain information to consumers. In practical terms, website operators should ensure that the fundamental ingredients of a contract (e.g., offer and acceptance) are appropriately dealt with on their websites. Certain prior information such as the identity of the supplier, price of the goods, delivery costs, delivery arrangements and cooling-off periods should also be provided on-screen prior to the submission of an online order.

Overseas Jurisdictions: Small enterprises are not in a position to obtain legal advice on all the jurisdictions in which their website is accessible. Insofar as it is possible therefore, website operators should seek to ensure that the laws and jurisdiction of their country of establishment apply to the website. Therefore, you should check the rules of the country where your website is hosted.

Advice Sheet 11: Web Security

Protecting information from unauthorised access is a critical Internet issue. It is also the case that the collection, storage and distribution of information via the Internet is increasingly governed by legal regulation.

The following points are an explanation of some basic security measures that can be installed in your computer or built into your website:

Authentication: A common security measure that requests the user to login with authorisation details before allowing access to restricted areas of a website. These details usually include a *username* and a *password.*

Email Security: It is possible to protect your email messages from snoopers, and ensure that email conversations remain private. One method is 'public key encryption'. This technology transmits email messages in a code or cipher, and decodes them at the other end, making it possible only for the recipient to read them. An encryption facility should be available as part of your email software (e.g., on MS Outlook Express).

Firewalls: These are security systems that protect the information contained in your computer system from outside hackers. Firewalls are particularly useful for protecting a business network that sends and receives emails, transfers data over the Internet or connects with outside computers.

Digital Certificates: A digital certificate is confirmation by a respected third party that the client company is legitimate and can guarantee security of a financial transaction. When a customer goes online and decides to buy something the web browser checks to see if a website has a digital certificate. If the required confirmation is detected, the vendor's site server is accepted and the visitor is able to shop with peace of mind.

Digital Signatures: A combination of services that allows you to electronically sign a document and affords the recipient the opportunity to authenticate the signature.

Another security problem is *viruses.* Computer viruses are passed from computer to computer via Internet downloads, email attachments, shared disks, and shared files. Caution should be exercised when exchanging information between computers and downloading from the Internet. Well-known suppliers of anti-virus software include Symantec or McAfee.

More advanced security measures become necessary when transactions are conducted over the Internet such as through the use of credit cards: These include *public key infrastructure (PKI)* and *Secure Sockets Layer (SSL).* These are methods of encryption whereby the recipient of a ciphered message unlocks the code by applying a mathematical key to it. In addition to standard authentication procedures, SSL uses encryption coding to lock in client information and is the industry standard where online credit card transactions occur.

Advice Sheet 12: Open Source Software

Open source typically means that the software code (the underlying computing instructions) can be read, re-distributed and modified, independent of the people that created it. A key benefit of the open source system is its potential ability to reduce software costs as it is usually free to obtain and saves on licence costs. It also allows you to upgrade your business software at your own pace, rather than having to keep up-to-date with commercial software upgrades.

The boundaries between open source and proprietary software (such as Microsoft) are becoming muddied, as proprietary software adopts some open source standards and often freely publishes its own formats. The choice between open source and proprietary systems comes down to what is right for your business: you may want to look at what other businesses in your field use but there are a number of eCommerce-related open source products now available.

Potential Benefits of Open Source Include the following:

- You can get some open source software free by downloading it from the Internet.
- Even if you purchase tailored packages from third parties the initial price can be much cheaper than for proprietary software.
- There are no copyright costs - you are free to copy and distribute open source software to additional users.

Potential Costs

- For commercial use, open source software may need more skill when it comes to installation and management than proprietary products. Also if a part of an open source system lets you down, it can be hard to know where to turn for help.

- Open source may save on some initial costs but for many business costs related to eCommerce - gathering data, training staff, changing the way you work - it has no cost advantage.
- The installed base of most open source software is smaller than for dominant proprietary packages, so it can be harder (or more costly) to obtain support and training.

Other factors depend on the particular software. For example, choosing open source may mean you are not tied to a particular software producer, but it may tie you in to one particular local support firm. Open source might provide greater reliability, attention to security, and capacity for customisation to your eCommerce needs. Or it might not - it all depends on which particular open source and which particular proprietary software you are comparing.

Overall, open source is a useful option that you should consider when implementing eCommerce. But you should gather information and local opinions about it first.

9

The Business Plan: Creating and Starting the Venture

Planning as Part of the Business Operation

(a) Planning is a Process that Never Ends

- In the early stages, the entrepreneur should prepare a preliminary business plan.
- The plan will be finalized as the enterprise develops.

(b) Many Different Types of Plans may be Part of Any Business Operation—Financial, Marketing, Human Resource, Production, and Sales Plans

- Plans may be short term or long term, or they may be strategic or operational.
- All of these plans have one purpose: to provide guidance and structure to management in a rapidly changing market environment

What is the Business Plan?

(a) A *business plan* is a written document prepared by the entrepreneur that describes all the relevant external and internal elements involved in starting a new venture.

- It addresses both short- and long-term decision making for the first three years of operation.
- The business plan is like a road map for the business' development.

(b) In developing the business plan the entrepreneur can determine how much money will be needed from new and existing sources.

Who Should Write the Plan?

(a) The business plan should be prepared by the entrepreneur; however, he or she may consult many sources.

- Lawyers, accountants, marketing consultants, and engineers are useful supplemental sources.
- Other resources are the Small Business Administration, Service Core of Retired Executives, Small Business Development Centers, universities, friends, and relatives.
- The Internet also provides outlines for business planning.
- Entrepreneurs can also hire or offer equity to another person to provide expertise in preparing the business plan.

(b) To help determine whether to hire a consultant, the entrepreneur needs to make an objective assessment of his or her own skills.

(c) Through this self-assessment, the entrepreneur can identify what skills are needed and where to obtain them.

Scope and Value of the Business Plan Who Reads the Plan?

(a) The business plan must be comprehensive enough to address the concerns of employees, investors, bankers, venture capitalists, suppliers, customers, advisors, and consultants.

(b) Three perspectives need to be considered:

- The *Perspective of the Entrepreneur* – the entrepreneur understands the new venture better than anyone.
- The *Marketing Perspective* considers the venture through the eyes of the customer.

- The *Eye of the Investor* – the investor looks for sound financial projections.

(c) The depth and detail of the business plan depends on the size and scope of the proposed venture.

(d) The business plan is valuable to the entrepreneur and investors because:
  - It helps determine the viability of the venture in a designated market.
  - It gives guidance to the entrepreneur in organizing planning activities.
  - It serves as an important tool in obtaining financing.

(e) Potential investors are very particular about what should be included in the plan.

(f) The process of developing a business plan also provides a self-assessment of the entrepreneur.
  - This self-evaluation is similar to role-playing, requiring the entrepreneur think. through obstacles that might prevent the venture's success
  - It also allows the entrepreneur to plan ways to avoid such obstacles.

How Do Potential Lenders and Investors Evaluate the Plan?

(a) Because the business plan should address the needs of all the potential evaluators, software packages and Internet samples should be used only to assist in preparation.

(b) As the entrepreneur becomes aware of who will read the plan, changes will be necessary.
  - Suppliers may want to see a business plan before signing a contract to supply products or services.
  - Customers may also want to review the plan before buying the product.
  - The business plan should consider the needs of these constituencies.

(c) Potential suppliers of capital will vary in their needs and requirements in the business plan.

- Lenders are primarily interested in the ability of the new venture to pay back the debt including interest within a designated period of time.
- Lenders focus on the four C's of credit:
    - The entrepreneur's credit history, or *character.*
    - Their ability to meet debt and interest payments (*cash flow.*)
    - The *collateral* or tangible assets being secured.
    - *Equity contribution,* or the amount of personal equity that has been invested by the entrepreneur.
- It is also important for the entrepreneur to develop a strong personal relationship with the loan officer of the bank.
- Investors provide large sums of capital for ownership (equity) and expect to cash out within 5 to 7 years.
    - They will often place more emphasis on the entrepreneur's character than lenders.
    - The venture capitalist will play an important role in management of the business and wants the entrepreneurs to be compliant and willing to accept this involvement.
    - These investors will also demand high rates of return and will thus focus on the market and financial projections.

(d) If the entrepreneur does not consider the needs of these sources, the plan may be an internalized document without consideration of the feasibility of meeting market goals.

(e) Most external advisors and potential investors are bound by a professional code of ethics regarding disclosure.

Presenting the Plan

(a) It is often necessary for an entrepreneur to orally present the business plan to investors.

- Typically the entrepreneur provides a short (20-30 minutes) presentation of the business plan.
- The entrepreneur must sell their business concept in a short time period.

(b) A venture capitalist or angel group may also ask the entrepreneur to present the plan to their partners before making a final decision.

Information Needs

(a) Before preparing a business plan, the entrepreneur should do a quick feasibility study to see if there are possible barriers to success.
   - The entrepreneur should clearly define the venture's goals, which also provide a framework for the business plan.
   - Goals that are too general or that are not feasible make the business plan difficult to control and implement.
   - The business plan must reflect reasonable goals.

(b) Market Information
   - It is important to know the market potential for the product or service.
     - The first step is to define the market.
     - A well defined target market makes it easier to project market size and market goals.
   - In order to build a strong marketing plan, the entrepreneur will need to gather information on the industry and market.
     - This process can be visualized as an inverted pyramid, starting with very broad based data and information.
     - This information can then be used in the industry analysis and marketing planning sections of the business plan.
   - The information gathering process.

- General environmental trends should be evaluated, including household income trends, population shifts, and employment trends.
- The next step is the assessment of trends in the national industry.
- The next two stages consider trends in the local market.
- General local economic trends should be considered.
- The final step is an analysis of the local competitive environment.
- After all of this analysis has been completed the entrepreneur is ready to clarify the product or service offering, actual market positioning, and market objectives.

– To assess the total market potential, the entrepreneur can use trade associations, government reports, and published studies.

(c) Operations Information Needs

– The entrepreneur may need information on:
- Location.
- Manufacturing operations.
- Raw materials.
- Equipment.
- Labor skills.
- Space.
- Overhead.

– Each item may require some research but is needed by those who will assess the business plan.

(c) Financial Information Needs.

– Before preparing the financial plan section of the business plan, the entrepreneur should prepare a budget, including possible expenditures and revenue sources for the first year.

    - Revenues from sales must be forecast from market data.
    - The entrepreneur will need to identify benchmarks in the industry that can be used in preparing the formal pro-forma statements.
  - The entrepreneur can use secondary sources that provide percentage norms for such costs in projecting operating costs.
  - Sources for benchmarks include:
    - Publications such as *Financial Studies for the Small Business.*
    - 10K reports for similar public competitors.
    - Trade associations and trade magazines.
  - Some investors require five-year projections.

Using the Internet as a Resource Tool

(a) Thanks to technology, entrepreneurs are able to access information efficiently, expediently, and at very little cost.
  - The *Internet* can serve as an important source of information in preparing the business plan.
  - Information on industry analysis, competitor analysis, and measurement of market potential can be located.

(b) In addition, the Internet also provides opportunities for marketing strategy through its website.
  - Online sales increased 52% in 2002.
  - The online audience has increased and represents a much broader cross section of consumers.

(c) An entrepreneur can also access competitors' web sites to gain knowledge of their strategy in the marketplace.

(d) The entrepreneur can also investigate *newsgroups.*
  - There are newsgroups of customers having the same interest in a topic.
  - The entrepreneur can use Usenet to identify the most appropriate newsgroups.

- Members of the newsgroup can be asked specific questions about their needs, competitive products, and potential interest in the new venture's products and services.

(e) All that is needed to use these sources is a small investment in hardware and software

Writing the Business Plan

(a) The business plan should be comprehensive enough to give a potential investor a complete understanding of the venture and will help the entrepreneur clarify his or her thinking about the business.
  - The business plan can take hundreds of hours to prepare.
  - Many entrepreneurs incorrectly estimate the length of time writing a business plan takes.

(b) Introductory Page
  - The title page provides a brief summary of the business plan's contents, and should include:
    - The name and address of the company.
    - The name of the entrepreneur(s), a telephone number, fax number, e-mail address, and website.
    - A paragraph describing the company and the nature of the business.
    - The amount of financing needed.
    - A statement of the confidentiality of the report.
  - It also sets out the basic concept that the entrepreneur is attempting to develop.

(c) Executive Summary
  - This section is prepared after the total plan is written.
  - It should be two to three pages in length.
  - The summary should concisely the key points in the business plan.
  - Questions that should be addressed include:

- What is the business concept or model?
- How is this business concept or model unique?
- Who are the individuals starting this business?
- How will they make money and how much?
- If strong growth is expected, the executive summary should also include an exit strategy such as an IPO.

– Any supportive evidence that might strengthen the case should be included.

– Remember that this section is only meant to highlight key factors and provide a strong motivation to the potential investor to read it in its entirety.

(d) Environmental and Industry Analysis.

– The entrepreneur should first conduct an *environmental analysis* to identify trends and changes occurring on a national and international level that may impact the new venture.

– Examples of environmental factors are:

- Economy.
- Culture.
- Technology.
- Legal concerns.
- All of the above external factors are generally uncontrollable.

– Next the entrepreneur should conduct an *industry analysis* that focuses on specific industry trends such as:

- Industry demand.
- Competition.

– The last part of this section should focus on the specific market.

- This would include such information as who the customer is and what the business environment is like.

- This information is significant to the preparation of the marketing plan section.

(e) Description of the Venture.

- The *description of the venture* should be detailed in this section.
- This should begin with the mission statement or company mission, which describes the nature of the business and what the entrepreneur hopes to accomplish with that business.
- Key elements should be described in detail, including the product or service, location, personnel, background of entrepreneur, and history of the venture.
- The emphasis placed on location is a function of the type of business.
  - In assessing the space the business will occupy, the entrepreneur should consider parking, access from the roadway, access to customers and suppliers, and zoning laws.
  - An enlarged local map is helpful.
- Maps that locate customers, competitors, and alternative locations can be helpful.
- If the building or site decision involves legal issues, the entrepreneur should hire a lawyer.

(f) *Production Plan*

- If a new venture is a manufacturing operation, a *production plan* is necessary.
- This plan should describe the complete manufacturing process, including whether or not the process is to be subcontracted.
- If the manufacturing is carried out by the entrepreneur, the plan should describe the physical plant layout and machinery and equipment needed.
- If the new venture does not include any manufacturing functions, this section would be eliminated.

(g) Operations Plan.

- All businesses – manufacturing or non-manufacturing – should include an operations plan as part of the business plan.
- This section goes beyond the manufacturing process and describes the flow of goods and services from production to the customer.
- This would be a convenient place to discuss the role of technology in the business transaction process.
- If the venture is not manufacturing, this section would be titled *operational plan.*
- The entrepreneur would need to describe the chronological steps in completing a business transaction.

(h) Marketing Plan

- The *marketing plan* describes how the products will be distributed, priced, and promoted.
- Potential investors regard the marketing plan as critical to the venture's success.

(i) Organizational Plan

- The *organizational plan* section is the part of the business plan that describes the venture's form of ownership.
- If the venture is a partnership, the terms of the partnership should be included.
- If the venture is a corporation, this should include the number of shares authorized, share options, and names and addresses of the directors and officers.
- It is helpful to provide an organization chart indicating the lines of authority.
- This chart shows the investor who controls the organization and how members interact.

(j) It is important that the entrepreneur make an *assessment of risk* in the following manner:

- The entrepreneur should indicate the potential risks to the new venture.

- Next should be a discussion of what might happen if these risks become reality.
- Finally the entrepreneur should discuss the strategy to prevent, minimize, or respond to these risks.

(k) Financial Plan

- The *financial plan* determines the investment needed for the new venture and indicates whether the business plan is economically feasible.
- Three financial areas are discussed:
    - The entrepreneur should summarize the forecasted sales and expenses for the first three years.
    - Cash flow figures for three years are needed, with the first year's projections provided monthly.
    - The projected balance sheet shows the financial condition of the business at a specific time.

(l) Appendix

- The appendix contains any backup material not included in the text of the document.
- Possible documents:
    - Letters from customers, distributors, or subcontractors.
    - Secondary or primary research data.
    - Leases, contracts, and other agreements.
    - Price lists from suppliers and competitors

Using and Implementing the Business Plan

(a) The business plan is designed to guide the entrepreneur through the first year of operations.

- It should contain control points to ascertain progress.
- There is a tendency among entrepreneurs to avoid planning.
- Planning should be a part of any business operation.
- Without good planning the employees will not understand the company's goals and how they are expected to perform their jobs.

- Bankers say that most businesses fail because of the entrepreneur's inability to plan effectively.
- The entrepreneur can enhance efficient implementation of the plan by developing a schedule to measure programs and to institute contingency plans.

(b) Measuring Plan Progress

- Plan projections will typically be made on a 12-month schedule, but the entrepreneur should check key areas more frequently.
- Inventory control. By controlling inventory, the firm can ensure maximum service to the customer.
- Production control. Compare the cost figures against day-to-day operating costs.
- Quality control depends on the type of production system used.
- Sales control. Information on units, dollars, and specific products sold should be collected.
- Disbursements. The new venture should control the amount of money paid out.

(c) Updating the Plan

- Environmental factors—such as the economy, customers, or competitors—and internal factors—such as loss of key employees—can change the direction of the plan.
- It is important to be sensitive to changes in the company, industry, and market.

Why Some Business Plans Fail

(a) A poorly prepared business plan can be blamed on:

- Goals set by the entrepreneur that are unreasonable.
- Goals that are not measurable.
- An entrepreneur who has not made a total commitment to the business.
- An entrepreneur who has no experience in the planned business.

- An entrepreneur who has no sense of potential threats to the business.
- No customer need was established for the proposed product.

(b) Setting goals requires the entrepreneur to be well informed about the type of business and the competitive environment.

- Goals should be specific.
- They should also be measurable and should be monitored over time.

(c) The entrepreneur who has not made a total commitment to the business will not be able to meet the venture's demands of the venture.

- Investors will not be positive about a venture that does not have full-time commitment.
- Investors will typically expect the entrepreneur to make significant financial commitment to the business.

(d) Lack of experience will result in failure unless the entrepreneur can gain the needed knowledge or team up with someone.

(e) The entrepreneur should also document customer needs before preparing the plan.

In Review: Summary

Learning Objective 1. To Define What the Business Plan is, Who Prepares It, Who Reads It, and How It is Evaluated

(a) A business plan is a written document prepared by the entrepreneur that describes all the relevant external and internal elements involved in starting a new venture.

(b) It should be prepared by the entrepreneur; however he or she may consult many sources.

(c) Three perspectives need to be considered:

- The perspective of the entrepreneur — the entrepreneur understands the new venture better than anyone.
- The marketing perspective considers the venture through the eyes of the customer.

- The eye of the investor—the investor looks for sound financial projections.

Learning Objective 2. To Understand the Scope and Value of the Business Plan to Investors, Lenders, Employees, Suppliers, and Customers

(a) Suppliers want to see a business plan before signing a contract to supply products or services.

(b) Customers want to review the plan before buying the product.

(c) Potential suppliers of capital will vary in their needs and requirements in the business plan.

(d) Business plan evaluation:

- Lenders are primarily interested in the ability of the new venture to pay back the debt plus interest focusing on the four C's of credit.
- Investors often place more emphasis on the entrepreneur's character than lenders.

Learning Objective 3. To Identify Information Needs and Sources for Each Critical Section of the Business Plan

(a) Market information: The first step is to define the market.

(b) Operations information needs: The entrepreneur may need information on location, manufacturing operations, raw materials, equipment, labor skills, space, and overhead.

(c) Financial information needs:

- Before preparing the finance section, the entrepreneur should prepare a budget, including possible expenditures and revenue sources for the first year.
- Revenues from sales must be forecast from market data.
- The entrepreneur needs to identify benchmarks in the industry that can be used in preparing the pro-forma statements.
- Some investors require five-year projections.

Learning Objective 4. To Enhance Awareness of the Ability of the Internet as an Information Resource and Marketing Tool

(a) The Internet can serve as an important source of information in preparing the business plan.

(b) Information on industry analysis, competitor analysis, and measurement of market potential can be located.

(c) Internet also provides opportunities for marketing strategy through its website.

(d) The entrepreneur can also access competitors' websites to gain knowledge of their strategy in the marketplace.

(e) Information can also be gained by participating in newsgroups.

Learning Objective 5. To Present Examples and a Step-by-step Explanation of the Business Plan

(a) The introductory page provides a brief summary of the business plan's contents.

(b) The *executive* summary should highlight the key points in the business plan.

(c) The environmental and industry analysis should include discussion of industry outlook, new project developments, and competitive analysis.

(d) The description of the new venture should be described in detail including the product, location, personnel, background of entrepreneur and history of the venture.

(e) If a new venture is a manufacturing operation, a production plan is necessary.

(f) The operations plan goes beyond the manufacturing process and describes the flow of goods and services from production to the customer.

(g) The marketing plan describes how the products will be distributed, priced, and promoted.

(h) The organizational plan section describes the venture's form of ownership.

(i) An assessment of risk is important to recognize the potential risks and prepare a strategy to deal with them.

(j) The financial plan determines the investment needed for the new venture and indicates whether the business plan is economically feasible.

(k) The appendix contains any backup material not included in the text of the document.

Learning Objective 6. To Present Helpful Questions for the Entrepreneur at Each Stage of the Planning Process

(a) Critical issues for environmental and industry analysis are included in Figure 7-5.

(b) Questions to consider in describing the venture are included in Figure 7-6.

(c) Issues to consider for the production plan are listed in Figure 7-7.

(d) Questions regarding the organization structure are given in Figure 7-8.

Learning Objective 7. To Understand How to Monitor the Business Plan

(a) The entrepreneur should develop a schedule to measure programs and to institute contingency plans.

(b) Plan projections are typically made on a 12-month schedule.

(c) Key areas should be checked more frequently.

- Inventory control.
- Production control.
- Quality control.
- Sales control.
- Disbursements. .

It is important to be sensitive to changes in the company, industry, and market.

Appendix

List of Incubation Centers in India

Here is a list of Incubation Centers in India. Hope this helps to give you a starting point if you intend to start your own company...

1. ABV-Indian Institute of Information Technology and management, Gwalior
2. NS Raghavan Center for Entrepreneurship Learning (NSRCEL), IIM Bangalore.
3. Technology Business Incubator, Birla Institute of Technology, Pilani
4. Center for Innovation, Incubation and Entrepreneurship, IIM Ahmedabad
5. Entrepreneurship Cell, IIT Kharagpur
6. Center for Entrepreneurship, SP Jain Institute of Management & Research
7. C-TIDES, IIT Madras
8. TeNeT, IIT Madras
9. Society for Innovation and Entrepreneurship, IIT Bombay
10. Nirma Labs
11. SIDBI Innovation and Incubation Center, IIT Kanpur
12. Entrepreneurial Development Cell, IIT Guwahati
13. Entrepreneurship Development Cell, IIT Delhi
14. Entrepreneurship Cell, FMS Delhi
15. Abhiyan, IIM Lucknow
16. E-Cell, IIM Kozhikode
17. Center for Entrepreneurship and Innovation, IIM Calcutta
18. Entrepreneurship Development Institute of India, Ahmedabad

19. ICFAI Center for Entrepreneurship Development, Hyderabad
20. MICA Entrepreneurship Development Center, Ahmedabad
21. Wadhwani Center for Entrepreneurship Development, Hyderabad
22. TIME IS, Delhi
23. Science & Technology Entrepreneurs Park, JSS Academy of Technical Education, NOIDA
24. National Institute of Industrial Engineering, Mumbai
25. Entrepreneurship Development Cell, IIT Roorkee

Reputed and Prestigious Institutes Offer Entrepreneurship Courses in India

Entrepreneurship as a career option has emerged due to the cut-throat competition and lack of opportunities in the formal sectors. Individuals with a dream to do something on their own are even leaving their secure jobs to pursue a business venture. There are several institutes that offer entrepreneurship courses in India. It is always considered to be a better idea to join a formal training before setting your foot forward as an entrepreneur.

1. Advanced Diploma in Enterprise Management
   - All India Management Association Centre for Management Education New Delhi
2. Certificate Course in Export Marketing
   - Indian Institute of Foreign Trade (IIFT), New Delhi
3. Certificate Course in International Business Language
   - Indian Institute of Foreign Trade (IIFT), New Delhi
4. Certificate Course in International Trade Logistics
   - Indian Institute of Foreign Trade (IIFT), New Delhi
5. Diploma/Certificate Courses in Entrepreneurship
   - Entrepreneurship Development Institute of India,Gujarat
   - FICCI, New Delhi
   - Small Industries Service Institute, New Delhi
   - National Science and Technology Entrepreneurship Development, New Delhi

6. Diploma in Entrepreneurship
   - National Institute for Entrepreneurship and Small Business Development (NIESBUD), New Delhi - 110020
   - ASEED and Entrepreneurship Development Institute of India (EDII), New Delhi
7. Diploma in Planning and Entrepreneurship
   - Indian Institute of Planning and Management (IIPM) New Delhi
   - Indian Institute of Planning and Management (IIPM) New Delhi
8. Executive Masters in International Trade
   - Indian Institute of Foreign Trade (IIFT), New Delhi
9. Executive MBA+M.Com/PGDBA
   - Institute of Marketing and Management (IMM) New Delhi
10. Executive Postgraduate Programme
    - Xavier Labour Relations Institute (XLRI), Jharkhand
11. Executive Postgraduate Diploma in Management
    - Xavier Institute of Management (XIM), Orissa
12. Fellow Programme in Management
    - Xavier Labour Relations Institute (XLRI),Bihar
    - Management Development Institute,Haryana
13. Fellow Programme in Management (Doctoral Level)
    - Management Development Institute,Haryana
14. Fellowship Programme (Doctoral Level)
    - Indian Institute of Information Technology and Management (IIITM), Madhya Pradesh
15. Master of Business Economics
    - Symbiosis Centre for Management,Maharashtra
16. Masters Diploma in Business Administration (MDBA) (Specialization in Marketing, Finance, HRM and HRD and International Trade)
    - Indian Institute of Modern Management (IIMM, Maharashtra
17. Masters in Own Business Management
    - Management

- Symbiosis Centre for Management and Human Resources Development (SCMHRD),Maharashtra

18. MBA (General-Human Resource Development Marketing, Operations Research and Finance) as well as online courses
    - Jamia Millia Islamia, New Delhi
19. MBA (pat-time)
    - Jamia Millia Islamia, New Delhi
20. Open Learing Programme on Entrepreneurship (OLPE) (Correspondence Course)
    - Aseed and Entrepreneurship Development Institute of India (EDII), New Delhi
21. Part-time course (Correspondence Course)
    - Postgraduate Diploma in Entrepreneurship Management, New Delhi
22. PG Diploma in Advertising and Communicaiton Management
    - Narsee Monjee Institute of Management Studies (NMIMS), Maharashtra
23. PG Diploma in International business/Enterpreneurship/ Small Business and Management of Services
    - Lal Bahadur Shastri Institute of Management Shastri Sadan, New Delhi
24. PG Diploma in Management of Small and Medium Enterprises
    - All India Management Association (AIMA), New Delhi
25. PG Diploma in Manufacturing and Operations Management
    - SP Jain Institute of Management and Research Munshi Nagar, Maharashtra
26. PGDBA (Marketing, Information Technology, Finance, HRM and Production and Operations Management)
    - Jaipur Institute of Managemtn Vineet Khand,Uttar Pradesh
27. PGDBM (Markeitng, Fianance, International Business, Information Systems, HRM, Operations Management)
    - Aisa-Pacific Institute of Management AIM, New Delhi
28. Postgraduate Diploma in Entrepreneurship Management (PGDEM)

- ASEED and Entrepreneurship Development Institute of India (EDII), New Delhi

29. PGDEM
    - ASEED and Entrepreneurship Development Institute of India (EDII), New Delhi
    - ASEED and Entrepreneurship Development Institute of India (EDII), New Delhi

List of Entrepreneurship Development Institutes

1. Shri A.K. Srivastave (Director)

   Institute of Entrepreneurship Development (UP) A 1 & 2 Sarojini Nagar, Industrial Area, Kanpur Road, Lucknow-226008 (UP)

2. Sh. G. Nagraju (Director)

   Centre for Entrepreneurship Development of Karnataka, "West View" UB Hills, Near D.C. office, Dharward-580007

3. Sh. B.V. Rathod (Director)

   Maharashtra Centre for Entrepreneurship Development A-38, MIDC near Railway Station, Aurangabad-431005

4. Sh. P.N. Mishra, (Executive Dir)

   Centre for Entrepreneurship Development, 60 Jail Road, Jahangirabad, Bhopal-462008

5. Sh. B.P. Rayaguru, (Director)

   Institute of Entrepreneurship Development, IEDO, Plot No. 123, Sector-A, Zone-A, Mancheswar Industrial Estate (near Postal Printing Press), Bhubneswar-751010 Orissa

6. Sh. P.A. Ramaswamy, (M.D.)

   Kerala Industrial & Technical Consultancy organisation Ltd., P.B. No. 1820, Ravipuram, M.G. Road, Cochin-682016

7. Sh. P.C. Gupta, (Executive Dir.)

   H.P.C.E.D., Udyog Bhawan, Bemloe, Shimla-171001

8. Dr. R. Jaya raman (Member Secy.)

   Centre for Entrepreneurs Development, CED SIPPO Campus No. 4, T.B. Road, Madurai-625010

9. Sh. Prasanna Kumar, (IAS)

   Haryana Institute of Public Administration, 76, HIPA Complex, Sector-18, Gurgaon-122001

10. Sh. D.K. Sharma, (Jt. Director)

    Entrepreneurship and Management Laboratory Building, 22 Godown, Industrial Area-1, Jaipur-302019

11. Smt. K. Rama Devi, (President,)

    CED an undertaking of Association Andhra Pradesh, 3-5-1091/15, Narayanaguda, Hyderabad-500029

12. Member Secretary,

    J&K Entrepreneurship Development Institute (J&K, EDI)

    O/o Directorate of Industries & Commerce, Exhibition Ground, Residency Road, J & K Govt. Jammu/ Srinagar

13. Sh. Lakshman Prasad (Executive Dir)

    IED Bihar, B.S.F.C. Building, 5th floor, Fraser Road, P.B. No. 114, PATNA-800 001

14. Dr. V.G. Patil, (Vice-President & Director,)

    EDII, (Near Village Bhat, Via Ahmedabad Airport, & Indira Bridge, P.O. Bhat, Ahmedabad-382428, Gandhi Nagar, Gujrat

References

Article by Tonia Hooper "How some successful young entrepreneurs got started".

Article by Shashank "Funding Resources for young Entrepreneurs".

Annette Smith "Break Studios Contributing Writer". www.mademan.com.

Young Turks: My Startup StoryYoung Entrepreneurs Society (YES, India)

Business week "Asia's Best Under 25".

www.sahajabschool.com/corporate_interface.html.

Case Code : LDEN013 "Women and Entrepreneurship" from IBS Center for Management Research

A Handbook for Entrepreneurs in Developing Countries "eCommerce for Small Enterprise Development" by Richard Duncombe & Richard Heeks IDPM, University of Manchester, Robert Kintu & Barbara Nakangu FIT (Uganda) and Sunil Abraham Mahiti.

A book titled "Entrepreneurship, 7th Edition by Irwin McGraw-Hill.

The Entrepreneur And Practice Of Innovation by MOhd. Arif working paper at "Social Science Electronic Publishing, Inc".

An online guide to business Success "Let's talk business".

An Article by suegold "An Entrepreneur Defined".

An Article by Tim Guy "Entrepreneur Defined".

An Article by MOHD ARIF "Origins and meaning of word 'Entrepreneur '. The Entrepreneur And Practice Of innovation.

An Article by Doug Gorman "Entrepreneurship/Business Environment".

An Article by Anne Wallingford on "characteristics_successful_entre.html".

An Article by A.J. Schuler, Psy. D. "Overcoming Resistance to Change: Top Ten Reasons for Change Resistance".

http://archive.prairiepublic.org/features/END/entrepreneur.htm

An Article by Hiatt, Jeff. "The definition and history of change management".

Filicetti, John (August 20, 2007). Project Management Dictionary". PM Hut.

"Leading Change" by John P kotter.

www.borland.com

www.businessballs.com

An e book on "Managing Change at work place" by Leslie Allan.

An Article by Clanzenetta Brown " Strategies For Overcoming Resistance To Organizational Change"

"Lewin's Change Management Model

Understanding the Three Stages of Change" by Lewin's.

An Article by Richar Grow "Entrepreneur : 7 Key Qualities of a Successful Entrepreneur".

Suggested Readings Material

A. Text Book Suggested

Robert D. Hisirich and Michael D. Peters: Entrepreneurship, Tata McGraw-Hill Edition, 2008.

Marc J. Dollinger :Entrepreneurship: Strategic and Resources , Pearson Education, 2008.

Mazzarol, T.W: Entrepreneurship and Innovation: A Manager's Perspective, Palgrave–Macmillan, 2006.

Gregory K.Ericksen:Net Entrepreneur Only, John Wiley and Sons Inc.2006.

Cynthia L. Greene: South Western Entrepreneurship Ideas in Action, South Western Educational Publishing, 2000.

P.F. Drucker: Innovation and Entrepreneurship: Practice and Principles, Heinemann, London, 1994.

J. Sundbo, The Theory of Innovation: Entrepreneurs, Technology and Strategy, Edward Elgar, Massachusetts, 1998.

M. Singh, D. Waddell, E-Business Innovation and Change Management, IRM Press, London, 2004.

T. Miller, Top Ten Lessons from the Internet Shakeout, Webmergers.com, 2002

H. Grupp, Managing New Product Development and Innovation: A Micro Economic Toolbox., Edward Elgar, Cheltenham, 2001.

A. Arora, A. Fosfuri, A. Gambardella, Markets for Technology: The Economics of Innovation and Corporate strategy, MIT Press, Cambridge, 2002.

P. Stoneman, Handbook of the Economics of Innovation and Technological Change, Blackwell, Oxford, 1995.

J. Schumpeter, The Theory of Economic Development, Harvard, New York, 1934.

B. Here are a Few Books for Brainstorming Ideas

What Business Should I Start: Seven Steps to Discovering the Ideal Business for You, by Scott Cook (Foreword), Rhonda Abrams. Planning Shop (June 1, 2004) ISBN: 096696358X This up-to-date book gets great reviews.

201 Great Ideas for Your Small Business: Revised & Updated Edition By Jane Applegate. Bloomberg Press (June 15, 2002). ISBN: 157660117X

101 Best Businesses to Start: the Essential Sourcebook of Success Stories, Practical Advice and the Hottest Ideas, by Russell Roberts. Broadway, 3rd Rev edition (August 15, 2000 ISBN: 0767906594

100 Small Business Ideas for Under $5000, by Corey Sandler, Janice Keefe John Wiley & sons (April 8, 2005) ISBN: 0471692875

Success for Less: Low Cost Businesses You Can Start Today, by Rob Adams, Terry Adams. Entrepreneur Press; First edition (September 1999) ISBN: 189194063

C. References List

The Young Entrepreneur's Edge: Using Your Ambition, Independence and Youth to Launch a Successful Business, by Jennifer Kushell Princeton Review; 1st edition (April 6, 1999) ISBN: 0375753494 (Good personal advice. For nuts and bolts, supplement it with others.)

The Young Entrepreneur's Guide to Starting and Running a Business: NEW: Use the Internet to jump-start your company; find out where the money is; Neat ideas from pet care to public relations, by Steve Mariotti Three rivers Press; Coml Rev edition (February 22, 2000) ISBN: 0812933060 (Geared toward young people.)

How to Start, Run, and Stay in Business, by Gregory F. Kishel, Patricia Gunter Kishel. Wiley; 3rd edition (September 11, 1998) ISBN: 0471247731 (Revision of best-selling classic.)

You Need to Be a Little Crazy: The Truth about Starting and Growing Your Business, by Barry Moltz. Dearborn Trade, a Kaplan Professional Company (October 1, 2003) ISBN: 079318018X (Rave reviews.)

Business Plans for Dummies, by Paul Tiffany, Steven D. Peterson, John B. Schulze. For Dummies (May 15, 1997). ISBN: 1568848684 (Good reviews. Shows how to use the plan to run the business, not just how to prepare the document.)

Small Business for Dummies, Second Edition, by Eric Tyson, Jim Schell. For Dummies; 2 edition (January 2, 2003) ISBN: 0764554816 (Excellent reviews.)

Business Start-Up Kit, by Steven D. Strauss. Dearborn Trade, a Kaplan professional Company (December 12, 2002). ISBN: 0793160278

The Small Business Start-Up Kit, by Peri Pakroo, Barbara Kate Repa (Editor). NOLO; 3rd Bk&Cdr Edition (April 1, 2004) ISBN: 1413300405

Steps to Small Business Start-Up: Everything You Need to Know to Turn Your Idea into a Successful Business, by Linda Pinson, Jerry Jinnett Dearborn Trade, a Kaplan Professional Company; 5th edition (October 1, 2003) ISBN: 0793179270 (More complete than inspiring.)

Small Business Solutions: How to Fix and Prevent the 13 Biggest Problems That Derail Business, by Robert Hisrich. McGraw-Hill Companies (January 26, 2004). ISBN: 0071414355

The Entrepreneur's Guide to Patents, Copyrights, Trademarks, Trade Secrets & Licensing, by Jill Gilbert. Berkeley Publishing Group (August 1, 2004). ISBN: 1425194094.

The Successful Business Plan: Secrets and Strategies, by Eugene Kleiner (Foreword), Rhonda Abrams. Planning Shop; 4th edition (September 1, 2003). ISBN: 0966963563

The Complete Book of Business Plans: Simple Steps to Writing a Powerful Business Plan (Small Business Sourcebooks), by Joseph A. Covello, Brian J. Hazelgren. Sourcebooks (April 1, 1994). ISBN: 0942061411 (The steps and advice are better than the examples.)

D. Recommended Reading Books on Entrepreneurship

Zero to One Million by Ryan P. M. Allis

Rich Dad Poor Dad by Robert Kiyosaki

Rich Dad's Guide to Investing by Robert Kiyosaki

New Venture Creation by Jeffrey Timmons

Zero to IPO by David Smith

Good to Great by Jim Collins

The E-Myth by Michael Gerber

The Young Entrepreneurs' Edge by Jennifer Kushnell

The Young Entrepreneur's Guide to Starting and Running a Business by Steve Mariotti

The Portable MBA in Entrepreneurship by William D. Bygrave

Innovation and Entrepreneurship by Peter Drucker

Good to Great by Jim Collins

At Work with Thomas Edison by Blain McCormick

Multiple Streams of Income by Robert G. Allen

On Entrepreneurship by Harvard Business Review

Entrepreneurship.com by Tim Burns

The Art of the Start by Guy Kawasaki

Fire in the Belly - an exploration of the entrepreneurial spirit by Yanky Fachler

The Anatomy of Buzz by Emanuel Rosen

The Tipping Point by Malcolm Gladwell

Obtaining a #1 Ranking in the Search Engines by Ryan Allis

What Clients Love by Harry Beckwith

Building Thousands of Links to Your Site by Ryan Allis

Net Results 2 by Rick E. Bruner

Permission Marketing by Seth Godin

Blink by Malcolm Gladwell

Guerilla Marketing by Jay Conrad Levinson

Principles of Marketing by Kotler and Armstrong

Think and Grow Rich by Napoleon Hill

The Seven Habits of Highly Effective People by Steven R. Covey

Succeed and Grow Rich Through Persuasion by Napoleon Hill

How to Win Friends and Influence People by Dale Carnegie

The Law of Success in Sixteen Lessons by Napoleon Hill

The Student Success Manifesto by Michael Simmons

Secrets of the Young & Successful Jennifer Kushnell

Soul of Money by Lynne Twist

Unlimited Power by Anthony Robbins

The Millionaire Mind by Thomas J. Stanley, Ph.D